Danielle Ancelet

CUISINE OF FRANCE

preface by Roland Magne

with 300 recipes illustrated in colour

W. H. ALLEN · LONDON
A Howard & Wyndham Company
1981

The dishes illustrated in this book were
prepared by Cavaliere Ernestino Magnani,
Commandeur de la Commanderie des Cordons-bleus.

The publisher thanks the Osteria del Binari of
Milan for its valued assistance.

Photographs by Vittorio Bobbi

Translated from the French by Adèle Dejey
English translation copyright © 1981 by Arnoldo Mondadori Editore S.p.A., Milan

Printed and bound in Italy by
Officine Grafiche Arnoldo Mondadori Editore S.p.A., Verona
for the Publishers, W.H.Allen & Co. Ltd,
44 Hill Street, London W1X 8LB

ISBN 0 491 02865 2

CONTENTS

PREFACE

Good food has always been an important consideration for French people, a fact borne out by the great number of works which have been written about traditional cookery by people such as Escoffier, Montagne, Taillevent, La Varenne, Grimod de la Reynière, to name but a few. In France, Western cookery attains the height of perfection. This achievement is due largely to France's fertile soil, varied terrain, moderate climate, abundant streams, hard-working farmers, high-quality vineyards, Cordon Bleu chefs and inspired teachers of cooking. The art of cooking evolves according to the demands made by the changes in taste which occur over the years. This taste is a result of the life-style of the age. Science has an ever-increasing part to play in the field of culinary art; but this art, which is the cornerstone of everyday life, has changed slowly over the years. The old recipes have proved their worth, but they have eventually been superseded by lighter, more streamlined and easily-prepared dishes which place less emphasis on elaborate presentation and more on wholesome ingredients. Our homes are comfortable and well-heated, cars have replaced coaches and horses and travel on foot, and our lives have become altogether more sedentary. All this means that we need a diet which is less rich and lower in calories.

The author of this book has succeeded in capturing the spirit of French cuisine, remaining faithful to old traditions, while incorporating the simplicity and high quality which we now regard as essential.

The book is presented clearly, avoiding technical terms and should be of use to anybody who understands the importance of a healthy, varied and enjoyable diet in the hectic age in which we live. To be a perfectionist is one way of improving the quality of life without necessarily increasing its cost. Those who consult this book will undoubtedly reap the rewards. Sitting down to a meal will become a relaxing experience, and eating will become a pleasure as well as a necessity. This cookbook, its recipes illustrated by photographs, shows you how the dishes you will want to try are going to look, and you will indeed want to try them, for successful cookery demands simple recipes which appeal to the heart as much as to the taste buds. Food which is lovingly prepared will give the best results, and you will make your table a popular venue for all your friends. As Dr. de Pomiane liked to repeat, "In order to succeed, more important than technique and intelligence, more important even than talent and artistry is love, a total commitment of heart and soul."

Roland Magne of Le Pactole
44 Blvd. St. Germain, Paris

SOUPS

The French can be proud
that those two things which can
distract us from our most pressing affairs
—*coquetterie* and *gourmandise*—
have both come to us from France.

CREAM OF ASPARAGUS SOUP
⚜ VELOUTE AUX POINTES D'ASPERGES

Serves 4

Time: *preparation 40 min.* • *cooking 25 min.*
Ingredients: *1 lb. (450 g) asparagus* • *2 cups (½ liter) milk* • *2 cups (½ liter) water* • *4 egg yolks* • *2 large potatoes cut in 3 or 4 pieces* • *4 tbsp. (55 g) softened butter cut into small pieces*

• Slice off the asparagus tips and set aside. • Wash and scrape the stems; slice. • Put into a large saucepan with the potatoes, milk and water. Bring to a boil, and simmer for about 25 min. or until the vegetables are cooked. • Put through a sieve or food mill; return to the saucepan and bring back to a boil. Lower the heat. • Add the asparagus tips and cook gently for a few minutes. • Meanwhile, in a large soup tureen beat the egg yolks and the butter together. This will thicken the soup and give it a creamy texture. • Let the vegetable mixture cool for 3-4 min. then very slowly pour it into the prepared egg yolks while beating with a whisk as fast as possible to avoid setting the eggs. • Serve at once.

CREAM OF SORREL SOUP
⚜ VELOUTE A L'OSEILLE

Serves 6

Time: *preparation 10 min.* • *cooking 30 min.*
Ingredients: *about 1 lb. (450 g) sorrel* • *3 medium-sized potatoes diced small* • *1 rounded tbsp* • *flour* • *8 cups (2 liters) water* • *1 sprig of chervil, chopped* • *3 tbsp (40 g) butter* • *1 egg yolk beaten* • *½ cup (1.2 dl) heavy cream* • *croutons*

• Set aside 4 or 5 leaves of sorrel. • Remove the stalk and the thickest ribs from the remaining leaves and cut the leaves into narrow slices. • Melt the butter in a large saucepan and put in the sorrel. • When it is sufficiently wilted, add the flour and stir well, making a roux. Cook for a few moments; then slowly add the water, stirring all the time, to make a smooth mixture. • Add the finely diced potatoes, and simmer for about 15 min. • When the potatoes are cooked, pass the soup through a sieve or food mill. • Add the remaining sorrel, chopped finely, and bring to a boil. • Remove from the heat and stir in the cream. Season to taste. • Slowly pour the soup onto the beaten egg, stirring rapidly all the time. • Serve with a side dish of croutons.

PUREE OF CHICKEN SOUP A LA REINE
❋ POTAGE A LA REINE

CREAM OF MUSHROOM SOUP
❋ POTAGE AUX CHAMPIGNONS

Serves 4

Time: *preparation 15 min. • cooking 10 min.*
Ingredients: *4 rounded tbsp. rice flour (or tapioca) • 4 egg yolks • 6 tbsp. cream • softened butter • 3 cups (¾ liter) chicken stock*

Serves 4

Time: *preparation 15 min. • cooking 50 min.*
Ingredients: *1 generous lb. (500 g) fresh mushrooms • 5 tbsp. (50 g) flour • 4 cups (1 liter) beef stock • ½ cup (1.2 dl) cream • 1 lemon • 1 shallot, finely chopped • 6 tbsp. (85 g) butter • salt, pepper*

• Moisten the rice flour (or tapioca) with a little milk and stir until smooth. • During this time heat the chicken stock and add a few spoonfuls to the flour mixture. • Pour the mixture into the rest of the stock, stirring well to avoid lumps. • Simmer over a low heat for 10 min. • Mix together the egg yolk, butter, and cream. • Slowly add the chicken stock to this mixture, stirring briskly all the time with a wooden spoon. • Serve immediately.

• Wash the mushrooms and dry thoroughly. Slice finely leaving on the stalks. Sprinkle with lemon juice to prevent blackening. • Cook the shallot gently in a saucepan with 2 tbsp. (30 g) butter. When the shallot has become transparent add the mushrooms. Season and cook over a low heat for 40 min. until all liquid has evaporated; take care not to let the mushrooms burn. • Meanwhile, melt the remaining butter in another saucepan; add the flour and stir with a wooden spoon to obtain a smooth roux. • Gradually add the stock and mix well. • Cook gently for 30 min. Pour over the mushrooms and simmer for 10 minutes more. • Put this mixture through a coarse sieve and pour into a soup-tureen. • Add the fresh cream. Check the seasoning and serve hot. • Croutons may be served separately if desired.

CAULIFLOWER SOUP
⚜ POTAGE DUBARRY

Serves 6

Time: *preparation 15 min.* • *cooking 20 min.*
Ingredients: *1 small cauiflower* • *7 tbsp. (100 g) butter* • *5 tbsp. (50 g) flour* • *1 cup (2.5 dl.) milk* • *2 egg yolks* • *½cup (1.2 dl) fresh cream* • *salt* • *croutons*

• Divide the cauliflower into flowerets and steam for 8-10 minutes. • Meanwhile, make a roux by heating 3 tbsp. (40g) of the butter until it begins to turn brown, adding the flour and stirring until smooth. • Gradually add 1½ quarts (1½ liters) and bring to boiling point. • Add the cauliflower and simmer over a low heat until cooked. • Purée the mixture in an electric blender or pass through a fine sieve. Add the milk to the pureé and return to the heat. • Beat the egg yolks with the cream. • Remove the purée from the heat as soon as it boils and add a few drops to the eggs and cream. Stir continously. Check the seasoning. Add the rest of the cauliflower pureé, continuing to stir. • Serve immediately with croutons fried in the remaining butter.

SPLIT PEA SOUP SAINT-GERMAIN
⚜ POTAGE SAINT-GERMAIN

Serves 6

Time: *preparation 5 min.* • *cooking 1½ hr.*
Ingredients: *1½ cups (300 g) split peas* • *1 onion stuck with 2 cloves* • *1 large carrot* • *7 tbsp.(100g) butter* • *small croutons* • *salt, pepper*

• Soak the split peas in a quart (1 liter) cold water for about 2 hours. • Chop the carrot coarsely. • Drain peas and refill pan with about 2 quarts (2 liters) fresh water. Add the carrot and the onion and bring to a boil. Skim. • Reduce the heat, cover the saucepan and simmer until all the water has evaporated (approximately 1½ hr.). • Rub through a fine sieve, adding a scant quart (1 liter) water until smooth; season. • Return to the heat; add half the butter piece by piece, stirring constantly. • Serve at once accompanied with croutons fried in the remaining butter.

FRENCH ONION SOUP
✳ GRATINEE AUX OIGNONS

Serves 6

Time: *preparation 20 min.* ● *cooking 20 min. + 10 min. for browning*
Ingredients: *6 medium-sized onions* ● *4 tbsp. (55 g) butter* ● *1 ⅔ cups (180 g) grated gruyère* ● *1 quart (1 liter) boiling water* ● *1 tbsp. flour* ● *12 slices French bread* ● *salt, butter, nutmeg*

● Slice the onions very finely. ● Melt the butter in a large saucepan without letting it brown and add the onions, stirring until they begin to turn transparent. Sprinkle with the flour and slowly pour the boiling water into the pan, stirring all the time. ● Add a little salt (remember, the cheese is salty), pepper and a pinch of grated nutmeg. ● Cook slowly for about 20 min. ● Toast the bread and put 2 slices into each individual soup tureen. Cover with some of the cheese. ● Fill up with the boiling soup. As soon as the bread rises to the top, sprinkle with the remainder of the cheese and put under the grill or into a hot oven to brown.

ONION SOUP WITH PORT WINE
✳ GRATINEE AU PORTO

Serves 4

Time: *preparation 30 min.* ● *cooking 25 min. + 10 min. for browning*
Ingredients: *4 medium-sized onions* ● *4 tbsp. (55 g) butter* ● *1 rounded cup (120 g) grated gruyère* ● *2 cups (½ liter) bouillon with the fat skimmed off* ● *8 slices toast* ● *1 egg yolk* ● *1 glass port wine* ● *salt, freshly ground black pepper, nutmeg*

● Slice the onions as finely as possible; cook gently until soft and slightly golden, in the butter. ● Add the water and bouillon, salt, pepper and a pinch of nutmeg. ● Boil quite briskly for 25 min. ● Meanwhile, line a flame-proof casserole with the toast from which the crusts have either been removed, or pounded soft. Sprinkle with two-thirds of the grated cheese. ● Pour the boiling bouillon and onions over the toast and sprinkle the rest of the cheese over the top. ● Place casserole in a hot oven until the surface is brown and crusty. ● Beat the egg yolk and port wine together with freshly ground black pepper. ● Just before serving, gently lift the edge of the cheese topping and slowly pour in the port and egg. Slip a spoon or fork beneath the crust and gently mix together. ● Serve at once.

● NB If you wish to serve more than 4 persons it is better to use 2 casseroles rather than 1 large one. The toast and gruyère can be arranged more evenly.

GRATINEE OF FISH SOUP WITH HERBS
✻ GRATINEE DE POISSONS AUX HERBES

FISHERMAN'S SOUP
✻ SOUPE DES PECHEURS

Serves 6

Time: *preparation 30 min.* • *cooking 20 min.* + *10 min for browning*
Ingredients: *1½ tb. (650 g) mixed fish (whiting, sole, haddock, carp)* • *1 quart (1 liter) mussels* • *1 quart (1 liter) white wine* • *1 cup (100 g) grated gruyère* • *12 small slices of bread with crusts removed* • *1 onion* • *parsley: chervil, chives, 2 or 3 stalks celery* • *1 bay leaf, 3 cloves* • *salt, white pepper*

Serves 6

Time: *preparation 30 min.* • *cooking 1¼ hr.*
Ingredients: *about 2 lb. (1 kg) various fishes (mullet, porgie, snapper, cod, sole, whiting, haddock, bass, plaice, etc.)* • *2 carrots* • *2 large tomatoes* • *2 onions* • *1 stalk celery* • *bouquet garni* • *2 cloves* • *2 cups (½ liter) dry white wine* • *3 tbsp. olive oil* • *4 tbsp. (55 g) butter* • *½ cup (60 g) grated gruyère* • *salt, pepper, saffron* • *croutons* • *½ - 1 quart (½ - 1 liter) shelled mussels (optional)*

• Wash and scrape the mussels carefully. • Place them in a large casserole with a small amount of water and steam them open over a high heat. • Remove from the shells and conserve their liquid by straining through cheesecloth or a fine sieve. • Chop the herbs and celery. • Peel the onion and insert the cloves; place in a large saucepan with the chopped herbs, the bay leaf, the liquid from the mussels, the white wine, a scant pint of water, salt and pepper, and bring to a boil. • Remove from heat and allow to cool. • Clean the fish and cut into pieces. • As soon as the court-bouillon has cooled, add the fish and bring to a boil once more. Simmer 15 min. • Remove the onion and the bay leaf, and add the mussels. Simmer gently for 15 min. then bring back to a boil. • Pour into individual soup bowls or tureens. • Place 2 slices of bread on each, sprinkle with gruyère and put under a grill or in a hot oven for a few minutes to brown.

• NB According to the season all types of fish may be used except oily fish like herring and mackarel, which will completely destroy the flavor of this delicate soup. Crayfish, prawns and lobster may also be added.

• Peel or scrape the vegetables and chop. • Clean the fish and cut in pieces. • Heat the oil and butter in a large pan; put in the vegetables and fish. Add the bouquet garni, cloves, wine, 1 quart (1 liter) of water, salt, pepper and saffron. • Cook for 1 hr., occasionally adding a little hot water to compensate for evaporation. Halfway through the cooking, add the mussels (if used). • When the soup is cooked, remove the mussels and pass the rest through a sieve or food mixer. • Pour into a serving dish with the mussels and croutons. • Serve the grated cheese separately.

• NB If desired the croutons can be rubbed with a clove of garlic.

MUSSEL SOUP
✻ POTAGE AUX MOULES

CRAYFISH BISQUE
✻ BISQUE D'ECREVISSES

Serves 6

Time: *preparation 20 min.* • *cooking 40 min.*
Ingredients: *2 quarts (2 liters) mussels* • *2 cups (5 dl) light cream* • *3 cups (¾ liter) dry white wine* • *1 generous lb. (500 g) small fish of different kinds (or mixed fish heads, bones, trimmings, etc.)* • *2 onions, chopped* • *parsley* • *salt, pepper*

Serves 6

Time: *preparation 1 hr.* • *cooking 30 min.*
Ingredients: *6 medium-sized carrots* • *2 onions* • *2 shallots* • *18 large crayfish* • *1¼ cups (3 dl) dry white wine* • *½ cup (1.2 dl) cognac* • *7 tbsp. (100 g) butter* • *½ cup (75 g) long grain rice (partly cooked for 7-10 min.)* • *bouquet garni* • *3 tbsp. tomato paste* • *¾ cup (2 dl) light cream* • *salt, pepper, cayenne* • *1 quart (1 liter) fumet, or stock, made from the following: 1 generous lb. (500 g) small fish* • *2 cups (½ liter) water* • *2 cups (½ liter) dry white wine* • *1 chopped onion* • *2 sprigs of parsley*

• First prepare the fish fumet (stock) in the following way: mix 2 cups (5 dl) of water with the same amount of white wine. Add the onions, 2 or 3 stalks of parsley, pepper, a little salt and the fish pieces. • Simmer for 25 min. • Meanwhile, thoroughly clean and scrape the mussels. • Cook in a little water over a high heat for 5-10 min. until the mussels open. Shell and put aside. • Pass their liquid and the stock through a fine sieve or the finest blades of a food processor. • Return to the heat, adding the cream while stirring constantly with a wooden spoon. Do not allow to boil. • Serve as soon as the soup is hot enough.

• First prepare the fumet using the fish, water, wine, the chopped onion and parsley. Simmer 25 min. • Meanwhile, chop the carrots, onions and shallots into small pieces and cook gently in the butter. • When soft, add the crayfish and sauté over a fairly high heat until they turn red. • Remove from the heat and allow to cool; then remove the flesh from the shells. Set aside. • Crush the remainder (claws, shells) and pass through a food processor and then through a fine sieve. • In a large casserole place a little butter, the bouquet garni, tomatoe paste, the white wine, the fish fumet, salt and pepper. Add the crayfish purée and the cognac. Bring to a boil and flame. • Put the rice into the saucepan and continue cooking for 15 min. Pass through a sieve or processor and mix with the cream and the crayfish meat which you have cut into cubes. Add a pinch of cayenne to taste. If not serving immediately, keep hot in a pan of hot water until wanted.

CRAB BISQUE
✣ BISQUE DE TOURTEAUX

SOUPE AU "PISTOU"

Serves 6

Time: *preparation 1 hr. • cooking 30 min.*
Ingredients: *3 large crabs, each about 1⅓ lb. (600 g) • 1 quart (1 liter) dry white wine • 9 tbsp. (130 g) butter • 5 tbsp. (50 g) flour • 2 egg yolks • 3 carrots • 3 onions • 1 stalk celery • thyme, 1 bay leaf, parsley, 1 clove garlic, pepper • 2 cloves • croutons*

Serves 6-8

Time: *preparation 40 min. • cooking 1 hr.*
Ingredients: *2 large potatoes • 3 carrots • 1 stalk celery • 3 leeks • 3 zucchini • 1 slice pumpkin or squash • 1 small lettuce • 2 onions • 1 generous lb. (500 g) canned navy beans • 3 large ripe tomatoes • 1 cup (125 g) little shells or similar pasta • 4 tbsp. chopped fresh basil (or 1 tbsp. dried basil) called "pistou" in Provençe • 6 cloves garlic • 1 wineglass olive oil • grated cheese (gruyère or parmesan)*

• To make the stock, melt 5 tbsp. (70 g) of the butter in a saucepan. • Add the onions studded with cloves and the carrots cut in rounds. • Cook slowly for 10 min. • Add 2 quarts (2 liters) of water and the white wine and cook for 20 min. • Scrub the crabs and place them in the stock. Simmer for 15 min. Drain them, without throwing away the cooking juices, and rinse them under cold water. • Remove the back, discard the gills, take out the spongy parts under the shell and pick out the solid meat. • Crack the claws and remove the meat, keeping some back to add to the soup before serving. • Crush all the remaining flesh in a mortar until it forms a pulp. Melt the rest of the butter in a saucepan; add the flour and stir with a wooden spoon until the mixture begins to turn golden. • Strain the stock (there should be about 1½ quarts (1½ liters) and add a little at a time to the butter. Allow the mixture to thicken, stirring continuously. • Force the pulped crab through a sieve using a pestle or put it through a food processor. Add to the soup. • Then add the crabmeat which had been kept back along with the chopped parsley. • Put the egg yolks into a bowl and beat with 2 or 3 tbsp. of the soup. Add to the rest of the soup and season with pepper. • Serve with croutons.

• Wash the vegetables; chop finely. • Peel the tomatoes but leave them whole. • Put 2 quarts (2 liters) cold water into a large saucepan; add salt and put in all the vegetables except the green beans and the tomatoes. • Simmer for 30 min. • Add the green beans and the tomatoes and simmer gently. • When the vegetables are almost cooked, add the pasta and cook until done. • Meanwhile, peel the garlic and crush in a mortar. • Chop the basil finely and add to the garlic. Pound to a smooth paste. • Very slowly add the olive oil in the same way as you would for mayonnaise. • Take the tomatoes from the soup; remove the seeds and crush the tomatoes thoroughly before putting them back. Put the "pistou" sauce in a tureen and slowly add the soup, stirring with a wooden spoon. • Serve the grated cheese separately as a garnish.

CHERRY SOUP
✳ SOUPE AUX CERISES

Serves 4

Time: *preparation 15 min.* ● *cooking 10 min.*
Ingredients: *1 generous lb.(500g) fresh or bottled cherries* ● *2 cups (½ liter) good red wine* ● *4 tbsp. (55 g) sugar (use no sugar with bottled cherries)* ● *1 piece of lemon peel* ● *1 cinnamon stick*

● Pit the cherries; crush the pits and boil in the wine for 10 min. ● Cook the fruit in 2 cups (½ liter) water with the sugar, the cinnamon and the lemon peel for 10 min. (If using preserved cherries cook them in their own juice with the cinnamon and lemon peel, but with neither water nor sugar.) ● Put the cherries into a bowl and pour the strained wine over the fruit. Serve hot with dry sweet cookies.
NB This ''soup'' is obviously a dessert but can be served as an after-theatre snack or aprés-ski or whenever a light, hot dish would be appropriate.

HORS-D'OEUVRES AND ENTREES

Good cooking is the true basis of happiness.

Escoffier

STUFFED AVOCADOES
❊ AVOCATS FARCIS

Serves 6

Time: *preparation 30 min.*
Ingredients: *3 large avocadoes (or 6 small ones) • 1 can crabmeat (14 oz.; 400 g) • 3-4 oz. (100 g) small mushrooms • 1 lemon • 1 tsp. Grand-Marnier • black olives • 1 recipe mayonnaise (recipe no. 281) • salt, pepper • olive oil • whole shrimps for garnish*

• Clean the mushrooms and slice thinly. Set aside in a marinade of lemon juice, 1 tbsp. olive oil, salt and freshly ground black pepper. • Make the mayonnaise and mix 1 tsp. Grand-Marnier into it. • Halve the avocadoes, remove the pits and scoop out the flesh without breaking the skins. Set aside but place an avocado pit in the dish, as this helps to prevent the flesh from turning black. • Drain the mushrooms and mix with the crabmeat; bind together with the mayonnaise. Fill the avocado skins with this mixture. • Mash the flesh of the avocadoes with a fork and mix with the marinade in which the mushrooms were soaked until you have obtained a smooth cream. Season with salt and pepper and pour over the stuffed avocadoes. • Garnish with black olives and shrimps. Keep in the refrigerator until serving time.
• N.B. It is better to prepare avocadoes at the last minute because of discoloration.

STUFFED TOMATOES " TAPENADE"
❊ TOMATES FARCIES A LA "TAPENADE"

Serves 6

Time: *preparation 30 min.*
Ingredients: *6 large tomatoes • 1 10 oz. (300 g) can tuna • 3½ oz. (100 g) anchovy fillets in oil • 7 oz. (200 g) black olives • 2 tbsp. (50 g) capers • 1 clove garlic • 2 tbsp. cognac • 3 eggs. • 1 cup (¼ liter) olive oil • 2 tbsp. vinaigrette (recipe no. 290)*

• Wash and dry the tomatoes; slice a little cap off the top of each and set aside. Scoop out the insides of the tomatoes with a small spoon (do not break the skins) and reserve the flesh on absorbent paper. • Hard-boil the eggs. • Pit the olives. • Purée together the olives, anchovies, capers and the peeled clove of garlic. • Add the olive oil drop by drop to this purée, stirring constantly with a wooden spoon, as though for a mayonnaise. Add the cognac. • Drain the tuna and crumble the flesh; mix it into this mixture. • Cover a serving dish with lettuce leaves and place the tomatoes among them. Put a little vinaigrette sauce into each tomato and then fill them with the tuna stuffing. Replace the little tomato caps. • Garnish with the halved hard-boiled eggs. • Keep in the refrigerator until just before serving.

HAM CORNETS WITH CARROTS
✹ CORNETS ROSES AUX CAROTTES

Serves 6

Time: *preparation 20 min.*
Ingredients: *6 thin slices lean ham • 6 carrots • about 2 tbsp. (50 g) dried currants • 1 cup (¼ liter mayonnaise(recipe no 281) • 1 lettuce*

• Clean the carrots and grate finely. • Wash and dry the lettuce. • Make the mayonnaise. • Mix together the grated carrots and currants in the mayonnaise. • Roll the slices of ham into cornets and hold together with wooden cocktail sticks or toothpicks; fill with the mayonnaise mixture. • Place the lettuce on a serving dish and arrange the cornets in a circle, the pointed ends towards the center. • Thin slices of carrots can be used as a garnish.

CREAM CHEESE "ESTIVAL"
✹ FROMAGE BLANC ESTIVAL

Serves 6

Time: *preparation 25 min.*
Ingredients: *1 generous lb. (500 g) cream cheese • 1 bunch radishes • 4-6 tbsp. (100 g) capers • 2 tomatoes • 1 small cucumber • black and green olives • salt, pepper • chives*

• Season with salt, pepper and chopped chives. • Cut the radishes and cucumber into thin slices and mix into the cheese. Add the capers and put the mixture into small ramekins. Put into the refrigerator until serving time. • Decorate the ramekins with small pieces of tomato, radish, olives and capers and a few chopped chives.

CHICKEN IN ASPIC
✲ CHAUD-FROID DE POULET EN GELEE

CROWN OF RABBIT
✲ COURONNE DE LAPIN

Serves 6

Time: *preparation 30 min.* • *cooking 2 hr.*
Ingredients: *1 chicken, approximately 3 lb. (1.5 kg)* • *1 egg yolk* • *½ cup (1.2 dl) cream* • *1 chicken bouillon cube* • *5 tbsp. (50 g) flour* • *4 tbsp. (55 g) butter* • *2 packets unflavored gelatine* • *bouquet garni* • *1 onion* • *2 cloves* • *tarragon* • *salt, pepper*

Serves 4

Time: *preparation 25 min. + chilling* • *cooking 1 hr.*
Ingredients: *1 rabbit, approximately 2-2½ lb. (1 kg)* • *1 packet unflavored gelatine* • *1 ⅔ lb. (750 g) baby carrots* • *about ½ lb. (250 g) small onions* • *1 cup (¼ liter) dry white wine* • *4 tbsp. (55 g) butter* • *chervil* • *gherkins* • *salt, pepper*

• Dissolve the chicken bouillon cube in 1 quart (1 liter water. • Put the chicken in the bouillon; add a little water if necessary so that it is almost covered. Add the bouquet garni, the onion stuck with the 2 cloves, some sprigs of tarragon and salt and pepper. • Cover and simmer for 1½ hr. • Remove the chicken from the bouillon; divide it into portions and remove as many bones as possible (they should lift out easily, but it is not essential to take them all out). Reserve the bouillon. • Melt the butter in a saucepan; stir in the flour and add a little bouillon to make a thick sauce. Cook, stirring constantly, for 10 min. • Away from the heat add the cream and the lightly beaten egg yolk. • Check the seasoning. • When the sauce is cool put each piece of chicken into it, turning them so that they are well covered. • Arrange the pieces on a serving dish and decorate with sprigs of tarragon. • Melt the gelatine in the reserved bouillon. Pour a little over the cold chicken and put into the refrigerator, to gel along with the remainder of the aspic in a bowl. • Just before serving cut up the aspic into small pieces and scatter over the chicken.

• NB This dish can be prepared several hours in advance, or even the previous day.

• Cut the rabbit into pieces and brown in a skillet in the butter. • Add salt, pepper, the little carrots, onions and white wine. • Cover and simmer gently over a low heat for 1 hr. Then allow to cool. • Meanwhile, prepare the gelatine. Rinse a ring mold in cold water; do not dry. Pour in about ½ in. (1 cm) gelatine and chill. • Allow the remaining gelatine to thicken but not set. • When the gelatine in the mold is set and the rabbit is cold, place the rabbit in the mold, alternating the pieces with layers of chervil, gherkins, carrots and gelatine. Finish with a layer of gelatine. • Put into the refrigerator until ready to serve. • Unmold either by dipping the mold for less than a second into a bowl of very hot water or by wrapping the mold with a towel soaked in hot water and wrung out, reversing it onto a plate and giving it a sharp jerk.

• NB This dish is more conveniently prepared the day before.

FISH "BREAD"
✽ PAIN DE POISSON

TUNA WITH GRIBICHE SAUCE
✽ THON GRIBICHE

Serves 6

Time: *preparation 20 min. • cooking 50 min.*
Ingredients: *1 generous lb. (500 g) whiting • 1 generous lb. (500 g) rainbow trout • 4 eggs • 5 oz. (150 g) stale bread • 1 glass milk • 1 onion • 2 tbsp. tomato paste • salt, pepper • 1 recipe mayonnaise (recipe no. 281) • 1 bouillon cube*

Serves 6

Time: *preparation 20 min. • cooking 20 min.*
Ingredients: *approximately 1 lb. (400 g) canned tuna • 1 scant lb. (400 g) potatoes • 3 eggs • 5 oz. (150 g) mushrooms • 1 cooked beetroot • 1 cup (1.2 dl) vinaigrette (recipe no. 290) • 1 lemon • parsley, terragon, gherkins*

• Simmer the fish for approx 10 min. in the bouillon. • Soak the bread in the milk; remove and press hard to remove all excess liquid. • Flake the fish as finely as possible and mix thoroughly with the bread. • Beat the eggs in a bowl with the salt, pepper and tomato paste. • Mix in with the fish mixture and add the finely chopped onion. Check the seasoning, then put the mixture in a buttered mold or cake tin, pressing it down firmly. • Place in a pan of hot water and bake for approximately 40 min. in a 375°F oven (190°C; 5). • When it is cold unmold the "bread" onto a serving plate. Keep in the refrigerator until serving time. • Decorate with a thick mayonnaise.

• Boil the potatoes in their skins. • Hard-boil the eggs. • Open and drain the can of tuna and break up the fish into fairly large pieces. • Clean the mushrooms and slice them thinly; sprinkle with lemon juice so that they do not turn black. • Peel and dice the beetroot. • As soon as the potatoes and the eggs are cooked, drain and put under running cold water. Shell the eggs. Peel the potatoes and slice. • Put all the ingredients (except for a few slices of egg) into a salad bowl, and over all pour the vinaigrette sauce • Decorate with slices of hard-boiled egg and sliced gherkins. Sprinkle with chopped parsley and tarragon. • Keep in the refrigerator until serving time.

TROUT IN ASPIC
❋ TRUITES EN GELEE

SEAFOOD COCKTAIL
❋ COCKTAIL DE POISSONS

Serves 4

Time: *preparation 25 min. + chilling • cooking 10 min.*
Ingredients: *4 small trout • 1 bouillon cube • 1 packet unflavored gelatine • a few stalks of parsley • 1 tomato • 1 lemon • truffle peelings (optional) • a few cooked shrimps (optional)*

Serves 4

Ingredients: *3 ½-4 oz. (100 g) each of two different white fish (burbot, cod, hake, halibut, pollack, whiting, etc.) • 2 fillets sole or other flat fish • 1 cup (¼ liter) mayonnaise • 2 oz. (55 g) cooked shrimps • shrimps for garnish • 1 bouillon cube*

• Slit open, empty and clean the trout carefully, without damaging the skin. • Put into a pan of bouillon; as soon as the water begins to simmer lower the heat and cook the fish very gently for 5 min. only. Leave to cool in the bouillon, then lift out carefully and place on absorbent paper to drain. • Make the aspic with the gelatine and some of the bouillon in which the trout has cooked. • Take the skins off the fish, but leave the heads and tails intact. • Lay the fish side by side on the serving plate and cover with a little of the gelatine. Put the remainder of the aspic in a cool place to gel. • Garnish the fish with stems of parsley, and (if you have them) truffle parings. Set aside in the refrigerator. • Just before serving, surround the dish with alternate slices of tomato and lemon and little clusters of shrimps. Dice the remainder of the aspic and scatter over the dish.
• NB Prepare this dish several hours in advance or even the day before.

• Dissolve the bouillon cube and poach the fish for approximately 10 min. • Leave covered to cool in the liquid. • Meanwhile, make the mayonnaise (recipe no. 281) • Remove the fish from the bouillon and set aside until completely cold, then cut into bite-size pieces and mix very carefully (so as not to crumble the flesh) into the mayonnaise along with the cooked shrimps. • Divide into individual dishes and garnish with the remaining shrimps. • Keep refrigerated until serving time.

DUCK LIVER MOUSSE IN ASPIC
✻ ASPIC DE MOUSSE DE FOIE DE CANARD

EGGS MIMOSA
✻ OEUFS MIMOSA

Serves 6

Time: *preparation 30 min. + refrigeration • cooking 5 min.*
Ingredients: *10 oz. (300 g) duck liver • 10 tbsp. (150 g) butter • 1 cup (2.5 dl) heavy cream • 1 small can truffle parings • 1 packet unflavored gelatine (or Madeira-flavored, if obtainable) • 1 tomato • 1 green pepper • black olives • fresh tarragon • salt, black pepper*

• Rinse individual jelly molds in cold water; do not dry. • Make up the gelatine (add a little Madeira or sherry to the water if using unflavored gelatine) When it has become tepid, pour a little into the bottom of each mould. Put in the refrigerator to set. Reserve the rest of the gelatine. • Cook the duck liver in butter; allow to cool. • Chop some of the truffle parings very finely. • Mash the livers in a mortar with the butter, and the chopped truffles. Season, using a lot of freshly grated black pepper. Add the cream and work the mixture to a thick, smooth paste or mousse. • Decorate the base of the molds with leaves of tarragon, a morsel of truffle and a small piece of tomato. • Fill each mold with the liver mousse; smooth the top with a spatula and cover with another thin layer of aspic. Leave in the refrigerator for several hours. • To serve, unmold the jellies onto a large dish covered with lettuce leaves and garnish with thin slices of tomato and green pepper. • Add the pitted olives and the remainder of the aspic cut into small cubes.

Serves 6

Time: *preparation 30 min. • cooking 10-15 min.*
Ingredients: *1 cup (¼ liter) mayonnaise • 6 eggs • 3 tbsp. fresh mixed herbs • 2 tomatoes • 1 fresh lettuce • salt, pepper*

• Hard-boil the eggs. • Make a thick mayonnaise (recipe no. 281). • Slice the tomatoes into rounds and sprinkle lightly with salt. • Wash the lettuce, reserving the best leaves. When the eggs are hard, place them under running cold water; remove the shells and slice in two lengthwise. • Scoop out the yolks and set 2 aside. Mash the other 4 with a fork, mixing in the mayonnaise and chopped fresh herbs (chives, tarragon, basil etc) until you have obtained a smooth cream. • Fill the whites with this mixture. • Cover the serving dish with the lettuce leaves; place the slices of tomatoes on top and put a filled egg white on each slice. • Put the reserved egg yolks through a coarse food mixer and sprinkle over the stuffed eggs (this resembles mimosa flowers). • Keep in a cool place until time to serve.

CHICKEN LIVER PATE
✻ TERRINE DE FOIES DE VOLAILLES

SAUSAGES SAINT-RESTITUT
✻ CAILLETTES DE SAINT-RESTITUT

Serves 6

Time: *preparation 30 min. + 24 hr. refrigeration • cooking 10 min.*
Ingredients: *2¼ lb. (1 kg) chicken livers • 1 scant cup (2 dl) port wine • 1¼ cup (3 dl) heavy cream • 4 tbsp. (55 g) butter • salt, freshly ground black pepper*

Serves 6

Time: *preparation 1 hr. • cooking 1 hr.*
Ingredients: *6 pigs cauls (at least 6 in.; 15 cm) • 1¼ lb. (600 g) lean pork • ½ lb. (225 g) bacon • 2 lb. (1 kg) spinach • 1 tbsp. lard • thyme, parsley, rosemary, sage, marjoram, salt, freshly ground black pepper*

• Remove all the fibers from the livers before putting them to marinate in the port wine for at least 2 hr. • Melt the butter in the largest frying pan available. Before it changes color empty the livers and port into it all together. Cook over a fairly high heat for 8-10 min., stirring frequently. • Remove from the heat and set aside a few whole livers. • When the rest of the mixture has cooled, purée in a food processor or pass through a sieve. • Beat the cream (which should be very cold) until it begins to form peaks. Mix gently into the puréed livers and season. • Put half this pate into a buttered terrine. Press it down firmly and lay the whole livers down the center in a row. Cover with the rest of the pâté. • Cover the terrine with a plate and put a weight (cans of food, or the iron) on top. Chill in the refrigerator for 24 hr before serving.

• Soak the pigs' cauls in cold water for 1 hr. • Meanwhile, thoroughly clean the spinach, removing the hard stalks. Cook for 8-10 min. in boiling, salted water. Drain well, removing all excess liquid. • chop the spinach finely with the lean pork, the bacon and the herbs and mix well. Season. • Drain the cauls and pat dry. • Divide the pork and spinach stuffing into 6 portions and stuff the cauls. Tie with thin white string or strong thread, making little packets. • Place in a baking dish which has been generously smeared with lard. • Cook in a moderate oven (375°F; 190°C; 5) for approx 1 hr. Allow to cool and serve as a pâté.

• NB This dish may also be served hot with a purée of fresh tomatoes.

RABBIT TERRINE "A LA SOLOGNOTE"
✳ TERRINE DE LAPIN "A LA SOLOGNOTE"

RABBIT RILLETTES
✳ RILLETTES DE LAPIN

Serves 6-8

Time: *preparation 1 hr + 24 hr. marinating ● cooking 2 hr*
Ingredients: *1 large rabbit ● ½ lb. (225 g) fat salt pork ● 6 oz. (200 g) lean pork ● 6 oz. (200 g) veal ● some wide strips of fat pork ● ½ calf's foot ● 1 egg ● 1⅓ cups (⅓ liter) dry white wine ● 1 liqueur glass cognac ● 1 tbsp. olive oil ● 2 onions ● 2 cloves garlic ● 2 carrots ● 2 cloves ● black peppercorns ● freshly ground black pepper ● thyme, parsley, 1 bay leaf*

● Make a marinade with the wine, oil, cognac, some peppercorns, the herbs, 1 carrot, 1 onion and 1 minced clove garlic. ● Remove the bones from the rabbit and slice the flesh of the back and haunches into long fillets. Put these with the remaining meat into the marinade and leave for 24 hr. turning occasionally so that all the pieces are impregnated. ● Put the bones, ½ calf's foot, a carrot, an onion, a clove garlic, peppercorns and herbs in a very little water and cook for a long time as slowly as possible (use an asbestos mat under the pan if necessary). Finally, reduce the liquid until only 1 cup remains. ● Drain the rabbit and set the fillets aside. Mince the remaining meat with the liver, veal, lean pork and fat salt pork. Season and bind together with the beaten egg and a little of the marinade. ● Line a terrine with flattened strips of fat pork and fill with alternating layers of the minced meat and the fillets, ending with the mince and covering the top with more strips of pork. Put the terrine into a pan of hot water. ● Cook for 2 hr. at 325°F (160°C; **2**) ● After 1 hr. add the cup of stock left from cooking the bones. ● Keep in a cool place.
● NB Terrines of this kind are usually made several days in advance and taste better after 2 or 3 days.

Makes 2-4 pots

Time: *preparation 25 min. + 12 hr. refrigeration ● cooking 3-4 hr.*
Ingredients: *1 rabbit, 3½-4 lb. (1.5-2 kg.) ● 1 generous lb. (500 g) lard ● 2 onions ● 2 sticks celery ● bouquet garni ● salt, nutmeg, mixed spices*

● Disjoint the rabbit and place in a saucepan with the bouquet garni, onions and celery, a pinch of nutmeg, ½ tsp. mixed spice and a little salt (pepper can be used in rillettes, if desired, but the taste can be obtrusive). ● Cover with water and bring to the boil. Immediately reduce the heat and simmer gently for 3-4 hr. until the flesh leaves the bones. The length of time depends on the rabbit's age. ● Drain through a sieve; keep the stock. Remove all the bones (some are very small) and put the meat in a terrine with a glassful of the cooking liquid and 14 oz. (400 g) melted lard which is still warm ● Put this preparation through a food processor and then pound it with a pestle or a wooden spoon until you have obtained a smooth, homogeneous paste. ● Check the seasoning and leave to cool. ● Put the mixture into little pots, pressing it down firmly and leave it in the refrigerator for 12 hr. ● Melt the remaining lard and pour it over the rillettes. When set, cover the pots tightly. ● Rillettes will keep for several days and can be served as an hors-d' oeuvres.

TOMATO MOUSSE
✳ MOUSSE FROIDE DE TOMATES

Serves 8

Time: *preparation 30 min. + 3 hr. refrigeration • cooking 30 min.*
Ingredients: *1 generous lb. (500 g) tomato pulp • 7tbsp. (100 g) butter • 4 tbsp. (40 g) flour • ½ cup (1.2 dl) milk • 1¼ tbsp. powdered gelatine • ¼ cup (.6 dl) heavy cream • salt, pepper, cayenne • juice of 1 lemon*

• Chop the tomato pulp into large pieces and cook gently in half the butter. • Make a Béchamel sauce (recipe no 272). • Dissolve the gelatine in a little cold water, then add the tepid Béchamel sauce; mix well. • Add the cooked tomatoes (which should be quite dry) to the sauce and stir briskly. • Beat the cream until it forms soft peaks (do not overbeat it, or it will turn grainy) and stir it into the tomato mixture. Add salt, pepper, a pinch of cayenne and several drops of lemon juice to taste. • Rinse a mold in cold water, but do not dry. Pour into it the tomato mousse. • Leave in the refrigerator for at least 3 hr. • At serving time unmold into a dish garnished with leaves of lettuce or water cress or the salad greens of your choice.

SALMON PATE WITH HERBS
✳ TERRINE DE SAUMON AUX FINES HERBES

Serves 6

Time: *preparation 30 min. • cooking 30 min.*
Ingredients: *1 salmon, approximately 3½ lb. (1.5 kg) • 2 packets gelatine • 1 bouillon cube • 1 bunch each parsley, chervil, tarragon, chives, water cress • 1 recipe mayonnaise (recipe no. 281)*

• Dissolve the bouillon cube in water and place the salmon in it. • Bring to the boil, but as soon as the water starts to simmer, lower the heat and poach the fish as gently as possible for 30 min. • Meanwhile, wash the herbs and put half of them aside. • Blanch the rest in boiling water for 2 min. only, drain and put under running cold water. Press out all the excess liquid in a tea towel. • When the salmon is cooked and cold, strip it from its bones and put it in a terrine, alternating layers of fish with layers of the uncooked herbs. • Dissolve the gelatin in sufficient water to just cover the salmon. Put the terrine in the refrigerator for several hours (preferably overnight). • Put the well-drained cooked herbs through the finest blade in the food processor. • Make a mayonnaise to which you add, at the last moment, the puréed herbs. Serve separately in a bowl with the salmon.
• NB The salmon may be served in the terrine, or unmoulded onto a dish of lettuce.

SWEETBREADS WITH ASPARAGUS
✳ RIS DE VEAU AUX ASPERGES

COLD ROAST LOTTE WITH HERBS
✳ ROTI DE LOTTE FROID AUX FINES HERBES

Serves 4

Time: *preparation 30 min.* • *cooking 20 min.*
Ingredients: *1 veal sweetbread, approximately 1½ lb. (700 g)* • *2¼ lb. (1 kg) asparagus* • *salad greens in season* • *1 small can truffle parings* • *olive oil, vinegar, salt, pepper* • *4 tbsp. (55 g) butter*

Serves 10

Time: *preparation 25 min.* • *cooking 15 min.*
Ingredients: *1 piece of lotte (burbot or eelpout), weighing about 7 lb. (3 kg) taken from the center of the fish* • *2 heaping tbsp. paprika* • *1 glass peanut oil* • *2 bouillon cubes* • *3 hard-boiled eggs* • *2 tbsp. chopped parsley* • *2 tbsp. chopped mixed herbs* • *olive oil, cider vinegar, mustard, salt, pepper for the vinaigrette*

• Clean the sweetbread by soaking in cold acidulated water for at least 2 hr. • Wash and scrape the asparagus; tie in a bunch and cook, standing upright with the tips uncovered, in boiling salted water for 15 min. • Meanwhile, wash the salad greens and make a vinaigrette (recipe no. 290). • When the asparagus is cooked, drain carefully and reserve the tips. • Drain and dry the sweet-bread and cut into thin slices. Cook the slices gently in the butter until they turn golden (approximately 12 min.). Season. • Divide the salad greens among 4 individual bowls; sprinkle with vinai-grette and place the asparagus tips on top. • Put the little slices of sweetbread on the asparagus and sprinkle with the truffle parings.

• Carefully take out the large bone from the middle of the fish. Remove all the gummy parts and rinse well under cold, running water. • Tie the fish up like a roast, after having carefully reshaped it. • Dissolve the bouillon cubes and plunge the fish into the boiling liquid; lower the heat at once and leave to cook with the water barely simmering for 15 min. • Cool, uncovered, in the bouillon. • Meanwhile, make a vinaigrette (recipe no. 290) and mix it well; add the finely chopped hard-boiled eggs, the parsley and the mixed herbs. • When the fish is cold, drain it on absorbent paper. • Mix the peanut oil and the paprika together in a deep bowl. Turn the fish around several times in this mixture until it is com-pletely covered. • Serve on a plate garnished with lettuce. Serve the vinaigrette-egg sauce separately.

SCALLOPS ST JACQUES
✣ COQUILLES SAINT-JACQUES

QUICHE LORRAINE

Serves 4

Time: *preparation 40 min.* • *cooking 30 min.*
Ingredients: *8 large scallops* • *5 oz. (150 g) mushrooms* • *7 tbsp. (100 g) butter* • *1 bouillon cube* • *3 tbsp. heavy cream* • *½ cup (55g) grated gruyère* • *1 clove garlic* • *1 shallot* • *flour* • *salt, pepper* • *breadcrumbs*

Serves 6

Time: *preparation 15 min.* • *cooking 35 min.*
Ingredients: *about 1 lb. (500 g) pie dough* • *1¼ cups (3 dl) light cream* • *3 oz. (85 g) unsmoked bacon* • *3 oz. (85 g) cooked ham* • *5 eggs*

• Dissolve the bouillon cube and poach the scallops and their corals, if available, in the liquid for 3-5 min. • Drain carefully and reserve the bouillon. • Wash and dry the mushrooms; chop and cook in half the butter. • Chop the scallops with a clove of garlic and a shallot. Mix with the mushrooms. • Melt the remaining butter and stir in the flour; add some of the reserved bouillon and stir with a wooden spoon until the sauce is smooth and thick. Add the cream and seasoning. • Put the mushroom mixture into the sauce and mix carefully; put into the scallop shells. • Sprinkle with gruyère and breadcrumbs and dot with morsels of butter. • Brown in a moderate oven for 15 min.

• Make the pastry at least 1 hr. in advance (recipe no. 252). • Beat 3 whole eggs and 2 yolks in a bowl; add a very little amount of salt and stir in the cream. • Roll out the pastry and line a 102' buttered pie pan with it, leaving approx ½ in (1 cm) pastry beyond the edge of the tin. • Prick all over with a fork. • Dice the bacon and the ham, and sprinkle over the pastry; pour the cream and egg mixture into the pie shell. • Place in a preheated oven: (375°F; 190°C; **4**) for approximately 30 min. • The surface of the quiche should be golden. If longer cooking is necessary and the top begins to burn, cover immediately with a piece of aluminum foil. • Serve straight from the oven.

MONT D'OR QUICHE
⚜ QUICHE DU MONT D'OR

Serve 4

Time: *preparation 15 min.* • *cooking 40 min.*
Ingredients: *10 oz. (300 g) pie dough* • *5 eggs* • *5/8 cup (1.6 dl) light cream* • *3½ oz. (100 g) roquefort* • *pepper*

• Prepare the pie dough at least 1 hr. in advance (recipe no. 252). • Hard boil 2 eggs; put under cold running water and shell. Slice into rounds. • Beat the remaining eggs and stir in the crumbled roquefort and the cream. Add a little pepper. • Line a buttered and lightly floured pie pan with the pastry. • Arrange the slices of boiled egg on the bottom and cover with the beaten egg mixture (be careful not to displace the sliced eggs) . • Put into a preheated oven (425°F; 220°C; **6-7**) for 30 min. If the top starts to burn cover with a piece of aluminum foil. • Serve straight from the oven; the quiche should be golden and puffed up.

CHEESE PUFFS
⚜ GOUGERE

Serves 6

Time: *preparation 30 min.* • *cooking 45 min.*
Ingredients: *3 eggs* • *1 ¼ cups (150 g) flour* • *7 tbsp. (100 g) butter* • *1 ⅓ cups (150 g) grated gruyère* • *salt, pepper*

• Put the butter in the top of a double boiler with ¾ cup (2 dl) water, salt and a large pinch of pepper. • Put over hot water on the top of the stove, and as soon as the mixture starts to boil, remove from the heat and add the flour • Stir with a wooden spoon until the mixture is thick and free from lumps. Cook over low heat, stirring all the time until the mixture comes away from the sides of the pan. • Leave to cool for a few minutes, then add the eggs, one at a time, beating hard. It is important to work the mixture well at this stage to accumulate enough air to make it as light as possible. • Add ½ the grated cheese to the paste; check the seasoning. • Using a tablespoon, place balls of the pastry in a circle on a buttered baking sheet, forming a kind of embossed crown. • Sprinkle the remaining cheese on the gougère and press lightly onto the surface of the paste. • Bake for approximately ¾ hr. in a moderate oven (350° F; 180° C; **4**).

MEAT PIE
✳ TOURTE

MEAT LOAF PARMENTIER
✳ HACHIS PARMENTIER

Serves 6-8

Time: *preparation 20 min. + 2 hr. marinating • cooking 1½ hr.*
Ingredients: *1 generous lb. (500 g) pie dough • 1 generous lb. (500 g) puff pastry • about ½ lb. (250 g) each of trimmed veal, boned loin of pork, bacon and cooked lean ham • 2 tbsp. olive oil • 1 egg • salt, pepper, nutmeg, thyme, parsley, 1 bay leaf*

Serves 6

Time: *preparation 20 min. • cooking 30 min.*
Ingredients: *14 oz. (400 g) cooked beef • 3 oz. (100 g) ham scraps • 1½ oz. (50 g) fat bacon • 3 shallots • 7 tbsp. (100 g) butter • 1 glass bouillon • 1½ cups (200 g) pureed potatoes • scant ½ cup grated gruyère • salt, pepper, nutmeg*

• Chop the meat, except the ham, into pieces ready to be minced. • Put all the pieces to marinate in a large dish with the oil, herbs and seasonings for at least 2 hr. • Meanwhile, prepare the pastry (recipes no. 252 and no. 253) or use frozen pastry. • Line a buttered pie plate with the pie dough letting the pastry overlap the edge by ½ in. (1 cm). Fill the pastry shell with the minced meat. • Roll out the puff pastry to a thickness of ¼ in. (½ cm), and cover the meat; moisten the edges of the pastry so that they will stick together. • Make a small hole in the center and insert a little funnel of rolled up grease-proof paper. • Brush the surface of the puff pastry with beaten egg and bake for 1½ hr. at 400 F (200 C; 5·6). Cover with aluminum foil if the top starts to burn.

• Grind or mince finely the meat, bacon, ham scraps and shallots. Mix well and season. • Moisten with the bouillon. • Mix the pureed potatoes with 6 tbsp. (80 g) melted butter. • Butter an oven-proof dish and spread the ground meat evenly over the bottom; cover with the pureed potatoes and sprinkle with the grated cheese. • Place in a preheated oven (400°F; 200°C; 6) for approximately 30 min. when the top should be golden brown. • Serve straight from the oven.

PICARDY LEEK PIE
❋ FLAMICHE PICARDE

Serves 6

Time: *preparation 35 min.* • *cooking 45 min.*
Ingredients: *1 generous lb. (500 g) puff pastry* • *1 ¾ lb. (800 g) leeks (white part only)* • *3 eggs* • *⅔ cup (1.6 dl) cream* • *salt, pepper, nutmeg* • *7 tbsp. (100 g) butter*

• Prepare the puff pastry (recipe no 253) or use the frozen variety. • Thoroughly clean the leeks; cut into 1-1½ in. (2-3 cm) slices. Throw into boiling salted water; boil for 5-6 min. • Drain on absorbent paper, then put into a saucepan with the melted butter and simmer for approximately 10 min. with salt, pepper and a pinch nutmeg. • Divide the pastry into two slightly unequal parts; roll out the larger and line a buttered pie pan. • Beat 2 egg yolks with the cream; add the leeks; check the seasoning and pour into the pastry shell. • Roll out the 2nd portion of pastry and place on top of the pie tin. Press the edges of the pastry together, moistening them with water to make them stick. • Beat the remaining egg and brush the surface of the pastry with it. • Place in a preheated hot oven (400°F; 200°C; 6) • Place in a preheated hot oven for approx ½ hr. • Serve straight from the oven.

CHEESE SOUFFLE
❋ SOUFFLE AU FROMAGE

Serves 6

Time: *preparation 15 min.* • *cooking 35-40 min.*
Ingredients: *2 cups (½ liter) milk* • *7 tbsp. (100 g) butter* • *1 scant cup (100 g) plain flour* • *1⅓ cups (150 g) grated gruyère* • *8 eggs* • *salt, pepper, nutmeg*

• Heat the milk until tepid with ¼ tsp. salt and a sprinkling of pepper. • Melt the butter in a saucepan without letting it change color; add the flour, stirring all the time with a wooden spoon. • Add the milk gradually, stirring until the mixture thickens and is free from lumps. When it reaches the boiling point, remove at once from the heat; add a pinch nutmeg and the grated cheese. Mix thoroughly and set aside to cool. • Add the yolks of 6 eggs, one at a time, beating hard after each one. • Beat 8 egg whites until stiff and fold very gently into cheese sauce lifting and turning, with a spatula. • Butter 2 soufflé molds (it is preferable to use 2 smaller molds rather than 1 large one) and divide the mixture equally between both. They should not be more than half full. • Put into a preheated oven (375°F; 190°C; 4) for approximately 35 min. Towards the end of the cooking time the heat may be raised a little. Serve without delay.

SEAFOOD SOUFFLE
* SOUFFLE AUX FRUITS DE MER

ALSATIAN ONION TART
* TARTE A L'OIGNON ALSACIENNE

Serves 6

Time: *preparation 40 min.* • *cooking 35 min.*
Ingredients: *12 scallops* • *18 medium shrimps* • *4 fillets of sole* • *⅔ cup (1.6 dl) cream* • *1 glass dry white wine* • *10 tbsp. (150 g) butter* • *2 shallots* • *¼ tsp. cornstarch or potato flour* • *2 tbsp. tomato paste* • *3 eggs* • *1 cup (¼ liter) milk* • *5 tbsp. (55 g) flour* • *salt, pepper.*

Serves 6

Time: *preparation 30 min.* • *cooking 1 hr. 10 min.*
Ingredients: *1 generous lb. (500 g) pie dough* • *1½ lb. (750 g) onions* • *3 eggs* • *4 tbsp. cream* • *4 tbsp. (40 g) flour* • *6 tbsp. (85 g) butter* • *salt, pepper.*

• Remove the tails from the shrimp and fry in butter for several minutes. Remove the shells. • Chop the scallops into 2 or 3 pieces. • Add another knob of butter to the pan in which the shrimp were cooked and simmer the chopped shallots until they become transparent; do not let them brown. • Add the lightly floured scallops and fry gently. Set aside. • Dice the sole; flour lightly and cook in the same pan until the flesh begins to turn white. Set aside. • Deglaze the pan with the white wine. Boil for 2 min. • Return all the fish to the pan and bring again slowly to the boil. • Season and take out a cupful bouillon to reserve for the soufflé. • Stir the cornstarch into the remaining pan juices. Add 1 tsp. tomato paste and the cream and stir with a wooden spoon. Simmer for 5 min. Remove from the heat. • Make the soufflé by melting 4 tbsp. (55 g) butter in a saucepan without letting it change color. Add the flour and stir with a wooden spoon to form a smooth roux. • Gradually pour the tepid milk and the cooking juices with the scraps into the pan, stirring all the time until the sauce is smooth and thick. Remove from the heat; allow to cool. • Add the egg yolks one by one, beating hard each time. • Beat the egg whites until stiff and fold gently into the sauce. • Put the fish into a buttered soufflé dish and pour in the soufflé mixture. • Put in a preheated oven (375°F; 190°C; **4**) for approximately 35 min. • Serve at once.

• Make the pastry 1 hr. in advance (recipe no. 252) or thaw out the frozen variety. • Slice the onions into rings; blanch in boiling salted water for 2 min.; drain. • Melt the butter in a large frying pan and let the onions cook gently (preferably covered) until they become transparent: approx 20-25 min. • Sprinkle with the flour and mash with a fork. • Beat the eggs; beat in the fresh cream then stir in the onions. Season. Line a buttered pie dish with the pastry and pour in the onion mixture. • Place in a preheated oven (445°F; 229°C; **7**) for 30-40 min. • Serve hot.

MUSTARD TART
❊ TARTE A LA MOUTARDE

Serves 6

Time: *preparation 25 min.* • *cooking 30-40 min.*
Ingredients: *14 oz. (400 g) puff pastry* • *5 oz. (150 g) gruyère* • *4 large tomatoes* • *strong mustard*

• Make the pastry in advance according to recipe no. 253, or thaw out the frozen variety. • Line a buttered pie tin with the pastry; spread a thick layer of mustard (½ in.; 1 cm) over the bottom. • Lay very thin slices of gruyère on top of the mustard. • Peel and seed the tomatoes and cut into thick pieces. Place on top of the cheese. • Put into a preheated hot oven: (425°F; 220°C;**7**). • After approx 20 min. look at the tart; it is ready to serve when the pastry has puffed up and begun to detach itself from the sides of the pan.

FISH-FILLED PANCAKES
❊ CREPES AUX FILETS DE SOLE

Serves 6

Time: *preparation 25 min.* • *cooking 30 min.*
Ingredients: *12 crêpes (recipe no. 250)* • *8 fillets sole* • *4 oz (2 cup; 125g) cooked shrimps* • *⅔ cup (140 g) butter* • *6 oz (1 cup generous; 150g) mushrooms* • *¼ pt (125g) cream* • *4 tbsp. (40 g) flour* • *1 bouillon cube* • *salt, pepper* • *shrimps for garnish*

• Make the crêpe batter in advance (leave out the rum) and when it has "rested" for the required time, make the pancakes. • Pile them on top of one another on a flat dish. • Dissolve the bouillon cube; poach the fish fillets in the liquid for 5 min., drain and cut into bite-size pieces. • Put a scant pint of the bouillon through a sieve and set aside. • Clean the mushrooms; slice finely and cook gently in butter. • Make a Béchamel sauce (recipe no. 272) with 4 tbsp. (55 g) butter, the flour and the filtered bouillon. Add a little salt, pepper to taste, and the cream. • Mix together ⅔ of the Béchamel sauce with the mushrooms, the sole and the shrimps. • Divide this mixture between the 12 crêpes and fold up to make little packets. • Lay them in a buttered ovenproof dish and cover with the remaining Béchamel sauce. • Dot with butter and place in a preheated oven: (425°F; 330°C;**7**) to brown for 15 min.

SEAFOOD RAGOUT
✳ SALMIS DE FRUITS DE MER

Serves 4

Time: *preparation 30 min.* ● *cooking 40 min.*
Ingredients: *2 medium sized crabs* ● *12 saltwater crayfish (or large shrimp)* ● *1 quart (1 liter) mussels* ● *1 quart (1 liter) clams or mixed shellfish* ● *1 cup (200 g) uncooked rice* ● *1 bouillon cube* ● *1 onion* ● *4 tbsp. (55 g) butter* ● *salt, pepper, saffron*

● Dissolve the bouillon cube in boiling water and add the crabs. Simmer for 10 min.; then add the crayfish and cook for 5-10 min. longer ● Remove the shells from the crayfish. ● Open the crabs; remove the spongy parts under the shells and pick out the meat. Crack the claws and take out the meat; chop coarsely. ● Cook the rice in a large pan of boiling salted water approximately 15 min. Drain and pass under running cold water for several minutes to remove the excess starch. ● Put the mussels and other shellfish into a large pan with a very little water and place over a high flame to open. Take from the shells. ● Cook the onions in a large pan with the butter; let them turn golden. ● Add the well-drained rice, 2-3 tbsp. bouillon, the crabmeat and all the shellfish. Season with a little salt, pepper and saffron to taste. ● Cover and heat over a low flame for a few minutes. ● Pile in a mound on a hot plate and serve at once.

HAM AND CHEESE FLANS
✳ FLANS GRATINÉS

Serves 6

Time: *preparation 15 min* ● *cooking 35 min*
Ingredients: *2 cups (½ liter) milk* ● *4 eggs* ● *5 oz. (150 g) ham in one thick slice* ● *1 cup (110 g) grated gruyère* ● *4 tbsp. (55 g) butter* ● *salt, pepper, nutmeg*

● Bring the milk to a boil; remove from the heat. ● Dice the ham. ● Beat the eggs in a large bowl and add the ham. ● Very gradually, so as not to cook the eggs, add the hot milk, beating continuously. ● Season and add a pinch of grated nutmeg and 2 tbsp. (30 g) grated gruyère. Mix well. ● Butter individual ramekins and fill with the egg mixture. Sprinkle with the rest of the gruyère. Put the ramekins in a pan of hot water and place in a hot oven: (425°F; 220°C; 7) for 30-35 min. ● Serve straight from the oven.

COD BRANDADE
❋ BRANDADE DE MORUE

BEET GATEAU
❋ GATEAU DE BETTES

Serves 6

Time: *preparation 25 min.* • *Make a day in advance*
Ingredients: *2½ lb. (1.2 kg) salt cod or 2 cans of fillets (1 lb. 1½ oz; 500 g each)* • *2 wine glasses olive oil* • *1 glass light cream* • *2-3 cloves garlic* • *1 potato boiled (optional)* • *1 small can truffle parings* • *pepper, nutmeg*

Serves 6

Time: *preparation 40 min.* • *cooking 40 min.*
Ingredients: *1½ lb (750 g) beetroot leaves* • *2 tbsp. lard* • *1 scant lb. (400 g) slightly salted bacon* • *3 shallots* • *3 eggs* • *3 egg yolks* • *1 cup (¼ liter) milk* • *5 tbsp. (50 g) flour* • *salt, pepper,* • *thyme, parsley, 1 bay leaf*

• Soak the cod in cold water for 24 hr. to remove excess salt (12 hr. is sufficient if canned fish is used). • Put the cod in a deep saucepan and cover with cold water. Place over a high flame; as soon as the water begins to simmer lower the heat to maintain the same temperature; cook for 10 min. • Remove from the heat but leave the fish in the hot water for a further 10 min. • Then, drain it well; carefully remove all the bones, and flake. • Pound the fish in a mortar with the garlic, until it is reduced to a creamy paste. • Put in a large saucepan and place over a low heat. • Gradually add the oil and the cream, stirring continuously and not allowing the mixture to boil. As soon as it has reached a purée-like consistency add no more liquids even if the stated amounts have not been used up. • Add pepper and a pinch of grated nutmeg. • If the brandade remains too thin gradually add a sieved, cooked potato to thicken the purée. • Stir in the truffle parings and serve very hot. • The dish may be garnished with garlic croutons.

• Wash the beetroot leaves and slice finely. • Chop the bacon into very small pieces. Melt the lard in a deep saucepan and cook the leaves over a high flame stirring all the time. • As soon as they soften, add the finely chopped shallots, 2 tbsp. of chopped parsley, a sprinkling of thyme and the bay leaf. • Away from the heat add the bacon, the eggs and the egg yolks and mix thoroughly. • Pour in the milk and season. • Put into a buttered gratin dish and place in a hot oven: (400 ˚F; 200 ˚C; 6) for approx 40 min. If the "cake" begins to burn, cover with aluminum foil. • Press the top of the gâteau with a finger-tip and if it feels quite firm it is ready to leave the oven. • Serve warm or piping hot.

CHEESE FLAN
✣ FLAN AU FROMAGE

Serves 6

Time: *preparation 10 min* • *cooking 35 min*
Ingredients: *6 eggs* • *2 cups (½ liter) milk* • *1⅓ cups (150 g) grated gruyère* • *2 tbsp. (20 g) flour* • *2 tbsp. (30 g) butter* • *salt, pepper* • *tomato sauce* • *3-4 oz. (100 g) mushrooms (optional)*

• Heat the milk. • Mix the grated cheese into the flour. Add the eggs one by one, beating after each. • Gradually add the hot milk stirring hard all the time, until the mixture is thick and shiny. • Pour into a buttered mold and place in a preheated moderate oven: (375°F; 190°C 5) for approximately 35 min. • Unmold and serve with a bowl of fresh tomato sauce (recipe no. 283). • If desired, a few chopped mushrooms lightly sautéed in butter, can be stirred into the flan just before it goes into the oven.

STUFFED MUSHROOMS
✣ CHAMPIGNONS FARCIS

Serves 6

Time: *preparation 40 min.* • *cooking 25 min.*
Ingredients: *12 very large mushrooms* • *6 medium-sized mushrooms* • *2 thin slices ham* • *generous ½ cup (60 g) grated gruyère* • *2 cups (½ liter) milk* • *1 cup (2.5 dl) cream* • *9 tbsp. (130 g) butter* • *2 egg yolks* • *1 lemon* • *flour* • *salt, pepper, nutmeg*

• Clean the mushrooms and remove the stems. • Put the caps into a frying pan with a large knob butter. Cook over a low flame; do not let them break. • Chop the stems and the 6 smaller mushrooms; sprinkle with lemon juice. • Cook gently in butter until all the juice has evaporated. Remove from the heat. • Chop the ham and mix with the chopped mushrooms. • Make 2 cups (½ liter) Béchamel sauce (recipe no. 272); add the cream; the egg yolks (beating after each one); salt; pepper and a pinch of nutmeg. • Pour half the Béchamel sauce into the ham and mushroom mixture and stir in half the grated cheese. • Fill each mushroom cap with this stuffing; heap it into small domes. • Spread the remaining stuffing over the bottom of a gratin dish and arrange the stuffed mushrooms on top. • Cover with the rest of the Béchamel sauce into which the rest of the gruyère has been mixed. If necessary, thin with a little milk. • Put into a hot oven to reheat and brown the surface.

PATE WITH NUTMEG
❋ LE PATE MUSCADE

Serves 8·10

Time: *preparation and cooking 1¼ hr.*
Ingredients: *about 1 lb. (500 g) puff pastry • 2¼ lb. (1 kg) shoulder of veal • 7 oz. (200 g) sausage meat • 1 slice bread • 3 eggs • salt, pepper, one nutmeg • butter*

• Make the pastry (see recipe no. 253). • Soak the bread in milk. • Grind the veal (discarding any bits of fat) and mix thoroughly with the sausage meat. • Add the bread which has been well-squeezed, 2 egg yolks, salt, pepper and half the nutmeg, finely grated. • Beat 2 egg whites until stiff and add to the mixture. • Form into the shape of a roast; place in a buttered oven dish and cook in a hot oven (400°-425°F; 200-220° C; 6·7) for approx 30 min. • Allow to cool. • Roll out the puff pastry into a rectangle and place the "roast" of meat in the center. • Fold the edges over and place a separate piece of pastry on top to act as a cover. • • Moisten the edges with water and stick together firmly. Paint the pastry with beaten egg yolk and cook in a hot oven for approximately 35 min, but do not allow to burn. • Serve while still warm and crisp.

PATTIES A LA REINE "A LA MAZILLE"
❋ BOUCHEES A LA REINE " A LA MAZILLE"

Serves 6

Time: *preparation 20 min. • cooking 45 min.*
Ingredients: *1 lb (500 g) puff pastry • 1 sweetbread approx 1½ lb (700 g) • 4 tbsp. (55 g) butter • 1 onion • 1 tbsp flour • 3½-4 oz. (100 g) mushrooms • 1 small tin truffle peelings • 3½-7 oz (100-200 g) cooked white chicken meat • 1 egg yolk • thyme*

• Make the puff pastry in advance (see recipe no. 253) or thaw out the frozen variety. • Soak the sweetbread in several changes of cold water for a few hours to soften the filaments covering it. • Pull off as much of the membrane as possible soaking the sweetbread again if necessary, until it is easy to separate the two lobes from the tube. • Blanch in boiling water for a few minutes; drain carefully and cut into bite size pieces. • Place these in a casserole with the butter, the finely chopped onion and the flour. Moisten with a little warm water or bouillon; season and simmer for ½ hr. • Clean the mushrooms; slice thinly. • Add to the sweetbread and, 5 min before the end of cooking time, add the truffle peelings and the finely sliced chicken meat. • Sprinkle with thyme and bind together with an egg yolk to which a little bouillon has been added. • Roll out the pastry ¼ in. (1/2 cm) thick. • Cut into circles 3½ 4 in (9-10 cm) across and place on a metal baking sheet. • Without cutting through completely, score circles 2 in. (5 cm) diameter in the center of the circles for covers. Bake in a hot oven for approx 20 min. • As soon as the "vol-au-vent" are cooked and have risen, use the point of knife to remove the "covers" and gently push the insides of the patties against the side with your finger. • Fill with the sweetbread; place the little covers on top, and keep hot until serving time.

• NB These patties or "vol-au-vents" can be bought ready-made at bakeries and cake shops, and only need reheating.

EGGS

The discovery of a new dish
adds more to the happiness of man
than the discovery of a new star.

SCRAMBLED EGGS WITH TRUFFLES
❋ OEUFS BROUILLES AUX TRUFFES

Serves 4

Time: *preparation 5 min.* ● *cooking 10 min.*
Ingredients: *8 eggs* ● *1 canned truffle (or truffle peeling)* ● *6 tbsp. (85g) butter* ● *4 tbsp. heavy cream* ● *several asparagus tips* ● *salt, black pepper*

● Break the eggs into a deep bowl; add the salt, freshly ground black pepper and 1 tbsp. water. Beat hard. ● Melt the butter in a saucepan without letting it color. ● Place the saucepan in a pan of water over low heat. Empty the eggs into the saucepan and cook, stirring all the time with a wooden spoon, until they are thick and creamy, but not hard. ● Remove from the heat while the eggs are still slightly liquid, as the heat of the saucepan will continue the cooking process. (Eggs should be served on unheated plates for this reason.) ● Add the cream, the asparagus tips and some of the truffle. ● Serve in individual ramekins and decorate with the remaining pieces of truffle.

EGGS MEURETTE
❋ OEUFS EN MEURETTE

Serves 4

Time: *preparation 5 min.* ● *cooking 25 min.*
Ingredients: *4 eggs.* ● *1 glass red wine (Bordeaux or Beaujolais)* ● *½ glass water* ● *3 tbsp. (40g) butter* ● *1 tbsp. flour* ● *1 onion* ● *1 clove garlic* ● *1 bay leaf* ● *parsley, salt, pepper*

● Put the wine, water, sliced onion, garlic, bay leaf, a stalk of parsley, salt and peper in a saucepan. ● *Boil over medium heat for 20 min.* ● Pour through a fine sieve; then pour the liquid back into the pan. ● When it begins to simmer (the liquid should barely ripple), gently slide the eggs in to poach (this is easier to do if each egg is broken into a saucer first). ● Put each egg into a small ramekin. ● Mix the softened butter with the flour to get a ''beurre manie'' ● Thicken the wine sauce by adding this mixture in small pieces, stirring all the time. Bring to a boil and pour over the eggs. ● Serve at once.

DARIOLES
✻ OEUFS EN DARIOLES

BOILED EGGS WITH SORREL
✻ OEUFS MOLLETS A L'OSEILLE

Serves 6

Time: *preparation 10 min. • cooking 20 min.*
Ingredients: *6 eggs • ¼ cups (.6dl) heavy cream • ⅔ cups (70g) grated gruyère • 5 tbsp. (70g) butter • salt, pepper • cooking oil • 6 slices bread from a sandwich loaf cut into rounds*

Serves 4

Time: *preparation 20 min. • cooking 1 hr.*
Ingredients: *1 ib. (450 g) sorrel • eggs • 6 tbsp. (85 g) butter • 1 level tsp. flour • ½ glass stock or bouillon • 1 egg yolk • 4 slices from a sandwich loaf toasted • salt, a pinch of sugar*

• Beat the eggs with the cream and the gruyère (reserve 1 tbsp. cheese). Season. • Butter 6 dariole molds (small cylindrical molds) and sprinkle with the remaining gruyère. • Pour the beaten eggs into the darioles (they should be ¾ full). • Place the darioles in a large flameproof dish and half fill with hot water. Cover (using aluminium foil if the dish does not have a lid) and simmer for 20 min. • When the mixture has risen to the tops of the darioles and no longer breaks under gentle pressure from your finger, it is cooked • Remove the darioles and unmold each onto a slice of toast which has been fried in a mixture of oil and butter. • Serve with a thick tomato sauce (see recipe no. 283).

• Remove the tough stalks from the sorrel and wash the leaves in several changes of water. • Put half the sorrel in a deep saucepan; heat gently and as the leaves begin to soften add the remainder, bit by bit. • Pour in ½ glass water, cover and cook on a low heat for 5 min. • Thoroughly drain the sorrel and purée • Melt a generous lump of butter in a saucepan, stir in the flour mixing to a smooth paste using a wooden spoon; then put in the sorrel. Mix well and add the bouillon. • Season with salt and a pinch of sugar. Stir constantly until the liquid boils. • Lower the heat; cover with a sheet of buttered greaseproof paper and place the lid of the pan on top. • Simmer as gently as possible for 1 hr. • At the end of the cooking time, beat 1 egg yolk with the milk and add to the sorrel away from the heat. • Fry the bread in butter. • Cook the eggs in boiling water for 6 min.; then shell them and put each one on a slice of fried bread. • Serve the sorrel heaped in the center of a dish surrounded by the eggs on toast.

POACHED EGGS CRECY
✻ OEUFS POCHES CRECY

EGGS WITH SHRIMPS
✻ OEUFS AUX CREVETTES

Serves 6

Time: *preparation 20 min.* • *cooking 35 min.*
Ingredients: *6 eggs* • *1 lb. (450 g) carrots* • *3tbsp. (40 g) butter* • *2 onions* • *1 recipe Béchamel sauce* • *1 egg yolk* • *3tbsp. heavy cream* • *salt, pepper, nutmeg* • *vinegar*

Serves 6

Time: *preparation 30 min.* • *cooking 30 min.*
Ingredients: *6 large hard-boiled eggs* • *½ lb. (225 g) shelled shrimps* • *¼lb. (110 g) shrimps for garnishing* • *⅓ lb. (150 g) small mushrooms* • *7 tbsp. (100 g) butter* • *a heaping tbsp. flour* • *2 tbsp. chopped mixed herbs (or 1 tbsp. dried herbs)* • *juice of 1 lemon* • *salt, pepper*

• Slice the carrots and onions. • Cook them in salted water for 20 min.; drain and purée in a food processor or through a sieve. • Season with salt, pepper and ¼ tsp. grated nutmeg; add the butter. • While the vegetables are cooking, make the Béchamel sauce (recipe no. 272). • Away from the heat, add the egg yolk and cream. • Heat some water in a large pan, adding 1 tbsp. vinegar per quart (liter) water. • When the water is barely simmering, slide in the eggs, one at a time, from a saucer (this helps them to remain unbroken and to keep their shape). • Cook for 3 min. and remove from the water with a slotted spoon or skimming ladle. • Drain on a tea towel. • Put the puréed carrots onto a serving dish with the eggs heaped on the top. Cover with the Béchamel sauce and serve immediately.

• Peel and chop the mushrooms and sprinkle with lemon juice. • Cook in a very small quantity of water with the remaining juice from the lemon for approx 10 min. • Drain, but save the cooking juices for the shrimps. • Put the shelled shrimps into the pan and cook for 10 min. over a low heat. Drain, this time pouring the cooking liquid through a fine sieve. • Chop ⅔ of the shrimp, reserving the rest for garnish. • Make a white sauce with the melted butter (do not let it brown), the flour and the strained liquid. Stir continuously with a wooden spoon. • Cut the eggs lengthwise and remove the yolks. • Chop these and add to the mushrooms, shrimps and herbs. Season. Bind together with half of the white sauce. • Fill the halved egg whites with this mixture; cover with the rest of the sauce and grill or put into a hot oven to brown for 5 min. • Decorate the dish with the shrimp garnish and slices of lemon.

HARD-BOILED EGGS WITH ONION SAUCE
✳ OEUFS A LA TRIPE

Serves 4

Time: *preparation 15 min.* • *cooking 30 min.*
Ingredients: *6 eggs* • *½ lb. (225 gr.) onions* • *6 tbsp. (85 gr.) butter* • *4 tbsp. (40 g) flour* • *2 cups (½ liter milk)* • *salt, pepper, nutmeg*

• Hard-boil the eggs. • Peel the onions, chop very finely and cook slowly in ⅔ of the butter. • As soon as they begin to turn transparent, moisten with 2 tbsp. hot water and continue cooking, taking care that they do not turn brown. • When the onions are soft, sprinkle with flour and stir well with a wooden spoon so that they are mashed to a soft pulp. • Add the milk, salt, pepper and a pinch of nutmeg. Cook for 10-12 min.; add the remaining butter. • Shell the eggs and cut into thick slices; add to the sauce. • Reheat for a few minutes being careful not to break the eggs. • Serve at once on a heated serving dish.

EGGS PRINTANIERE
✳ OEUFS A LA PRINTANIERE

Serves 6

Time: *preparation 10 min.* • *cooking 10 min.*
Ingredients: *6 eggs* • *1 cup (2.5 dl) heavy cream* • *1 generous handful fresh herbs (chives, chervil, sorrel, etc.) chopped finely* • *4 tbsp. (55 g) butter* • *salt, black pepper*

• Reserve 2 tbsp. finely chopped fresh herbs. • Mix the cream with salt and freshly ground black pepper (add a pinch of nutmeg if desired) and the rest of the herbs. • Generously butter 6 oven-proof ramekins and put 1 tbsp. cream in each. • Break an egg into each dish and cover with the remainder of the cream and herbs. • Place the ramekins together in a large pan of water and put into a preheated oven (400˚F; 200˚C; 6-7). • Cook for approx 8-10 min. • Remove from the oven when done; sprinkle with the herbs which were set aside, and serve immediately.

POACHED EGGS NIMES STYLE
✳ OEUFS POCHES NIMOISE

EGGS WITH SPINACH
✳ OEUFS MOLLETS AUX EPINARDS

Serves 6

Time: *preparation 30 min. • cooking: a few minutes.*
Ingredients: *6 slices bread 1 inch (2½cm.) thick • 7 eggs • 1¼ cup (250g) brandade of salt cod (recipe no. 50) • 1 cup(2.5 dl.) cream • 2 tbsp. (30 g) butter • 2 tbsp. (20g.) flour • 1 lemon • oil, vinegar • salt, pepper*

Serves 6

Time: *preparation 30 min. • cooking 25 min.*
Ingredients: *6 eggs • 9 oz. (250 g) cooked drained spinach • 4 oz. (110 g) sorrel • 7 tbsp. (100 g) butter • 1 cup (¼ liter) Béchamel sauce • ½ cup (1.2 dl) cream • ½ cup (55 g) grated gruyère • salt, pepper, nutmeg*

• Cut the crusts off the bread. Scoop an indentation (But not a hole) in the center of each piece. • Fry gently in a little cooking oil and drain on absorbent paper while keeping warm (this can be done in a preheated oven which has been turned off). • Poach 6 eggs for about 3 min. in water to which a little vinegar has been added. • Put them aside in tepid water so that they do not continue to cook. • Meanwhile, have the *brandade de morue* heating in a double boiler (stir frequently). • Make a Béchamel sauce (recipe no. 272) with the butter and flour but use the cream in place of milk. • If necessary add a little water; season with salt and pepper and stir in the yolk of the remaining egg with several drops of lemon juice. • Fill the hollowed-out toasts with the hot brandade; place a poached egg on each and cover with the Béchamel sauce. • Serve at once.

• Boil the eggs for 6 min. in salted water; then immediately put under cold running water. • Shell and set aside to cool. • Chop the sorrel coarsely and cook in 1 tbsp. butter. When the leaves have softened, add the cooked chopped spinach and continue to cook over a low heat until all the liquid has evaporated. • Season with salt, pepper and a pinch of mustard and add some cream. • Heap the vegetables on an ovenproof dish and press the eggs into the mound so that they stand upright. • Cover with Béchamel sauce (recipe no. 272) to which you have added the rest of the cream and half the grated gruyère . Sprinkle the remainder of the cheese over the top and dot generously with butter. • Put into a very hot oven for a few minutes to brown. • Serve immediately.

PIPERADE

Serves 6

Time: *preparation 40 min.* • *cooking 40 min.*
Ingredients: *6 eggs* • *about 2 lbs. (1 kg) tomatoes* • *4 sweet peppers (red or green)* • *6 slices Virginia or Bayonne ham* • *1 onion* • *clove garlic* • *olive oil* • *salt, black pepper*

• Sear the peppers over a flame so that their skins can be peeled off. • Chop coarsely and remove the seeds. • Peel and seed the tomatoes and put through a sieve or food mill. • Chop the onion finely and cook in 2 tbsp. olive oil until transparent. • Add the peppers and, when they are almost cooked, put in the puréed tomatoes and the crushed garlic. Season, and cook slowly until all the vegetables are soft. • Meanwhile, brown the ham in a frying pan and keep in a warm place. • Deglaze the frying pan with 2-3. tbsp. of the vegetable purée. • Beat the eggs as for an omelette and, away from the heat, mix into the vegetables. • Return to the stove and cook slowly, stirring constantly. • As soon as the mixture begins to thicken and become fluffy, turn out onto the serving dish and garnish with the slices of ham. • Serve immediately.

EGGS TOUPINEL
❋ OEUFS TOUPINEL

Serves 6

Time: *preparation 30 min.* • *cooking 1 hr. + 20 min. for browning*
Ingredients: *6 large potatoes* • *6 small eggs* • *7 tbsp. (100 g) butter* • *1 cup (¼ liter) Béchamel sauce* • *4 oz. (110 g) ham* • *5 slices bacon* • *½ cup (55 g) grated gruyère* • *salt, pepper, cayenne*

• Wash and dry the potatoes carefully. • With the point of a knife cut lid-like opening in the skin of each potato, but do not detach it completely (see illustration). • Bake in a hot oven until cooked (approximately 1 hr.). • Remove from the oven; lift up the "lids" and scoop out the pulp without breaking the skins. • Season the insides of the potatoes and put in a knob of butter. Break an egg into each one. • Chop the ham and the bacon finely and mix into the Bévhamel sauce (recipe no. 272); add the potato pulp; mash with a fork and add more butter. • Season lightly with a little salt and a pinch of cayenne. • Fill the potato shells with this mixture; sprinkle with grated gruyère and return to the oven long enough for the eggs to cook and the cheese to brown (about 10 min.).

EGG TART
✳ TARTE AUX OEUFS

MUSHROOM HASH WITH EGGS
✳ HACHIS DE CEPES AUX OEUFS

Serves 6

Time: *preparation 15 min.* • *cooking 45 min.*
Ingredients: *1 lb. (450g) pie dough* • *½ can corn* • *2 eggs* • *1 scant cup (100 g) grated gruyère* • *1 cup (¼ liter) milk* • *salt, pepper*

Serves 4

Time: *preparation 20 min.* • *cooking 45 min.*
Ingredients: *4 oz. (110 g) fat bacon* • *4 large mushrooms* • *6 eggs* • *clove garlic* • *2 shallots* • *7 tbsp. (100 g) butter* • *salt, pepper* • *parsley chopped* • *peanut oil (optional)*

• Make the pie dough, following recipe no. 252, or use the frozen variety. • Combine the corn with the eggs, cheese, milk, salt and pepper. Mix well. • Line a buttered pie pan with the pastry and pour in the egg mixture. • Place in a hot oven (400°F; 200°C; **7**) for 15 min. Lower the temperature to (350°F; 180°C; **4**) and cook for another 30 min. • Serve immediately.

• Wash and dry the mushrooms; chop finely with the shallots and garlic. • Dice the bacon. Put altogether in a pan with half the butter or an equal amount of peanut oil and cook, covered, over a very low heat for approx ½ hr. • Towards the end of the cooking time, melt the remaining butter in the top of a double boiler. • Beat the eggs and pour them into the melted butter, stirring constantly. Remove the pan of eggs from the boiling water while the eggs are still a little liquid. • Put the cooked mushroom mixture into an ovenproof dish and cover with the scrambled eggs. • Season; put into a hot oven for 5-7 min. • Sprinkle with chopped parsley and serve at once.

HERB OMELETTE
❋ OMELETTE AUX FINES HERBES

MUSHROOM OMELETTE
❋ OMELETTE FORESTIERE

Serves 6

Time: *preparation 10 min.* • *cooking 20 min.*
Ingredients: *12 eggs* • *3 heaped tbsp. fresh herbs (chives, chervil, tarragon, parsley etc)* • *4 tbsp. (55 g) butter* • *salt, pepper* • *clove garlic (optional)*

Serves 4

Time: *preparation 10 min.* • *cooking 20 min.*
Ingredients: *6 eggs* • *4 tbsp. (55 g) butter* • *about 4 oz. (125 g) mushrooms* • *4½ oz. (130 g) smoked bacon* • *1 lemon* • *salt, pepper* • *parsley chopped*

• Chop the herbs finely. • Beat the eggs; add salt, pepper and herbs. Melt the butter in a large pan and pour in the eggs and herbs. • As the eggs cook, lift them gently at the edges and in the center with the prongs of a fork so that the uncooked mixture can run underneath to the heat. • When the eggs have almost set and are pale gold, turn off the heat and cover the pan with a large plate for 1-2 min. This helps the eggs to set while remaining soft in the center. • Fold the omelette over with a wooden spatula and slide onto the serving dish.

• NB: Never use more than 12 eggs in making an omelette. It is preferable to cook more than one omelette.

• Dice the bacon. • Clean the mushrooms in a mixture of water and lemon juice; dry and chop finely. • Melt half the butter in a saucepan and cook the bacon and mushrooms together for 10-12 min., stirring constantly with a wooden spoon or spatula. • Beat the eggs; season. • Remove the bacon and mushrooms from the pan with a slotted spoon, and drain on absorbent paper. Above all, do not pour out the juices in the pan. • Add the rest of the butter to the cooking juices in the pan and pour in the beaten eggs. • After cooking for a few minutes, return the bacon and mushroom mixture. • While the omelette is still creamy in the center, fold it in two with the spatula and slide onto the serving plate. • Sprinkle with chopped parsley before serving.

SOUFFLEED CHEESE OMELETTE
❊ OMELETTE MOUSSEUSE AU FROMAGE

Serves 4

Time: *preparation 15 min.* • *cooking 6-8 min.*
Ingredients: *6 eggs* • *¼ cup (0.6 dl) heavy cream* • *scant ½ cup (60 g) grated gruyère* • *3 tbsp. (40 g) butter* • *salt, pepper*

• Separate the whites from the yolks of the eggs. • Lightly beat the yolks with the cream. Season. Add the grated cheese and beat again. • Beat the whites until they form stiff peaks. Put 2 tbsp. whites into the egg yolks and beat hard. Then fold in the remaining whites very gently without breaking them up. • Melt the butter in a pan and carefully pour in the eggs. • At the start of the cooking, use a wooden spatula to move the edge of the omelette away from the pan and to raise the omelette to allow the eggs to reach the heat; as the eggs begin to set, lift only the edge • Slide the cooked omelette onto the serving plate and take to the table immediately.

OVEN-BAKED OMELETTE
❊ OMELETTE MOULEE AU FOUR

Serves 6

Time: *preparation 15 min.* • *cooking 20-30 min.*
Ingredients: *8 eggs* • *7 oz. (200 g) smoked pork belly* • *2 onions* • *2 cloves garlic* • *1 small can whole tomatoes* • *4 tbsp. (55 g) butter* • *1 tsp. dried herbs (basil, oregano, rosemary, savory etc)* • *salt, pepper*

• Dice the pork into small pieces and chop the onion finely. • Cook together in the butter; add the crushed garlic. • Drain the tomatoes and remove the seeds; add to the saucepan and mix with the pork and onions until they are almost puréed. • Beat the eggs and pour into the saucepan stirring at the same time. • Butter a round, shallow mold and empty the egg mixture into it. • Put into a hot oven (400°F; 200°C; **6**) for 20-30 min. but do not let the eggs burn. • Unmold and serve at once.

TUNA FISH OMELETTE
❊ OMELETTE AU THON

OMELETTE WITH TRUFFLES
❊ OMELETTE AUX TRUFFES

Serves 6

Time: *preparation 10 min.* ● *cooking 15 min.*
Ingredients: *12 eggs* ● *7 oz. (200 g) fresh tuna* ● *½ cup (1.2 dl) cream* ● *7 tbsp. (100 g) butter* ● *1 shallot* ● *2 tbsp. chives, chopped* ● *1 lemon* ● *½ glass dry white wine*

Serves 4

Time: *preparation 10 min.* ● *cooking 25 min.*
Ingredients: *8 eggs* ● *4 oz. (110 g) truffles or truffle skins* ● *1 cup (¼ liter) Madeira or white wine* ● *bouquet garni* ● *salt, pepper* ● *butter* ● *fat salt pork, chopped finely*

● Finely chop the shallot and cook slowly in a generous amount of butter. ● Add the wine, raise the heat and cook until the liquid is reduced by almost half. ● Meanwhile, mash the tuna fish with a fork and mix in the cream. Add the juice of ½ lemon and ⅓ of the chives. ● Cook over a low heat stirring constantly. ● Beat the eggs and add ⅓ chives. ● Melt the butter in a saucepan, pour in the beaten eggs and make an omelette in the usual fashion. ● Just before the end of the cooking time put the fish into the center of the omelette; heat for a minute or two; fold over with a spatula and slide onto a serving dish. Sprinkle with melted butter and the remaining ⅓ of the chives. ● Serve at once.

● Carefully wash the truffles using a brush; peel, and slice thinly. ● Slowly melt the finely chopped salt pork; add the truffles, salt, bouquet garni and wine. ● Cook for 10-15 min., depending on whether you are using fresh truffles or the skins. ● Meanwhile, make the omelette: Beat the eggs and pour into the pan in which the butter has been melted. Use a fork or a wooden spatula to raise the eggs in order to let the uncooked mixture underneath to the hot surface of the pan. ● When the omelette is still fairly liquid in the center, empty the truffles into it and fold it over (save a few slices of truffle for a garnish). ● Slide onto the serving dish and decorate with the reserved pieces of truffle.

MEAT

The delicacy of the human tongue
and its surrounding membranes
is proof of the sublimity
of the work for which it is designed.

PEPPER STEAK
✳ LE STEAK AU POIVRE

Serves 1

Time: *preparation 35 min. • cooking 10-12 min.*
Ingredients: *1 thick slice fillet of beef • 1 tbsp. coarsely ground pepper-corns • butter • 1 tbsp. cream • 1 liqueur glass cognac • salt*

• Spread the pepper out on a plate and put the steak on top of it. Press down firmly to make the pepper stick to the meat. • Turn the steak over and repeat. Let the steak absorb the flavor for 30 min. • Melt a large lump of butter in a frying pan and, when it is sizzling hot, put in the steak. • As soon as the meat is "sealed," turn it to the other side. Salt. Pour in the cognac and flame. Cook 5-10 min. longer according to taste. • Put the fillet onto a hot plate, add the cream to the cooking juices and heat gently so that the cream does not curdle. • Pour over the fillet and serve at once.

GRILLED ENTRECOTE
✳ ENTRECOTE GRILLE

Serves 6

Time: *preparation 5 min. • cooking to taste*
Ingredients: *2 thick entrecotes (or rib steaks) approximately 2 lb. (900 g) each or 1 weighing 3¾ lb. (1.6 kg) • Salt, pepper • 7 tbsp. (100 g) butter • pars-ley*

• 30 min. before cooking, lightly coat both sides of the steak with butter, salt and pepper. • Score the fat around the side in a few places to prevent the meat from curling. • Preheat the grill for about 15 min. to make it as hot as possible. • Put the steak on a grid and grill; turn over and grill on the other side. The cooking time depends on individual taste (6-8 min. each side for a rare steak, and a few more minutes for medium rare). • Serve with several knobs of parsley butter (butter softened with a fork and mixed with chopped parsley).

TOURNEDOS WITH MARROW
✳ TOURNEDOS A LA MOELLE

FILLET OF BEEF "EN PATE"
✳ FILET DE BOEUF EN PATE

Serves 6

Time: *preparation 10 min.* • *cooking 7-12 min.*
Ingredients: *6 tournedos (or sliced fillet of beef) 6-7 oz. (180-200 g) each* • *5-6 oz (150 g) beef marrow* • *4 tbsp. (55 g) butter* • *salt, pepper* • *3 tbsp. chopped parsley*

Serves 8

Time: *preparation 20 min.* • *cooking 40 min.*
Ingredients: *fillet of beef 3-3½ lb. (1.500 kg)* • *14 oz (400 g) pie dough* • *1 egg* • *4 tbsp. (55 g) butter* • *thyme, 1 bay leaf* • *salt, pepper* • *1 egg yolk*

• 30 min. before cooking, smear the tournedos with butter, salt and pepper; cut the marrow in ½ in. (1 cm.) slices. • Cook the tournedos for a few minutes on each side, either under a very hot grill or in a pan of sizzling butter (cook 3-6 min. according to taste). • Put onto a hot plate to keep warm. • Meanwhile, poach the beef marrow in 1 cup boiling, salted water; simmer 3-4 min. • Place a piece of marrow on each tournedos; sprinkle with chopped parsley and serve at once.

• The tournedos may also be served with a Bourguignonne sauce (recipe no. 276).

• Choose a piece of beef fillet, oblong and regular in shape. Do not lard it, but tie neatly with thin white string. • Smear all over with butter and cook in the oven for 15-20 min. (375°F; 190°C; **4**) with a sprig of thyme and a bay leaf. • Halfway through the roasting sprinkle with salt and pepper. Do not let the fillet overcook. • Take from oven; remove the herbs and untie. • While the meat is cooling roll out the pastry (recipe no. 252 or use the frozen variety) in the shape of a rectangle. • Place the roast in the middle and fold the pastry over to cover the meat completely; seal the edges with water. Make a few incisions on the top to let out the steam. • Paint the pastry with a slightly beaten egg yolk and put into a hot oven: (470°F; 243°C; **7**) for approx 20 min. • Serve immediately.

• NB: The meat may be cooked several hours in advance.

BEEF BOURGUIGNON
✤ BOEUF A LA BOURGUIGNONNE

Serves 6

Time: *preparation 20 min.* • *cooking 2-3 hr.*
Ingredients: *about 3 lb. (1.5 kg) round beef top or top rump.* • *½ lb (25g) salt pork.* • *4 tbsp (55 g) butter.* • *4 tbsp. olive oil.* • *1 bottle dry red wine* • *12 pearl onions.* • *2 tbsp. flour.* • *1 bouquet garni.* • *1-2 cloves garlic.* • *1 small glass cognac (optional)* • *salt, pepper, nutmeg*

• Dice the salt pork and cut the beef into large cubes. • Put the pork into a heavy-bottomed saucepan and as the fat begins to melt add the whole onions. • As soon as they begin to turn golden remove them with a slotted spoon. • Add the olive oil and butter and put in the beef to brown over a gentle heat (do not let the butter turn brown). Turn the meat with a wooden spoon so that it browns on all sides. • Sprinkle with flour; stir again. Pour over the warmed cognac and flame (this is optional). • Add the wine (if there is not sufficient to just cover the meat add a little water). • Season with salt, pepper and a pinch of nutmeg; put in the bouquet garni and the garlic and bring to a boil. • Immediately lower the heat. Add the diced pork and onion: cover and simmer over a very low heat for 2-3 hr. (the longer the better). • Serve the meat in its own sauce accompanied by steamed or boiled potatoes.

• NB: As with many dishes of this type, the flavor improves with reheating, so it is better made the day before.
• This recipe calls for an ordinary red table wine. However, if a good Burgundy is used the result is much more delicate.

STEAK A LA BORDELAISE
✤ ENTRECOTE BORDELAISE

Serves 6

Time: *preparation 10 min.* • *cooking 20 min.*
Ingredients: *1 thick steak 3½lb. (1.6 kg)* • *approximately 4½ oz. (125 g) beef marrow.* • *6 shallots.* • *½ cup (1.2 dl) red wine.* • *7 tbsp. (100 g) butter.* • *salt, crushed peppercorns.*

• Melt a large piece of butter in a frying pan (oval if possible) without letting it brown. • Put in the steak and brown for 5 min. on both sides but do not let the butter turn black. • Remove the meat and keep it hot but not cooking. Season. • Meanwhile, poach the marrow in a little hot water for 1-2 min.; cool and slice. • Add more butter to the pan and put in the chopped shallots. When they turn transparent, pour in the wine and bring to a boil over a high flame, stirring and scraping the bottom of the pan. • Lower the heat and cook, still stirring, until the liquid has reduced a little, and the sauce has thickened. • Away from the heat, add the remaining butter bit by bit, stirring with a fork. • When the sauce is smooth, check the seasoning and put in the poached marrow. • Pour over the steak and serve at once.

VEAL CHOPS FLAMBE
❋ COTES DE VEAU FLAMBEES

Serves 6

Time: *preparation 10 min. • cooking 35 min.*
Ingredients: *6 thick veal chops 7-8 oz. (180-200 g) each • 1 lb. (450 g) mushrooms • 4 tbsp. (55 g) butter • 2 tbsp. oil • 1 scant cup (2.5 dl) cream • scant ½ cup (1 dl) cognac • ½ tsp. cornstarch • salt, pepper*

• Ask your butcher to trim the chops and cut out the bone. • Brown the chops 3 at a time using 1 tbsp. oil each time. • Meanwhile, clean the mushrooms. Reserve 6 of the best-looking to use as a garnish and slice the rest. • Cook all the mushrooms in butter but do not allow the butter to turn brown. • Cook the chops in another pan in butter; do this slowly to prevent the meat from shrivelling. • When they are hot enough, add the cognac and flame. • Add the sliced mushrooms with their juices and half the cream. Bring slowly to a boil and simmer very gently until the cream begins to change color. • Mix the cornstarch into the rest of the cream; stir till smooth. Add to the meat and season. • Simmer for a few minutes. • Garnish each chop with a whole mushroom. Serve very hot.

MEDALLIONS OF VEAL
❋ GRENADINS AU POIVRE VERT

Serves 6

Time: *preparation 20 min. • cooking 20 min.*
Ingredients: *6 medium-sized medallions of veal • 3-4 tsp. green peppercorns • 7 tbsp. (100 g) butter • 1 scant cup (2 dl.) dry white wine • 1¼ cup (3 dl) cream • 1 tsp. cornstarch • 1 liqueur glass cognac • salt • ½ tsp. tomato paste • flour*

• Lightly flour each piece of meat. • Cook the pieces gently in butter until they are light brown, but take care not to let the butter burn. • Place them in a dish; pour in the cognac and leave to marinate, covered. • Deglaze the frying pan with the white wine, scraping up all the pan scraps with a wooden spoon or spatula. Add the peppercorns, coarsely crushed. • Boil until the liquid is reduced by half. Pour over the meat. • Mix the cornstarch into the cream; add ½ tsp. tomato paste for coloring (sweet paprika could be substituted) and pour over the meat. • Return the meat and the sauce to the pan and cook for 20 min. over a very low heat; turn the grenadins once through the cooking. • Serve very hot accompanied by rice; sautéed potatoes; French beans, etc.

STUFFED SHOULDER OF VEAL
❋ EPAULE DE VEAU FARCIE

VEAL BIRDS
❋ PAUPIETTES DE VEAU

Serves 8

Time: *preparation 30 min. • cooking 3 hr.*
Ingredients: *1 boned shoulder of veal 2 ½ lb. (1.2 kg). about 14 oz. • (400 g) sausage meat • 9-10 slices (150 g) bread • 3 eggs • about ¾ cup (100 g) pitted green olives • 2 shallots • 2 carrots • 1 large onion • several strips pork fat • 2 cups (½ liter) bouillon • bouquet garni • salt, pepper*

Serves 6

Time: *preparation 30 min. • cooking 50 min.*
Ingredients: *8 escalopes (cutlets) of veal pounded very thin (about 3 ½-4 oz.; 100 g each) • 9 oz. (250 g) ham • 7 oz. (200 g) veal neck meat • 1 egg • 4 tbsp. (55 g) butter • parsley • 3 shallots • 2 onions • 4 tomatoes • 1 glass port wine • ⅔ cup (1.6 dl) cream • salt, pepper • powdered thyme, powdered bay leaves • bouquet garni*

• Hard boil 2 eggs and chop. • Soak the bread in a little bouillon; squeeze as dry as possible. • Make a stuffing with the sausage meat; bread; hard-boiled eggs; chopped shallots and coarsely chopped olives. Bind together with a lightly beaten egg. Season. • Spread the stuffing over the boned shoulder of veal; roll up and tie securely, placing two strips of pork fat at either end to prevent the stuffing from escaping during cooking. • Line an ovenproof casserole with the remaining pork strips and put in the meat. Add the carrots cut in rounds, the chopped onion, the bouquet garni, salt, pepper and half the bouillon. • Cover and cook in a slow oven: (290°F; 143°C; **1**) for 3 hr. • Just before serving, tke out the bouquet garni and untie the veal. Place on a meat dish and serve the sauce separately.

• Trim 6 escalopes to make them rectangular. • Chop up the trimmed scraps, the 2 remaining escalopes, the ham, the neck meat and the parsley. Season and sprinkle lightly with thyme and bay. • Add the lightly beaten egg and 2 tbsp. cream. Mix well and divide among the 6 escalopes. Roll into little packets or "birds" and tie securely. • Melt the butter in a large frying pan and let the "birds" brown slowly (about 20 min.) turning occasionally. Take care not to let the butter burn. • Moisten with the port wine, add the halved tomatoes, chopped onions and shallots, bouquet garni and salt and pepper. Cover and simmer for 30 min. • Put the veal onto a hot serving dish. Pour the remaining cream into the pan; heat without boiling and pour through a sieve over the meat. • Serve immediately.

VEAL JARDINIERE
✳ VEAU JARDINIERE

Serves 6

Time: *preparation 20 min.* • *cooking 2½ hr.*
Ingredients: *about 3 lb. (1.5 kg) breast of veal* • *6-7 lb. (3kg) fresh new garden peas (petits pois)* • *1 lb. (450 g) very small white onions* • *1 ¼-1 ½ lb. (600g) baby carrrots* • *bouquet garni* • *4 tbsp. (55 g) butter* • *½ glass cooking oil* • *salt, pepper, sugar*

• Cube the veal and brown lightly in a frying pan with the oil. When it is nicely golden, transfer to a saucepan with the bouquet garni. • Season and just cover the meat with boiling water. • Simmer, covered, for 1 ½ hr. over a very low flame. • Meanwhile, shell the peas, wash the carrots and peel the onions. • When the meat has cooked 1 ½ hr., add the vegetables and 2 small lumps of sugar. Continue cooking over a low flame. • When the vegetables are cooked (approximately ½ hr.) remove the bouquet garni and add the butter. • Serve at once or keep hot but not boiling.

BLANQUETTE OF VEAL
✳ BLANQUETTE DE VEAU

Serves 6

Time: *preparation 15 min.* • *cooking about 2 hr.*
Ingredients: *about 3½ lb. (1.500 kg) cubed veal (neck, breast, etc)* • *1 lemon* • *2 onions each stuck with 2 cloves* • *2 cloves garlic* • *1 carrot, 1 stick celery, 1 leek (white part only)* • *bouquet garni* • *1 cup (¼ liter) dry white wine* • *½ cup (1.2 dl) cream* • *3 egg yolks* • *10 oz. (300g) mushrooms* • *20 small white onions* • *salt, pepper* • *1 truffle (optional)*

• Sprinkle the veal with lemon juice and put the pieces into a large saucepan with the onions and the finely chopped carrot, celery and leek. • Pour the wine over the meat and add just enough water to cover; add the bouquet garni, garlic, salt and enough pepper to taste. • Bring to a boil; skim; cover; lower the heat and simmer for approximately 1½ hr. • Peel the onions and clean the mushrooms. • When the meat is cooked, take it out of the bouillon and set aside. Strain the bouillon; skim if necessary, and add the onions and mushrooms.Cook, uncovered for ¼ hr.
• Lightly beat the cream and egg yolks together; add the juice of ½ lemon and pour into the hot bouillon, stirring constantly with a wooden spoon. • Check the seasoning (more will be necessary) and return the meat to the pan. Add the chopped truffle (optional). • Heat gently without allowing the blanquette to boil and serve at once accompanied by a dish of rice.

PORK WITH PRUNES
✱ ROTI DE PORC A L'AGENAISE

Serves 6

Time: *preparation 20 min. + 1 ½ hr. marinating • cooking 2 hr*
Ingredients: *1 pork tenderloin about 2¾ lb. (1.2 kg) • ½ lb. (225 g) large prunes • 4 tbsp. (55g) butter • 2 cups (½ liter) bouillon • salt, pepper • bouquet garni • 1 small glass Madeira*

• Soak the prunes for 1 hr. in hot water. Drain and dry carefully.
• Pit 12 prunes and put to marinate in the Madeira for ½ hr. Save the marinade. • Make a cut in the fillet and stuff the marinated prunes into the meat. Close up the opening and tie securely. • Melt the butter in a deep saucepan and brown the pork on all sides. Add the bouquet garni, salt, pepper and 2 tbsp. bouillon. Cover and simmer for ½ hr. • Cook the remaining prunes in the bouillon for 20 min. then add to the meat before the end of the cooking time. • Place the pork on a serving dish and surround with the prunes. • Remove the bouquet garni and decrease the sauce; add the Madeira in which the prunes have marinated and, if necessary, 1 or 2 tbsp. cooking juices from the prunes. • Serve separately, very hot.

PORK CHOPS CHARCUTIERE
✱ COTES DE PORC CHARCUTIERE

Serves 6

Time: *preparation 20 min • cooking 40 min*
Ingredients: *6 rib pork chops • 1 large onion • 3 tbsp. (40g) lard • 1 tbsp. flour • 2 glasses white wine • 1 glass bouillon • 1 tsp. mustard • 3-4 oz. (100g) gherkins • salt, pepper, nutmeg*

• Chop the onions and cook gently in 1 tbsp. lard until transparent. Add the flour and cook for a few minutes stirring all the time. • Away from the fire, add the wine and bouillon together, then the bouqet garni, salt, pepper and a pinch nutmeg. Return to the heat; bring to a boil; then immediately lower the heat and leave to simmer for approximately 30 min. • Brown the chops on both sides in the rest of the lard; reduce the heat and cook for about 15 min. • When they are cooked, drain them and put onto a warm plate. • Away from the heat, thicken the sauce (which should have reduced during cooking) with the mustard; remove the bouquet garni and add the gherkins cut in rounds. • Pour the sauce over the chops and serve.

LOIN OF PORK WITH SAGE
✤ ECHINE DE PORC A LA SAUGE

RAGOUT OF PORK
✤ RAGOUT DE PORC

Serves 6

Time: *preparation 10 min. (begun the previous day)* • *cooking 1¼ hr*
Ingredients: *approximately 3 lb. (1.5 kg) loin of pork, boned* • *3 cloves garlic* • *6 leaves sage* • *1 onion* • *3 glasses dry white wine* • *1 tbsp. olive oil* • *1 tbsp. lard* • *1 branch thyme* • *salt, pepper*

• The day before, make a marinade with the wine, oil, thyme, finely chopped onion, salt and pepper. Let the meat marinate all night. • The next day, drain and dry the meat; make incisions all over and insert the cloves garlic split lengthwise and the sage leaves. Smear all over with the lard and put in a baking dish. • Sprinkle with some of the marinade and place in a pre-heated oven (390°F; 200°C; 5). Cook for about 1 hr. 10 min. • Turn off the oven and leave the roast inside for 5 min. before serving.

Serves 6

Time: *preparation 20 min.* • *cooking 2 hr.*
Ingredients: *1½ lb. (700 g) boned pork cut in 1 in. (2.5 cm) cubes* • *1¾ lb. (800 g) loin of pork with bone* • *2 large tomatoes* • *3 onions* • *6 large potatoes* • *bouquet garni* • *salt, pepper, flour*

• In a frying pan (cast iron is best), but without fat, gently brown the pork. When it is golden, remove and put into a large saucepan. • Cut the loin in pieces and brown in the fat which has run from the pork. • Put into the saucepan and sprinkle with 1 heaping tbsp. flour. Stir so that all the meat cubes are coated. • Add the whole tomatoes, onions, bouquet garni and enough water to just cover the meat and vegetables. Bring quickly to a boil; lower the heat, season and simmer for 1½ hr. • Add the peeled potatoes and cook for another 20-30 min. • As soon as the potatoes are cooked, the ragout is ready to serve.

SMOKED SHOULDER OF PORK WITH LENTILS
❖ PALETTE DE PORC AUX LENTILLES

Serves 6

Time: *preparation 5 min. + 12-24 hr. soaking • cooking 2 hr.*
Ingredients: *1 smoked pork shoulder • 1 lb. (450 g) lentils • 1 large onion stuck with 2 cloves • bouquet garni*

• The day before, soak the shoulder of pork in cold water. • The next day, wash the lentils and put into a saucepan; cover with cold water; add the onion and bouquet garni. Do not add salt. • Bring to a boil and put in the drained smoke shoulder. Simmer gently for 2 hr. • Serve very hot with mustard on the side.

HAM WITH NAVY BEANS
❖ JAMBONNEAU AUX FLAGEOLETS

Serves 6

Time: *preparation 15 min. + 3-4 hr. soaking • cooking 1¼ hr.*
Ingredients: *1 fresh hock or foreleg of ham • 1¼ lb. (600 g) small dried white kidney beans (navy beans) • bouquet garni • 3 cloves garlic • 1 onion stuck with 2 cloves • salt, pepper • chopped parsley*

• Soak the beans for 3-4 hr. Then drain, and put into a large saucepan with the ham; cover with cold water and bring slowly to a boil. • Skim; add the bouquet garni, onion, garlic, salt and pepper. Cook for at least 1 hr. If possible, cook longer, as this improves the flavor of the beans. • To serve, remove the bouquet garni, drain the ham, slice and arrange on a serving dish surrounded by the beans and sprinkled with chopped parsley.

LAMB WITH SORREL
❋ SAUTE D'AGNEAU A L'OSEILLE

LEG OF LAMB "EN CROUTE"
❋ GIGOT D'AGNEAU EN CROUTE

Serves 6

Time: *preparation 10 min.* • *cooking 35 min.*
Ingredients: *2¼ lb. (1 kg) cubed lamb (breast and shoulder)* • *½ lb. (225 g) sorrel* • *2 cups bouillon* • *2 onions* • *1 tbsp. flour* • *1 egg yolk* • *6 tbsp. (85 g) butter* • *oil, salt, pepper*

Serves 4

Time: *preparation 30 min.* • *cooking 40 min.*
Ingredients: *1 small leg of lamb approx 3-3½ lb. (1.5 kg)* • *2 lamb kidneys* • *¾ cup (150 g) butter* • *1 glass Madeira* • *about ¼ lb. (100 g) mushrooms* • *1 egg* • *1 lb. (450 g) puff pastry* • *salt, pepper* • *thyme, rosmary, tarragon*

• Heat the butter with some oil (to prevent the butter from burning) in a large frying pan. Add the cubes of lamb to brown. Stir so that the pieces brown on all sides and, as they are ready, remove them from the pan but keep them warm; season. • Wash the sorrel carefully. • Chop the onions; put them into the frying pan; sprinkle with flour and stir while they brown lightly. • Pour in the bouillon; season and add the sorrel. • Return the lamb to the pan and simmer, covered, over a low heat for approximately 30 min. • To serve, put the meat and vegetables in a heated dish. Away from the heat, beat 1 egg yolk into the cooking juices in the pan and pour over the meat.

• Ask your butcher to bone the lamb. • Make the pastry beforehand (see recipe no. 253) or thaw the frozen variety. • Remove the thin skin and fibres from the kidneys, and cut into small pieces. Cook in 6 tbsp. (85 g) butter for a few mintues. • Deglaze the pan with Madeira and throw in the finely sliced mushrooms. • Add salt, pepper and a branch each of rosemary and thyme along with 1 tsp. chopped tarragon. Cook gently for several minutes. • Stuff this mixture into the cavity left in the leg of lamb by the removal of the bone. Close up the opening and secure firmly with skewers. • Smear the meat with the remaining butter then put into a preheated oven (425°F; 220°C; 7-8) • Roll out the pastry to ¼ in. (½ cm.) thickness; wrap it around the meat sealing the edges with water; brush the pastry with the lightly beaten egg yolk and return to the oven for 15-20 min. Serve very hot, without delay.

ROAST RACK OF LAMB PRINTANIER
✻ CARRE D'AGNEAU PRINTANIER

Serves 6

Time: *preparation cooking 25 min.*
Ingredients: *rib roast of lamb • salt, pepper*

• Ask your butcher to trim the lamb. • Set your oven to the maximum heat. • Put the meat, fat side down, on a rack in a baking or dripping pan, and place in the oven. As soon as the ends of the bones start to blacken turn the meat over. • Season with salt and pepper and judge when the lamb is ready by the crispy golden appearance of the fat. • Turn off the oven and leave the lamb inside for another 5-8 min. • Carve the lamb into chops (cutlets) and serve at once on very hot plates.

SPRING LAMB POULETTE
✻ AGNEAU DE LAIT POULETTE

Serves 6

Time: *preparation 15 min. • cooking 50 min.*
Ingredients: *about 3¼ lb. (1.5 kg) spring lamb (shoulder, neck, chuck) • 5 tbsp. (70 g) butter • 9 oz. (250 g) mushrooms • bouquet garni • 3 onions • ¾ cup (2 dl) dry white wine • ½ cup (1.2 dl) cream • 2 egg yolks • 1 lemon • flour, salt, pepper*

• Cut up the meat and brown the pieces in a heavy-bottomed pan without adding any extra fat. When the meat is half-cooked, set aside to drain. • Melt the butter in a saucepan and cook the onions until transparent but do not let them brown. • Put in the meat and sprinkle with flour (about 2 tbsp.); stir well and add the white wine and a little water. Season; put in the bouquet garni; cover and simmer 30 min. • At the end of this time, add the cleaned mushrooms and let the "poulette" simmer for a further 15 min. over a very low heat. • Beat the cream lightly with the egg yolks and a little lemon juice. Stir in some of the cooking juices but do not let the eggs cook. • Away from the heat, remove the bouquet garni and pour the egg mixture into the pan. Stir well while reheating but do not let the sauce come to a boil. • Serve immediately.

RAGOUT OF MUTTON AND BABY TURNIPS
⚜ RAGOUT DE MOUTON AUX NAVETS

Serves 6

Time: *preparation 30 min* • *cooking 1¾ hr.*
Ingredients: *4½ lb. (2 kg) mutton chops* • *4½ lb. baby turnips* • *2 tbsp. lard* • *4 onions* • *bouquet garni* • *1 clove garlic* • *salt, pepper, flour* • *6 large potatoes*

• Brown the chops in a heavy-bottomed pan without adding extra fat. • Transfer them to a deep saucepan and sprinkle with flour. Move the chops around a little so that the flour cooks in the meat juices, add the chopped onion, garlic bouquet garni and 1 cup water, (2.5 dl). • Bring to boiling point then lower the heat at once. Simmer, covered, over a very low heat. • Peel and quarter the turnips. Brown the pieces in a frying-pan in the lard. Drain and put into the stew. • Season and cook slowly for a further 1¼ hr. • Meanwhile, peel the potatoes and lay them on top of the stew 1¼ hr. after the turnips. • The ragout is ready when the potatoes are cooked: approx ½ hr., but test with a pointed knife to be sure.

MUTTON WITH SHELL BEANS
⚜ HARICOT DE MOUTON

Serves 6

Time: *preparation 15 min.* • *cooking 2½ hr.*
Ingredients: *2¼lb. (1 kg) white haricot or shell beans* • *1 shoulder mutton* • *2 carrots* • *2 onions* • *2 cloves garlic* • *bouquet garni* • *4 tbsp. lard*

• Choose fresh white beans. Wash but do not soak them. • Put them into a large quantity of cold water and bring to boiling point. Boil for 10 min. Throw away the water and add the same quantity of boiling salted water. Cook until tender. • Meanwhile, brown the cubed meat in the lard in a large saucepan. Turn to brown on all sides and add the carrots cut into rounds, the chopped onion, garlic and bouquet garni. • Cover and simmer over a very low heat for 40 min. • Drain the cooked beans, reserving a few tbsp. of the water, and add them to the meat. Moisten with the reserved cooking liquid and cover. • Simmer for at least another hour.

LAMB's KIDNEYS CHARENTAISE
✳ ROGNONS D'AGNEAU A LA CHARENTAISE

CREAMED VEAL KIDNEYS
✳ ROGNONS DE VEAU A LA CREME

Serves 4

Time: *preparation 25 min* • *cooking 10 min.*
Ingredients: *4 fresh young lamb's kidneys* • *7 tbsp. (100 g) butter* • *3 tbsp. cognac* • *2 cloves garlic* • *9 oz. (250g) mushrooms* • *1 lemon* • *½ cup (1.2 dl) cream* • *salt, black pepper*

Serves 6

Time: *preparation 5 min* • *cooking 25 min.*
Ingredients: *2¼lb. (1 kg) veal kidneys* • *4 tbsp. (55 g) butter* • *scant ½ cup (1 dl) cognac* • *1 scant cup (2.2 dl) cream* • *1 tsp. potato flour or cornstarch* • *1 tsp. strong mustard* • *salt, pepper, nutmeg*

• Clean the mushrooms in a mixture of lemon juice and water. Cut into thick slices and allow to cook for a few minutes in half the butter, a small spoonful lemon juice and a little water. • Meanwhile, remove the thin outer skin from the kidneys and take out the gristly center filament and clot of blood from the middle without, however, separating the two halves. Heat the remaining butter and brown the kidneys slowly on both sides. Season with salt, freshly ground black pepper and minced garlic. • Sprinkle with warmed cognac and flame. • Put the kidneys onto a hot plate. • Empty the mushrooms and their cooking juices into the pan in which the kidneys were cooked; add the cream and stir carefully. • Reheat without boiling, pour over the kidneys and serve at once.

• Remove the thin outer skin and the center filament from the kidneys. • Melt the butter in a pan and cook the kidneys on both sides for a few minutes only; do not let the butter brown. Add the cognac; cover the pan and heat for a minute or two. • Remove from the heat and leave for 10 min. for the kidneys to marinate. Take them from the pan and keep them hot. • Reduce the cooking juices by half; add salt, freshly ground black pepper and a pinch nutmeg. • Mix the potato flour or corn starch into the cream and pour into the cooking juices. Simmer, uncovered, for a few minutes. • Add the kidney but be careful that they do not overcook. They should still be a little pink but neither too raw nor too cooked. • Just before serving stir the mustard into the sauce, pour over the kidneys and serve hot.

BRAINS WITH CAPERS
❊ CERVELLES AUX CAPRES

CALF'S LIVER COCOTTE
❊ FOIE DE VEAU COCOTTE

Serves 4

Time: *preparation 15 min. + ½ hr. soaking • cooking 15 min.*
Ingredients: *4 lamb's or calves' brains • 7 tbsp. (100 g) butter • 4 tbsp. capers • 1 lemon • 2 tbsp. flour • bouquet garni • vinegar • parsley • salt, pepper*

Serves 10

Time: *preparation 45 min. • cooking 1 hr.*
Ingredients: *1 whole calf's liver 4¼-5 lb. (2-2.5 kg) • ¾ cup (2 dl) Madeira • 3 cups (¾ liter) dry white wine • 3 shallots • 2 onions • 1 carrot • bouquet garni. • 6 tbsp. (85g) butter • salt, pepper, nutmeg, potato flour or cornstarch. • 1 clove • 1 small can truffles*

• Soak the brains in cold water and a little vinegar for 30 min. Remove the membranes and fatty filaments. • Put the brains into a large saucepan of water mixed with vinegar (2 tbsp. vinegar to every quart water); add the bouquet garni, salt and pepper. • Bring to a boil and lower the heat at once. Simmer gently for approx 10 min. • Drain and, when cool, slice the brains and dip in flour; brown for a few minutes on each side, in butter. • Arrange on a hot dish; sprinkle with lemon juice and the butter in which the brains were browned; decorate each slice with chopped parsley and a few capers.

• Ask the butcher to lard the liver lengthwise with 5 or 6 strips of pork fat and to wrap it in a thin covering of fat and tie in the shape of a long oval roast. • Melt the butter in a heavy-bottomed casserole and cook the chopped onions, shallots, carrots and bouquet sliced in rounds and bouquet garni until the vegetables start to soften. • Add the Madeira and white wine. Season with salt, pepper, nutmeg and 1 clove. • Cover and allow to simmer over a low heat for 30 min. • Sieve or put through a food mill to extract all the juices. • Place the liver in an ovenproof casserole and pour the sauce over it (it should reach halfway up the side). Cover and put in a preheated oven: (425˚F; 220˚C; 7) for 30 min. Then turn the liver over and cook for a further 30 min. • It is very important that the sauce should simmer gently and not actually boil. • Remove the liver at the end of the cooking time; untie and take off the thin covering of fat. • Degrease the sauce and thicken with 1 tbsp. potato flour or cornstarch moistened in a little water. Simmer for a few minutes; season. • Serve the liver garnished with truffles with the sauce on the side.

SWEETBREADS JARDINIERE
❋ RIS DE VEAU JARDINIERE

Serves 6

Time: *preparation 45 min. + 3 hr. soaking • cooking 45 min.*
Ingredients: *2 sweetbreads about 1½ lb. (700 g) each • 7 oz about (200 g) fat salt pork • 2 shallots • 2 onions • 1 glass Madeira • 1¼ lb (600 g) new peas (petits pois) • 8 baby carrots • bouquet garni • 6 tbsp. (85 g) butter • 1 small sugar lump • salt, pepper, nutmeg*

• Soak the sweetbreads in 3 or 4 changes of cold water for 3 hr. until the blood has disappeared. Put into a pan of fresh cold water and bring slowly to a boil; boil for 3 min. • Plunge into cold water and remove the fibrous bits but not the thin membraneous skin surrounding the sweetbreads. • Dice the salt pork and put into a thick-bottomed pan to melt over a low heat. • Remove, and brown the sweetbreads in the resulting fat. When they are a golden color all over, take them out, throw away the cooking fat and carefully clean the pan before putting the butter in it to melt. • Add the diced pork, the sweetbreads, the finely chopped shallots and onions and the bouquet garni. Season with salt, pepper and a pinch of nutmeg. • Place, uncovered, over a very low flame for 10 min. • Add the Madeira; cover the pan and leave to simmer for 25 min. • Meanwhile, boil the carrots and peas separately, then add them to the sweetbreads with 1 small sugar lump. Simmer for a further 15 min. • Serve the sweetbreads cut in slices, surrounded by the vegetables.

SWEETBREADS FINANCIERE
❋ RIS DE VEAU FINANCIERE

Serves 4

Time: *preparation 30 min. + 3 hr. soaking • cooking 50 min.*
Ingredients: *1¾ lb. (800 g) sweetbreads • ¼ lb. (110 g) mushrooms • about 3 oz. (100 g) green olives • 1 small can veal quenelles (available in specialty stores) • 1 small can truffle peelings • 5 tbsp. (50 g) flour • 1 glass dry white wine • 1 carrot • 1 onion • 2 cups (½ liter) bouillon • salt, pepper*

• Soak the sweetbreads in 3 or 4 changes of cold water for 3 hr. • Plunge into cold salted water and bring slowly to the boil; simmer 4-5 min. • Drain; rinse in cold water; remove the fibrous threads, wrap in a piece of muslin and place under a heavy weight until they are completely cold. • Meanwhile chop up the carrot and onion and brown slowly in half the butter; sprinkle with a little flour and stir until browned. • Add the sweetbreads and truffle peelings; moisten with white wine; season and cook over a low heat for 30 min. If necessary, add a little bouillon. • Melt the remaining butter and stir in the rest of the flour; then stir in the bouillon until the mixture is perfectly smooth. • Season and add the quenelles, the pitted olives and the sliced mushrooms. • When the sauce is hot arrange the sweetbreads on a heated serving dish with the vegetables and sauce.

POULTRY AND GAME

Do we not even today see people
who have discovered
the particular savor
of the thigh
on which the partridge leans, sleeping?

DEVILLED CHICKEN
❋ POULET A LA DIABLE

CHICKEN WITH MUSHROOMS
❋ POULET AUX CHAMPIGNONS

Serves 4

Time: *preparation 50 min. • cooking 30 min.*
Ingredients: *1 tender chicken • 2 eggs • 2 tbsp. Dijon mustard • I large carrot • 1 onion • 2-4 oz. (50-100 g) ham, finely chopped • dried breadcrumbs • 1 glass white wine • 1 glass Madeira • oil, salt, pepper • bouquet garni*

Serves 6

Time: *preparation 30 min. • cooking 1¼ hr.*
Ingredients: *1 chicken 3-4 lb. (1.5 kg) • 5 oz. (150 g) salt pork or bacon • 7 tbsp. (100 g) butter • 2 tbsp. cooking oil • 1 lb. (450 g) large mushrooms • 12 small onions • 1 glass dry white wine • 1 glass chicken bouillon • bouquet garni • 1 lemon • ½ cup (1.2 dl) light cream • 2 tbsp. chopped parsley • 1 clove garlic • salt, pepper*

• Divide the chicken into 4 portions and flatten each piece by beating with a pestle or steak mallet. • Beat the eggs. • Mix the mustard in a bowl with the salt and pepper and gradually stir in the eggs to get a creamy consistency. • Dip each chicken piece in this mixture turning so that they are well covered, then coat with the breadcrumbs, patting them on so that they will adhere. • Place the chicken in an ovenproof dish with a little olive oil and roast for 30 min. at 350°F (180°C; **4**) or until the juices run yellow when pricked with a fork. • Meanwhile, prepare the accompanying sauce: • Chop the carrot and the onion and mix with the ham; brown in a little oil with the bouquet garni and seasonings. The mixture should turn slightly golden without burning. • Add a glass of white wine and a sherry glass of Madeira, and simmer gently until the liquid has reduced slightly. Serve in a sauce boat accompanying the chicken.

• Divide the chicken in 12 portions (or buy 12 chicken pieces). • Cut the pork or bacon into small pieces and sauté until golden in a mixture of 3 tbsp. (40 g) butter and some oil. • Remove the pork bits with a slotted spoon, draining carefully and put aside. • Put the chicken pieces in the pan and brown on all sides. • Remove and put in the onions. • Put the chicken and the pork (or bacon) back in the pan, add the wine, bouillon, salt, pepper and bouquet garni. • Cover and simmer gently for about 1 hr. • Meanwhile, clean the mushrooms and rinse quickly in water to which you have added the juice of a lemon. • Cut the largest in pieces and cook all of them in a covered saucepan for a few minutes until their juices run. • Drain, and put back on the stove with the remainder of the butter, the crushed garlic and some of the parsley. Cook on a low heat for 10 min. • When the chicken is cooked, take it from the pan; put the pieces on a heated serving dish and arrange the mushrooms around them. • Add the cream and the garlic-mushrooms butter to the juices in the chicken pan; heat without boiling. • Pour this sauce along with the onions and the pork morsels over the chicken; sprinkle with the rest of the chopped parsley and serve at once.

CHICKEN WITH GARLIC
✳ POULET A L'AIL

CHICKEN AURORA
✳ POULARDE A L'AURORE

Serves 4

Time: *preparation 15 min. • cooking 50 min.*
Ingredients: *1 chicken 2½-3 lb. (1.5 kg) • scant ½ cup (1 dl) white wine • 5 oz. (150 g) bacon • 6 cloves garlic • 7 tbsp. (100 g) butter • 2 tbsp. oil • 1 tbsp. flour • bouquet garni • salt, pepper • small croutons • 1 extra chicken liver*

Serves 6

Time: *preparation 20 min. • cooking 3 hr.*
Ingredients: *1 large capon, 6-7 lb. (3 kg) • 2 carrots • 2 leeks • 1 large stalk celery • bouquet garni • 2 eggs • 1 heaped tbsp. soft breadcrumbs • 6 tbsp. tomato purée • 2 shallots • ½ cup + 3 tbsp. (150 g) butter • ¾ lb. (350 g) tomatoes • 4 tbsp. (40 g) flour • 2 tbsp. light cream • salt, pepper*

• Cut the chicken into several pieces, keeping the liver aside. • Melt half the butter and some of the oil in a flameproof casserole and brown the chicken on all sides. • Add the wine, garlic, bouquet garni, salt and pepper. Cover and simmer gently for 40-50 min. • Cut the bacon into 1-½ in. (3 cm) pieces and brown in the rest of the oil. • Sear the chicken livers in a little butter and then mash them. • Fry the croutons. • Prepare a "beurre manié" with the flour and remaining butter (form small balls of softened butter and flour to be used in the sauce later). • Just before the end of the cooking, carefully remove the garlic from the chicken (do not throw away) and add the bacon. • Mash the garlic with the chicken livers and spread onto the croûtons. • Arrange the pieces of chicken on a heated serving dish and surround with the croûtons. • Keep hot while you quickly drop the "beurre manié" into the remaining sauce in the casserole, and mix well until it is smooth. • Pour over the chicken and serve hot.

• Boil the vegetables together in 3-4 quarts (3-4 liters) salted water in a very large saucepan. • Meanwhile, prepare a stuffing with the breadcrumbs, the finely chopped shallots, half the tomato purée, the chopped chicken liver, 3-4 tbsp. (50 g) butter, 1 egg slightly beaten, salt and pepper. • Stuff the chicken with this mixture and sew up the opening or fasten very securely with skewers. • Carefully plunge the chicken into the boiling vegetables; lower the heat; cover and simmer for 2½-3 hr. • Halve the tomatoes, sprinkle with salt and leave for 30 min. Then scoop out the seeds and drain off the salted juice. • Make a roux with the flour and 3-4 tbsp. (50 g) butter. Using the liquid in which the chicken has been cooking, stir into a smooth sauce. • Add the cream and the beaten egg, stirring briskly all the time. Add the rest of the tomato purée. • Sauté the halved tomatoes in the remaining butter. • Take the chicken from the pan; divide into portions and arrange on a serving dish with the stuffing piled in the center; put the tomatoes around the edge of the dish. • Cover the chicken with some of the sauce and serve the rest separately.

NORMANDY SQUAB
❊ COQUELETS A LA NORMANDE

COQ·AU·VIN

Serves 6

Time: *preparation 10 min.* • *cooking 30 min.*
Ingredients: *3 squabs or baby chickens 1-1½ lb. (500 g) each* • *3 glasses dry cider* • *1 small glass Calvados (or apple brandy)* • *6 tbsp. (85 g) butter* • *3 tbsp. oil* • *2 carrots* • *4 shallots, bouquet garni* • *1 tsp. cornstarch* • *¾ cup (1.8 dl) cream* • *salt, pepper, nutmeg*

Serves 6

Time: *preparation 20 min. + 1 hr. for marinating* • *cooking 50 min.*
Ingredients: *1 4½ lb. (2 kg) chicken* • *6-7 oz. (180 g) bacon* • *20 pearl onions* • *4 shallots* • *4 tbsp. (55 g) butter* • *1 small glass cognac warmed* • *1 bottle (1 liter) red wine* • *12 button mushrooms* • *bouquet garni* • *1 clove garlic* • *1 cube sugar* • *3 tbsp. (30 g) flour* • *salt, pepper, nutmeg* • *2 heaping tbsp. finely chopped parsley*

• Cut each squab (or chicken) in two. • In a flameproof casserole melt 4 tbsp. (55 g) butter and 2 tbsp. oil. Let the chicken halves cook gently in this mixture until they turn golden. • Remove from the pan and discard the fat. • Put the rest of the butter and the oil into the same pan and add the whole shallots and the carrots coarsely cut in 3 or 4 pieces. • Replace the chicken halves in the pan; sprinkle with the Calvados and cover. • Leave for 3-4 min. for the chicken to absorb the flavor of the brandy, then add the cider, bouquet garni, seasonings and a pinch of nutmeg, and simmer gently for 20-25 min. • Meanwhile, stir a little of the cream into the cornstarch and work to a smooth paste. Add the rest of the cream gradually. • As soon as they are cooked through, place the squabs on a serving dish and keep hot. • Skim as much fat as possible from the surface of the sauce remaining in the casserole. Add the cream sauce and a few drops of lemon juice. • Heat but do not allow to boil or the cream will separate. • Pour some of the sauce through a sieve over the chicken and serve the remainder separately. • Sliced apples sautéed in butter make a good accompaniment to this dish.

• Heat the chopped bacon in a heavy frying pan without any extra fat. • When the pieces begin to melt, add the peeled, whole onions and the well-washed mushrooms. • When bacon, onions and mushrooms are golden, remove with a slotted spoon, and keep warm. • Meanwhile, cut the chicken into serving pieces; add to the pan and brown gently on all sides. • Add the warmed brandy and set it alight. When the flames have died down add the finely chopped shallots and bouquet garni. • Cover and simmer very gently for 20 min. • Reheat the chopped bacon in a saucepan and pour in ¾ of the wine. • Bring to a boil and pour over the chicken. Add more wine until the chicken is completely covered. • Season with salt and pepper, add the sugar cube and a little grated nutmeg. • Put in the onions and mushrooms and simmer for 30-40 min. • Make a "beurre manié" by rolling the softened butter into little balls with the flour. • Arrange the chicken, onions and mushrooms on a heated serving dish and keep warm in the oven. • Quickly stir the "beurre manié" into the sauce remaining in the casserole. Transfer to a sauce boat. • Sprinkle the chicken with the parsley and serve.

CHICKEN IN WHITE SAUCE
✽ POULET AU BLANC

Serves 6

Time: *preparation 10 min.* • *cooking 1½ hr.*
Ingredients: *1 chicken 3-4 lb. (1.6 kg)* • *about ½ lb. (250 g) mushroom caps* • *2 carrots* • *10 small onions* • *¾ cup (2 dl) light cream* • *bouquet garni* • *2 egg yolks* • *3 lemons* • *2 rounded tbsp. flour* • *6 tbsp. (85 g) butter* • *1 glass white wine.* • *salt, pepper, nutmeg.*

• Run cold water through the cavities of the chicken after removing the giblets etc. Rub carefully inside and out with lemon juice; truss. • Melt the butter in a flameproof casserole and add the flour. Stir for 2 min. to make a smooth paste. • Slowly add 2 large glasses of cold water stirring constantly to prevent lumps. • Bring to a boil and add seasonings. • Place the trussed chicken in the casserole and add the white wine, peeled onions, the carrots sliced into rounds and the bouquet garni. • Simmer over a low heat for 1¼ hr., but after ¾ hr. add the mushroom caps to the casserole, having previously rinsed them in cold water mixed with lemon juice and cut the larger ones into 2-3 pieces. • Beat the egg yolks with the cream, then slowly add the juice of 1 lemon, beating all the time. • To serve, remove the chicken and vegetables from the casserole but keep hot. Take out the bouquet garni. • Add the beaten egg yolks and cream very gradually to the stock in the casserole. Stir well. • Check the seasoning and reheat but do not boil. • Cut the chicken into serving pieces and arrange with the vegetables on a heated serving dish. Cover with some of the sauce and pour the remainder into a sauce-boat to be served separately. • Rice is a good accompaniment to this dish.

RABBIT WITH MUSTARD
✽ LAPIN A LA MOUTARDE

Serves 6

Time: *preparation 10 min.* • *cooking 2 hr. 20 min.*
Ingredients: *1 tender rabbit, about 2½ lb. (1.2 kg)* • *1 small glass Dijon mustard + 1 tsp. English mustard* • *1 glass white wine* • *4 tbsp. (55 g) butter* • *1¼ cups (3 dl) light cream* • *bouquet garni (if cooked on top of the stove) or ¼ lb. (100 g) fat salt pork thinly sliced (if cooked in oven)* • *salt, pepper*

• There are 2 ways of cooking this dish:
(1.) *On top of the stove in a flameproof casserole.* • Mix the butter and the mustard until smooth and spread it both inside and all over the outside of the rabbit with a spatula. • Brown rabbit all over in a little oil in the casserole. • Cover and cook very gently for 15 min. on an asbestos mat. • Add a glass of white wine and the bouquet garni; cover and simmer for 2 hr. • Remove the rabbit from the casserole and throw away the bouquet garni. • Cut the meat into serving pieces and arrange on a hot serving dish; keep warm. • Stir the cream into the stock and heat without boiling. Pour over the rabbit and serve.
(2.) *In the oven:* • prepare the rabbit as in the previous recipe, but when it is smeared all over with mustard, wrap it in a covering of thinly sliced pieces of salt pork. If necessary tie these on with thin twine. • Place on a rack over a dripping pan and put into a slow (300˚F, 150˚C; 1·2) oven. • Roast for about 1¼-1½ hr. • Cut in pieces and keep hot on a heated serving dish. • Skim the top layer of fat from the dripping-pan and add the white wine and cream, stirring all the time. • Pour the sauce over the rabbit and serve.

BLANQUETTE OF RABBIT
❋ BLANQUETTE DE LAPIN

Serves 6

Time: *preparation 20 min.* • *cooking 1½ hr.*
Ingredients: *1 large rabbit 3¼ lb. (1. kg)* • *2 carrots* • *2 leeks* • *2 turnips* • *2 onions* • *1 large clove garlic* • *½-¾ lb. (250 g) button mushrooms* • *bouquet garni* • *1 lemon* • *1 egg yolk* • *1 generous cup (¼ liter) white wine* • *4 tbsp. (55 g) butter* • *3 tbsp. (30 g) flour* • *salt, pepper, cayenne*

• Thoroughly clean, then cut into small pieces, the carrots, leeks and turnips, and plunge into boiling salted water for 5 min. • Drain carefully and put into a deep dish sprinkled with lemon juice. • In a flameproof casserole put the rabbit cut into serving pieces, the vegetables, the peeled chopped onions, the bouquet garni, chopped garlic, salt, pepper and a pinch of cayenne. • Cover with cold water and bring to a boil; skim; lower the heat, cover the pot and leave to simmer for about 1¼ hr on an asbestos mat. • Meanwhile, sauté the carefully wiped mushrooms for about 10 min. in a pan with ½ the butter and a little water and lemon juice. • Fifteen minutes before the rabbit is cooked, add the mushrooms and their juices to the casserole. • In another saucepan melt the rest of the butter and mix with the flour to a smooth paste without letting it brown. • Gradually stir in 2 cups (½ liter) of liquid made in equal parts of white wine and the stock taken from the rabbit. • Take off the heat and add by the tsp. to the beaten egg yolk stirring constantly until a smooth sauce is obtained without the egg cooking. Then add the rest of the liquid in a thin stream, still stirring. • Season and pour over the rabbit and vegetables which you have drained of the remaining juices.

STUFFED RABBIT
❋ LAPIN FARCI

Serves 6

Time: *preparation 25 min.* • *cooking 1½-2 hr.*
Ingredients: *1 rabbit 3¼ lb. (1.kg)* • *2 chicken livers* • *approximately ½ lb. (200 g) sausage meat (or a mixture of minced raw pork and veal)* • *7-8 oz. (200 g) smoked bacon or streaky pork* • *5-6 oz. (150 g) button mushrooms* • *1 onion* • *1 shallot* • *3 cloves garlic* • *several green olives pitted* • *4 tbsp. (55 g) butter* • *olive oil* • *bouquet garni* • *½ cup (1.2 dl) white wine* • *salt, pepper*

• Cut the pork into small "lardons" about 1½ in. long by 1 in. (2.5 × 3 cm) and melt them gently in a pan over a low heat without any extra fat. • When they are golden on all sides, remove with a slotted spoon, put aside and brown the sausage meat in the pan. • Repeat the process with the chicken livers and the liver from the rabbit. • Remove the livers and replace with the finely chopped onion and shallot. Pour their juices onto the sliced mushrooms. • Blanch the olives for 5 min. in boiling water. • Coarsley chop the lardons, livers and olives and mix with the mushrooms, onion, crushed garlic and shallot. Add the sausage meat and mix well. • Stuff the rabbit with this mixture and sew up the openings with thin white string. • Put the rabbit into a flameproof casserole just large enough to hold it, so that it is coiled round; add 2 large tbsp. olive oil and the bouquet garni. • Let the rabbit brown over a moderate heat then add the wine. • Simmer over a gentle heat for 1½-2 hr. • Serve the rabbit covered with the cooking juices which you have thickened with the butter and a little flour, added bit by bit away from the fire.

RABBIT IN PAPILLOTES
❋ LAPIN EN PAPILLOTE

RABBIT CHASSEUR
❋ LAPIN CHASSEUR

Serves 4

Time: *preparation 15 min.* ● *cooking 1 hr.*
Ingredients: *1 loin of large rabbit or hare* ● *4 thin slices bacon* ● *4 tbsp. (55 g) butter* ● *marjoram, rosemary, thyme, oregano, chervil* ● *salt, pepper* ● *aluminum foil*

Serves 6

Time: *preparation 15 min.* ● *cooking 1¼ hr.*
Ingredients: *1 rabbit 2½–3 lb. (1.3 kg)* ● *2 onions chopped* ● *2 shallots chopped* ● *1 clove garlic* ● *bouquet garni* ● *2 large glasses white wine* ● *1 small glass cognac* ● *7-8 oz. (200 g) mushrooms* ● *4 oz. (100 g) fat salt pork* ● *4 tbsp. (55 g) butter* ● *1 tbsp. chopped parsley* ● *flour* ● *salt, pepper, nutmeg* ● *1 lemon*

● Cut the meat into 4 pieces and wrap each one in a slice of bacon. ● Place on a piece of aluminum foil cut in the shape of a heart approximately 10 in. (25 cm) long. ● Season and sprinkle generously with the herbs. ● Fold the foil over and roll the edges together sealing tightly to keep in the juices; be careful not to tear. ● Place in a fairly hot oven (437˚F; 225˚C; **6·7**) for 50 min. ● Turn off the oven and leave the casserole inside for a further 10 min. ● Serve in the papillotes.

● Cut the rabbit into serving pieces and the salt pork into small ''lardons.'' ● Melt the ''lardons'' in a pan over a low heat without any extra fat. When they begin to turn golden put in the rabbit and brown the pieces gently on all sides. ● Pour the warmed cognac into the pan and flame. ● Sprinkle lightly with flour and turn the pieces until the flour begins to brown. Add the wine slowly, then the onions and shallots, the bouquet garni, the crushed garlic, salt, pepper and a ¼ tsp. grated nutmeg. ● Bring to the boil; skim if necessary; lower the heat; cover and simmer 1 hr. ● Clean the mushrooms in a mixture of water and lemon juice and, if large enough, cut into quarters. Add to the rabbit and simmer for 15 minutes. ● Prepare a ''beurre manie'' by making little balls of softened butter and flour. ● Arrange the rabbit on a heated serving dish and remove the bouquet garni. Keep the rabbit hot. ● Keeping the casserole off the heat, quickly add the ''beurre Manié'' to the remaining sauce and stir until smooth. ● Pour over the rabbit, sprinkle with chopped parsley and serve.

RABBIT WITH OLIVES
❋ LAPIN AUX OLIVES

RABBIT IN MADEIRA
❋ LAPIN AU MADERE

Serves 6

Time: *preparation 25 min. ● cooking 1 hr.*
Ingredients: *1 rabbit 2½–3 lb. (1.3 kg) ● about 30 pitted black olives ● ½ cup (1.2 dl) white wine ● 3 tbsp. olive oil ● 2 large onions coarsely chopped ● 6 cloves garlic chopped ● 2 tbsp. tomato paste ● bouquet garni ● salt, pepper ● 2 heaping tbsp. chopped parsley and fresh basil ● powdered thyme, rosemary, chervil, sage etc.*

Serves 6

Time: *preparation ½ hr. ● cooking 1½ hr.*
Ingredients: *2 loins of rabbit cut into pieces ● 7 tbsp. (100 g) butter ● 2 onions ● 2 shallots ● 3 carrots ● 2 turnips ● the white parts of 2 leeks ● 1 small stalk celery ● 3-4 oz. (100 g) salt pork ● 1 rounded tbsp. (10 g) flour ● bouquet garni ● ½ cup (1.2 dl) stock ● ½ cup (1.2 dl) Madeira ● salt, pepper ● chopped parsley*

● Cut the rabbit into serving pieces. ● Warm the oil in a flame-proof casserole and lightly brown the onion and rabbit pieces on all sides. ● Remove the pieces from the pan. ● Skim the fat off the surface of the pan and add the wine. Boil for 1 min. ● Replace the rabbit and add the onions, garlic, tomato paste, bouquet garni, salt and pepper; sprinkle the powdered herbs over the surface. ● Simmer gently, covered, for 45 min. ● Add the olives and cook for another 15 min. ● Before serving, place the rabbit on a hot serving dish, remove the bouquet garni and sprinkle the olives over the meat along with the chopped parsley and basil.

● NB: If the sauce looks too dry during the cooking some water can be added to keep the casserole moist and simmering.

● Clean and finely chop all the vegetables. ● Cut the rabbit into smallish pieces and slice the salt pork into "lardons" about 1 in. x 1½ in. (2.5 x 3 cm). ● Melt the butter in a flameproof casserole. ● Brown the vegetables gently and then add the "lardons" and, as they begin to melt, add the rabbit. ● When the pieces are nicely browned on all sides, remove from the casserole with the "lardons" and vegetables. Keep warm. ● Sprinkle the flour into the casserole and stir with a wooden spoon until you have a smooth brown roux. Gradually add the stock stirring all the time. ● Season and add the bouquet garni. ● As soon as the stock reaches the boiling point, return the rabbit, pork and vegetables to the pot. Cover and simmer gently over a low heat for about 1 hr. ● Remove the bouquet garni and pour the Madeira into the pot. Simmer for a further 10 min. and serve on a heated dish, sprinkled with chopped parsley.

YOUNG GUINEA FOWL WITH MUSHROOMS
⚜ PINTADEAUX AUX CHAMPIGNONS

Serves 6

Time: *preparation 10 min.* • *cooking 30 min.*
Ingredients: *3 young guinea fowl, a little over 1 lb. (500 g) each* • *½ lb. (225 g) fresh mushrooms* • *7 tbsp. butter* • *1 heaping tbsp. flour* • *1¼ cups (3 dl) light cream* • *salt, pepper* • *1 lemon*

• Slowly melt ½ the butter in a flameproof casserole. • Brown the birds on all sides over a low heat. Season and cook for 15 min. • Meanwhile wash the mushrooms in a mixture of water and lemon juice; cut into 3 or 4 pieces and add to the casserole. Pour in a little water and continue cooking. • Melt the remaining butter in a saucepan. • Add the flour and cook for a few minutes stirring continuously to obtain a smooth roux. Do not let the flour brown. • Gradually add a glass of water stirring all the time. • Add the cream, salt and pepper and pour in the liquid from the guinea fowl. Heat gently. • Divide the birds into serving pieces and arrange on a heated serving dish with the mushrooms in the center. • Cover with the sauce and serve very hot.

• NB Guinea fowl can be termed "young" for only six months. After this they must be cooked for a longer time, and can be prepared in any way suitable for chicken.

GUINEA FOWL STUFFED WITH RAISINS
⚜ PINTADE FARCIE AUX RAISINS

Serves 4

Time: *preparation 30 min. + marinating* • *cooking 50 min.*
Ingredients: *1 guinea fowl 2½ lb. (1.2 kg)* • *5 oz. (150 g) sausage meat* • *7 tbsp. (100 g) butter* • *½lb. (225 g) dried raisins* • *1 egg* • *3 liqueur glasses brandy* • *2 slices stale bread* • *1 lemon* • *2 tbsp. fresh herbs, chopped* • *salt, pepper, nutmeg*

• Soak the raisins in the brandy for several hours or, preferably, all night. • Make a stuffing with the sausage meat, the bread (which has been soaked in a mixture of water and the brandy in which the raisins were soaked and squeezed dry), the remaining brandy, some of the raisins, the chopped herbs (chives, tarragon, parsley, chervil) and the lightly beaten egg. • Season with salt, pepper and nutmeg. • Stuff the guinea fowl and sew up the openings carefully. • Melt the butter in an earthenware pot or ovenproof casserole and brown the bird gently on all sides in a moderately hot oven (400° F; 205°C; **5**). Season, cover and cook for approx 50 min. • Halfway through the cooking add the remaining raisins to the casserole and, if needed, a little water so the bird will not become dry. Serve surrounded with raisins and quarters of lemon.

TURKEY BRAISED IN CHAMPAGNE
✳ DINDONNEAU BRAISE AU CHAMPAGNE

FILLETED DUCK WITH GREEN PEPPERCORNS
✳ FILETS DE CANARD AU POIVRE VERT

Serves 6-8

Time: *preparation 30 min.* • *cooking 2-3 hr.*
Ingredients: *1 fine young turkey about 5½ lb. (2.5 kg)* • *5-6 oz. (150 g) sausage meat* • *scant ¾ cup (150 g) chestnut purée* • *5-6 oz. (150 g) mushrooms* • *1 egg* • *1 small can truffles* • *scant ½ lb. (200 g) butter* • *several strips of fat pork* • *3 carrots* • *2 onions* • *bouquet garni* • *1 cup (2.5 dl) light cream* • *4 cups (1 liter) dry champagne* • *salt, pepper, nutmeg*

Serves 6

Time: *preparation and cooking 1½ hr.*
Ingredients: *2 ducklings, 4 ½ lb. (2 kg) each* • *1 heaping tbsp. green peppercorns* • *2 shallots* • *4 tbsp. (55 g) butter* • *4 tbsp. brandy* • *1 glass dry white wine* • *1 rounded tbsp. cornstarch* • *¾ cup (1.8 dl) cream* • *salt*

• Mix together the sausage meat, the chestnut purée and the truffles. • Season, add a generous pinch nutmeg and bind together with the lightly beaten egg and 4 tbsp. (55 g) softened butter. • Chop the carrots and onions finely and cook gently in butter in a large pan, until they begin to soften. • Stuff the turkey with the sausage meat mixture; lay strips of fat salt pork over it and secure firmly with string or skewers. • Brown it for several minutes in the ''julienne'' of vegetables, turning frequently. • Add the champagne, the bouquet garni and seasonings. Cover and simmer over a low heat for 2-2½ hr (25 min. for each lb. or .5 kg). • Half an hour before the end of the cooking time, wash the mushrooms and cook for a few minutes in butter; add to the turkey. • When the bird is cooked (approx 3 hr.), remove the pork fat and bouquet garni; arrange the turkey on a hot serving dish with the mushrooms. • Thicken the sauce with the cream, reheat without boiling and serve separately.

• Roast the ducks in a moderate oven (375°F; 190°C; 4) for 40 min. turning 2 or 3 times until they are golden. Take from the oven; reserve the juices. • First cut off the legs, then the wings, then turn the duck onto its side, its tail facing you, and remove the skin. • Cut long thin slices of meat diagonally, starting from the tail, cutting towards the breastbone. Do the same on the other side, cutting in the opposite direction. • The flesh should be faintly pink and the juices rosy; in France, duck is preferred slightly underdone. It may, however, be left in the oven for 20 min. longer. • Keep the slices of breast warm but do not let them overcook. • Cut the carcass into small pieces removing any fat that may remain. • Chop the shallots finely and cook slowly in butter; add the chopped carcass. • Pour in the wine and brandy, cover and cook over a fairly high heat for 20 min. • Put through a sieve to obtain as much of the cooking juices as possible. Leave for a few minutes to cool before skimming off the surplus fat. • Crush the green peppercorns coarsely and add to the sauce. • Mix the cornstarch to a smooth paste with the cream and stir into the sauce. Simmer gently for 10-12 min. • Pour over the slices of breast and serve.

PIGEONS BORDELAISE
✳ PIGEONNEAUX BORDELAISE

Serves 6

Time: *preparation 45 min.* • *cooking pigeons 40 min. vegetables 50 min.*
Ingredients: *3 large pigeons (or squabs)* • *2 lb. (1 kg) potatoes* • *6 medium-sized artichokes* • *1 ½ lb. (600 g) small onions* • *4 tbsp. (55 g) butter* • *2 tbsp. cooking oil* • *8-10 tbsp. goose fat (a mixture of butter and oil can be substituted)* • *1 small glass brandy* • *2 rounded tbsp. chopped parsley* • *6 slices of soft bread* • *salt, pepper, sugar* • *1 lemon*

• Cut the pigeons in half down the center and flatten with a steak mallet. Keep the livers aside. • Season the pigeons with salt and pepper and brown in butter or goose fat in a heavy pan. Cover and let them cook over a low flame in their own juice for 35-40 min. • Away from the heat, pour the brandy over the birds and leave covered so that they may draw in the flavor. • Meanwhile, remove the stalks and base leaves of the artichokes, sprinkle with lemon juice and slice. • Cook in butter or goose fat but do not let them brown. If no goose fat is used, add a tsp. oil to prevent the butter from burning. • Salt and pepper. • Peel and dice the potatoes and sauté them in another pan in butter or goose fat. • Peel the onions and blanch them in boiling salted water for 5-8 min. • Drain well, then glaze in butter and 2 tsp. sugar over a moderate heat. • Fry the bread in a mixture of oil and butter. • To serve, heap the potatoes and artichokes in the center of a dish; place each halfpigeon on a slice of fried bread and arrange around the vegetables; arrange the onions in small clusters between the slices of toast. • Mash the livers and cook quickly in the juices in which the pigeons were cooked. • Adjust the seasoning and serve in a sauce boat.

GOOSE ROASTED WITH APPLES
✳ OIE ROTIE AUX POMMES

Serves 6-8

Time: *preparation 25 min.* • *cooking 1 ½ - 2 hr.*
Ingredients: *1 young goose, 6-7 lb. (3 kg)* • *2 chicken livers* • *2oz. (60 g) cooked ham, chopped finely* • *1 onion* • *2 shallots* • *1 bunch parsley, chopped* • *2 small sprigs of sage* • *2 sour apples* • *1 egg.* • *1 cup (150 g) breadcrumbs* • *7 tbsp. (100 g) butter* • *salt, pepper*

• Slice the apples coarsely and put to simmer gently in a pot with some butter while you mix the ham, chopped chicken livers, finely chopped onions and shallots and the herbs. • Cook this mixture lightly in butter. • Stir together thoroughly the apples, the stuffing mixture and the breadcrumbs which have been moistened in enough milk just to hold them together. • Bind together with the lightly beaten egg. • Remove the neck and wing tips from the goose and sew up the neck opening. • Season the stuffing and insert into the goose. Truss. • Mash the remaining butter with salt and pepper and smear over the goose • Place the bird on a rack and put into a preheated oven (425°F; 220°C; 6-7). • Turn after 10 min. to brown the other side. After a further 10 min. turn again and 10 min. later reduce the heat to 325°F (160°C; 3) • Pour a cup of boiling salted water into the pan and baste the goose frequently. The fat should not be allowed to collect in the pan. • At the end of the cooking time, cover the goose with aluminum foil and leave without further cooking for 15 min. • To serve, carve in the usual manner, reserving the juices and mixing them with the sauce in the bottom of the pan to be served separately. • Goose is excellent accompanied by baked apples stuffed with prunes and nuts.

PARTRIDGE CAMARGUE STYLE
✳ PERDREAUX A LA CAMARGUAISE

STUFFED QUAILS WITH CROUTONS
✳ CAILLES FARCIES AUX CROUTONS

Serves 6

Time: *preparation 20 min.* • *cooking 1 ½ hr.*
Ingredients: *3 partridges • 3 ½ oz. (100 g) smoked pork • 3 wide slices bacon • 1 ½ cups (300 g) rice • 1 egg • ¾ cup (2 dl) Madeira • 5-6 oz. (150 g) mushrooms • ½ cup (1.2 dl) light cream • ½ cup + 1 tbsp. (130 g) butter • salt, pepper • breadcrumbs.*

Serves 6

Time: *preparation 30 min.* • *cooking 20 min.*
Ingredients: *6 quail • 1 egg • 1 cup (150 g) breadcrumbs • 3 shallots • 1 clove garlic • 3 strips salt pork • 6 slices of fried bread (crusts removed) • 1 glass white wine • 7 tbsp. (100 g) butter • 1 small can foie gras • salt, pepper, tarragon*

• Dice the smoked pork and brown in a little butter. • Wrap each partridge in a good slice of bacon and brown on all sides in the pan with the diced pork. • Add Madeira, salt and pepper; cover and cook over a very low heat for 1 hr. • Remove the bacon barding but leave the birds in the pan. • Add the finely chopped mushrooms and the cream and leave to cook, covered, for another 20 min., turning the birds 3 or 4 times so that they are completely covered in the sauce. • Meanwhile, wash the rice in a sieve to remove some of the starch, and cook in boiling salted water. • Divide the rice into portions the size of an egg, pat into flat cakes, dip into melted butter, then into beaten egg and finally in flour, then fry lightly in butter until golden. • Cut the partridges in two and arrange on a hot serving dish with the rice cakes between them and the mushrooms and fried ''lardons'' sprinkled on top. • Serve the sauce separately after checking the seasoning.

• Finely chop the shallots and garlic and cook till soft in a little butter. • Soak the breadcrumbs in a little chicken stock or milk, but make sure they are squeezed dry. • Make a stuffing with the crumbs, the shallots and garlic and the lightly beaten egg. Season and add a tsp. of chopped fresh tarragon (or slightly less if you have to use dried herbs). • Stuff the quail with this mixture, wrap in the salt pork and tie securely with thin white string. • Cook on a rack in an open pan in a 375°F (190°C; **5**) oven for 20 min. (If you prefer your game less rare than it is eaten in France, cook for about 10 min. longer.) • Remove the salt pork; deglaze the sauce by adding the white wine and scraping the bottom and sides of the pan over a low heat while the wine heats. • Check seasoning. • Spread the slices of fried bread liberally with the foie gras, and arrange on a hot serving dish with the quail. • Pour the sauce over the birds before serving.

THRUSHES FLAMED IN GIN
✣ GRIVES FLAMBEES AU GENIEVRE

Serves 4

Time: *preparation 20 min.* ● *cooking 40 min.*
Ingredients: *8 thrushes* ● *½ cup (115 g) butter* ● *2 cups (½ liter) chicken stock* ● *¼ lb. (100 g) smoked pork* ● *½ lb. (250 g) mushrooms* ● *2 liqueur glasses of gin or juniper liqueur* ● *25 dried juniper berries* ● *1 lemon* ● *pepper*

● Wash the mushrooms in water to which some lemon juice has been added and cut the largest ones in pieces. ● Dice the smoked pork and cook gently in some of the butter in a heavy-bottomed pan. When golden, remove. ● Add the remainder of the butter to the pan and brown the birds, turning constantly. ● Pour the warmed liqueur over the birds and flame. ● Add the diced pork, the mushrooms, and the juniper berries. Heat the stock and pour into the pan. ● Check the seasoning; be careful with the salt as both the stock and the pork will add salt to the flavor. ● Cook gently for 30 min. ● Arrange the birds on a hot serving dish, surround with the mushrooms and cover with the sauce.

● NB Small game birds, in season, may be substituted for the thrushes. Cooking time will vary depending on the fowl chosen.

CHRISTMAS TURKEY
✣ DINDE DE NOEL

Serves 8-10

Time: *preparation 10 min.* ● *cooking 2½ hr.*
Ingredients: *1 turkey, 7-8 lb. (3.6 kg)* ● *1 large pear* ● *4 tbsp. (55 g) butter* ● *salt, pepper*

● Cut the pear into quarters but do not peel. ● Roll the pieces in a mixture of salt and freshly ground pepper and insert into the turkey, from which you have removed the liver, the neck and the wing tips. ● Sew up all the openings and truss securely. ● Place on a rack in an open pan with no extra fat and roast in a 350°F (180°C; 4) oven allowing about 20 min. per pound. Keep turning the bird so that it browns evenly on all sides. ● Halfway through the cooking pour a cup of water into the baking pan. ● When the turkey is ready, take it from the oven, wrap it up completely in aluminum foil and keep it warm without allowing it to cook, until it is time to serve. ● While the turkey is cooking, mince the liver and cook gently in butter; season. ● When carving the bird, collect the juices which run from it and add to those in the baking pan together with the bird's liver. If the quarters of pear are still whole, place them on the serving dish with the turkey. ● Serve the sauce separately. Chestnuts cooked in butter or puréed, or baked apples are good accompaniments to turkey.

PHEASANT GRENOBLE
✻ FAISAN A LA GRENOBLOISE

Serves 4

Time: *preparation 30 min.* • *cooking 1½ hr.*
Ingredients: *1 pheasant* • *1 small can foie gras* • *5 tbsp. (45 g) bread-crumbs* • *1 egg* • *3 liqueur glasses cognac* • *1 cup (2.5 dl) milk* • *4 tbsp. (55 g) butter* • *1 large thin slice of pork* • *1 generous lb. (500 g) walnuts* • *1 large carrot* • *1 large onion* • *bouquet garni* • *salt, pepper*

• Put aside some whole walnuts to use as a garnish, and mince or finely chop the rest. • Soak the breadcrumbs in the milk and then squeeze as dry as possible. • Beat the egg. • Make a stuffing of the foie gras, the liver and heart of the bird, the breadcrumbs, 1 glass cognac, the minced nuts, salt, pepper, and the beaten egg to bind the whole together. • Mix very thoroughly with a fork before inserting into the pheasant; then wrap the slice of pork around the bird and tie securely. • Melt the butter in a casserole and add the pheasant with the carrot and onion sliced into rounds, and the bouquet garni. • When the bird has browned a little, put the pan into a moderately hot oven (425°F; 220°C; **7**). Halfway through the cooking cover the pan. • To serve place the pheasant on a hot plate, pour over the warmed cognac and flame. Add the cognac which remains in the dish after the flaming, to the sauce in the pan and stir well before transferring to a sauce-boat. • Decorate the pheasant with the whole walnuts just before serving.

HARE STEW
✻ LIEVRE EN DAUBE

Serves 8

Time: *preparation 20 min. + 24 hr. for marinating* • *cooking 3-4 hr.*
Ingredients: *1 hare* • *1 bottle dry red wine* • *7 oz. (200 g) bacon* • *4 tbsp. (55 g) butter* • *1 liqueur glass cognac* • *1 calf's foot* • *3 onions* • *3 tomatoes* • *2 cloves garlic* • *oil* • *thyme* • *1 bay leaf, salt, pepper*

• The day before make a marinade with the wine, cognac, 3 tbsp. olive or vegetable oil, salt, pepper, herbs and garlic. • Bring to a boil, simmer for 20 min. and leave to cool. • Pour it into the casserole in which you have arranged the portions of hare, and allow to marinate overnight (the longer the better). • The next day remove the hare draining each piece. • Melt the butter in a pan and put in the diced bacon to brown. • Remove, and replace with the portions of hare. When these are nicely golden on all sides add the chopped onions and cook until they have melted slightly. • Pour in the marinade and add the calf's foot cut in pieces. • Cover and simmer gently for at least 3 hr. • Then add the tomatoes cut in quarters; but back the chopped bacon and simmer for a further 30 min. Remove the pieces of calf's foot. • When the hare is well cooked, take out the bay leaf and the sprig of thyme; check the seasonings. • Put the hare onto a serving dish and serve with boiled potatoes or rice or pasta.

TURBAN OF WILD BOAR CUTLETS
✳ COTELETTES DE MARCASSIN EN TURBAN

Serves 6

Time: *preparation 30 min. + 24 hr. marinating • cooking 45 min.*
Ingredients: *6 wild boar cutlets (chops) • 6 slices bread with the crusts removed • 2 lbs. (1 kg) chestnuts • 1 cup + 2 tbsp. (250 g) butter • 2 cups (½ liter) stock • bouquet garni • 2 cups (½ liter) good red wine.; 6 tbsp. oil • 5 tbsp. wine vinegar • 3 onions • 1 clove garlic • 1 stick celery • black peppercorn • 2 carrots • thyme, 1 bay leaf • 3 tbsp. (30 g) flour • salt, pepper*

• The day before, prepare the marinade: in a large casserole mix the red wine, oil, vinegar, chopped celery, bouquet garni, peppercorns, 1 sliced onion and mashed garlic. • Put the boar meat in this marinade and turn from time to time so that all parts become tender. • The following day, remove the cutlets, draining them thoroughly, and cook them in a large pan in butter for 8 min. on each side. • Meanwhile, slice the remaining 2 onions, and the carrots and let them soak in the marinade with the thyme and bay leaf for 30 min.; then pass through a meat grinder or food processor. • Melt 7 tbsp. (100 g) butter in a saucepan and add the flour. Stir to a smooth paste, allowing it to color slightly. • Gradually add the stock, stirring constantly to avoid lumps. • Season, and add the carrot mixture. • Deglaze the pan in which the cutlets have cooked with a few tbsp. of marinade; then stir in the sauce. Bring it to a boil and simmer gently for 10 min. • Cook the chestnuts in butter while you are frying the bread in butter in another pan. • Place the chestnuts in the center of a hot serving dish and arrange the cutlets and slices of fried bread alternately around them. • Cover with a little sauce and serve the rest of the sauce separately.

LEG OF VENISON WITH THREE PUREES
✳ CUISSOT DE CHEVREUIL AUX TROIS PUREES

Serves 8

Time: *preparation 20 min. + 24-48 hr. marinating cooking 1¼ hr.*
Ingredients: *1 leg of venison, about 4 lb. (1.5-2 kg) • 4 oz. (125 g) salt pork • 2 carrots • 2 onions • 1 quart (1 liter) white wine • 2 liqueur glasses Grand-Marnier • 1¼ cup (3 dl) cream • bouquet garni • several green peppercorns • 2 tbsp. oil • 1 tbsp. vinegar • 3 tbsp. (30 g) flour • salt, pepper • about 1 lb. (500 g) each of dried beans (haricots), celeriac, chestnuts.*

• The venison must be left to marinate for 24-48 hr. according to its age. Use the following marinade: All but 1 glass of the wine, the oil, the vinegar, the bouquet garni, the carrots and onions chopped small, salt and pepper. • Cut the pork into small pieces and marinate in the Grand-Marnier for 1 hr. • Take the venison from the marinade, make small incisions all over it with a sharp-pointed knife and insert the bits of pork. • Brush lightly with the oil and roast in a preheated moderate (350˚F; 180˚C; **4**) oven for a good hour. • Take the vegetables from the marinade and drain, saving the marinade; remove the bouquet garni. • Cook the vegetables in a little oil and, when they have softened slightly, sprinkle with flour. • When the flour has browned, gradually add the marinade, stirring gently all the time; simmer for 1 hr. • Skim the grease from the pan in which the venison is roasting. • Spoon some of the brown juices into another pan. • All this must be done quickly to prevent your oven from cooling. If it does cool down cook the meat for 5 min. longer. • Add the glass of white wine, the Grand Marnier, the marinade which has been cooked and sieved, the cream and the slightly crushed green peppercorns. • Let this sauce boil for 5 min. • While the venison is cooking, cook separately, the beans, the celeriac and the chestnuts. When cooked, pass through a sieve to obtain the three purées. • Serve the venison by itself on a hot platter, with the sauce served separately and the purées in three side dishes.

LOIN OF VENISON WITH HUCKLEBERRIES
✽ SELLE DE CHEVREUIL AUX AIRELLES

WILD DUCK WITH CHERRIES
✽ CANARD SAUVAGE AUX CERISES

Serves 8-10

Time: *preparation 10 min. + 2 hr. marinating • cooking 1½ hr.*
Ingredients: *1 loin of venison, 4 lb. (2 kg) • 1 cup (¼ liter) meat stock • ½ cup (1.2 dl) heavy cream • 1 onion • oil • salt, pepper • huckleberry jam (or jelly)*

Serves 4

Time: *preparation 20 min. • cooking 1½ hr.*
Ingredients: *1 duck, 4–4½ lb. (1.2–1.5 kg) • 9 tbsp. (125 g) butter. • 1 wineglass Madeira • 1 glass stock • 1 carrot • 1 onion • bouquet garni • 1 tbsp. flour • 1 bottle preserved cherries (approximately 14 oz.; 400 g) • salt, pepper*

• In a bowl put several tbsp. oil, the bouquet garni, salt and pepper. • After letting this stand for several minutes, brush it carefully all over the meat. Leave for 2 hr. to impregnate. • Put the meat in a deep dish with the finely chopped onion, the bouquet garni and the stock. • Place in a preheated oven (350°F, 180°C; **3-4**) and cook for 1½ hr., basting frequently with the juices in the pan. • Place on a hot serving dish, and keep warm. • Take out the onion and bouquet garni and thicken the sauce with the cream. • At the last moment add 2 tbsp. of huckleberry jam or jelly and stir well. Serve the gravy in a sauceboat.

• Cut the onion and carrot into rounds. • Melt half the butter in a large saucepan and brown the duck on all sides with the vegetables (be sure to cut away all excess fat and prick the duck all over with a fork). • When the duck is nicely golden, add the Madeira, stock, bouquet garni and salt and pepper. • Cook over a gentle heat for approximately 1 hr 20 min. • Meanwhile drain the cherries. • Take the duck from the pan. • After a few minutes, skim the surface fat from the top of the pan. • Return the duck with the cherries to the heat and cook for another 15 min then place the duck on a serving dish surrounded by the cherries. • While the duck and cherries are cooking, remove the bouquet garni from the sauce. • Melt the remaining butter and stir in the flour. Add a few tbsp. sauce and make a smooth roux. • Return this to the sauce and stir well. • Check the seasoning. • Serve separately.

FISH
AND SHELLFISH

Fishes, believed by most to be all the same species,
are, for the philosopher,
a subject full of wonder and speculation.
Prepared by the hand of a skillful acolyte, they are
an inexhaustible source of delight to the palate.

PIKE FILLETS IN WHITE WINE
❉ FILETS DE BROCHET AU POUILLY

Serves 6

Time: *preparation 25 min. + 1 hr. for marinating • cooking 45 min.*
Ingredients: *1 pike, 4-5 lb. (2-2.5 kg) • 1 bottle dry white wine • 6 shallots • ½ lb. (225 g) mushrooms • ⅔ cup (150 g) butter • ⅔ cup (1.6 dl) cream • 6 large crayfish or prawns • toasted breadcrumbs • bouquet garni • 1 lemon • salt, pepper*

• Ask your fishmonger to fillet the pike. Carefully remove any bones which might remain. • Finely chop the shallots and the cleaned mushrooms. • Melt 1 tbsp. (15 g) butter in a large saucepan; add the shallots and cook until soft but do not let them brown. Add another tbsp. butter and the mushrooms. • When some of the liquid from the mushrooms has evaporated, pour in half the white wine, add the bouquet garni and boil for a few minutes; then add the crayfish which have already been boiled for 5 min. • Season, and leave to cool, uncovered. • Remove the crayfish and put aside. • Lay the pike fillets in a buttered ovenproof dish, which can also be used on the table; add the cooked wine and seasonings and leave to marinate 1 hr. • Cover with buttered greaseproof paper or aluminium foil, and place in a preheated oven (400°F, 200°C; 6) • As soon as the liquid has evaporated (take care not to let the fish burn), add the cream with salt and pepper. • Cover with a thick layer of toasted breadcrumbs and put back in the oven at 300°F (150°C; 1·2). • Baste occasionally. • Serve in the baking dish, garnished with the crayfish.

EEL SOUP
❉ MATELOT D'ANGUILLES

Serves 6

Time: *preparation 10 min • cooking 1 hr*
Ingredients: *4 lb. (2 kg) eels • 1 bottle dry white wine • 1 small glass armagnac or brandy • 20 small onions or shallots • 20 button mushrooms • 7 tbsp. (100 g) butter • 2 tbsp. (20 g) plain flour • bouquet garni • 1 lemon • salt, pepper, sugar • 6 slices crustless bread*

• Slice the cleaned and skinned eels into finger-length pieces and roll in flour. • Melt 1 tbsp. (15 g) butter in a pan and let the eels cook a little until the flesh looks firm but not brown. Add the armagnac and take the pan away from the heat while the fish absorbs the flavor. • Cover with the wine; add salt, pepper and the bouquet garni. Return to the heat and bring to a boil • After approximately 4 min. remove the eels and keep warm. • Let the wine sauce simmer gently for 20 min. • Add the washed mushrooms and cook for a further 15 min. • Meanwhile cook the onions in butter without letting them brown, then sprinkle with sugar and glaze them over a very low heat. • Make a beurre manié with softened butter and the rest of the flour and add gradually to the sauce away from the heat, stirring all the time. • Bring to the boil, replace the eels, and simmer for another 10 min. • Add the onions. • Fry the bread in butter. • In a deep dish arrange the eels, mushrooms, and onions, and cover with the sauce. • Serve with triangles of fried bread.

• NB If you use red wine eels must be cooked 10 min. longer.

TROUT IN CHAMPAGNE
✻ TRUITES AU CHAMPAGNE

SHAD IN SORREL
✻ ALOSE A L'OSEILLE

Serves 6

Time: *preparation 20 min.* ● *cooking 35 min.*
Ingredients: *6 trout, about 7 oz. (200 g) each* ● *2 shallots* ● *1 tbsp. tomato paste* ● *Several sprigs parsley* ● *7 tbsp. (100 g) butter* ● *2 egg yolks* ● *1 lemon* ● *1 tbsp. cornstarch* ● *½ bottle dry champagne* ● *salt, pepper* ● *1 bay leaf*

Serves 6

Time: *preparation 30 min.* ● *cooking 1 hr. 15 min.*
Ingredients: *1 shad 3-4 lb. (1.5 kg)* ● *2 lb. (1 kg) sorrel* ● *⅔ cup (150 g) butter* ● *½ cup (1.2 dl) heavy cream* ● *2 eggs* ● *1 cup (150 g) stale breadcrumbs* ● *2 shallots* ● *sea salt, pepper* ● *1 lemon*

● Have the trout cleaned by the gills in order to keep the fish whole. Preheat the oven to 325° F (160° C; 2-3) 15 min. beforehand. ● In an ovenproof dish put the chopped shallots, parsley, bay leaf and the trout taking care that they do not overlap. Season. ● Cover with champagne. ● Place a layer of aluminium foil over the dish and put in the oven for 20 min. ● Take out the trout, but keep warm, while you gently remove their skins. ● Put the skins and the cooking liquid in a saucepan and simmer for 5 min. before passing through a food processor or sieve. ● Add the tomato paste and reheat. ● Mix the cornstarch to a smooth paste with a little water. Add to the sauce and bring to a boil. ● Away from the heat add the butter in little pieces to the sauce. ● Beat the egg yolks with the juice of half a lemon. ● Add a few tbsp. sauce to this mixture then combine with it the rest of the sauce. Check the seasoning. ● Return the trout to the baking dish and cover with the sauce. ● Place a clean sheet of aluminium foil over the dish and put back into the oven; at a lower heat (250°F, 120°C; ¼-½) for 10 min. before serving.

● Clean the sorrel; remove the coarse center vein of the leaves. ● Using only the water still clinging to the leaves after their final washing, cook the sorrel in a saucepan with a pinch of sea salt over a very low heat. ● After 15 min. drain whatever liquid remains and cook the sorrel for another 10 min in 2-3 tbsp. (30-40 g) butter. ● Meanwhile, split and bone the shad, cutting off the head; scrape off the scales. ● Crush the roe with the raw eggs, the breadcrumbs which have been soaked in a little milk, 2 tbsp. of sorrel, the chopped shallots, ¼ of the cream; salt and pepper. ● Stuff the shad with this mixture and sew the opening together. ● Brush both sides of the fish with lemon juice and leave to soak for 1 hr. ● Drain; lay in an ovenproof dish and cover with 7 tbsp. (100 g) melted butter. Put into a preheated oven (400°F, 200°C; **6**). ● After 15 min. remove the fish from the oven; turn it over very carefully and cover it with sorrel. ● Pour the remainder of the cream on top and return to the oven at a reduced temperature (350°F; 180°C; **3-4**) for ¾-1 hr.

SALMON WITH SHRIMPS
✱ SAUMON AUX BOUQUETS

SEA BREAM STUFFED WITH ALMONDS
✱ DAURADE FARCIE AUX AMANDES

Serves 6-8

Time: *preparation 25 min. + 1 hr. for the court-bouillon • cooking 1½ hr.*
Ingredients: *1 salmon 4–4½ lb. (2 kg) • 2 cups (½ liter) dry white wine • about ½ lb. (200 g) carrots • 1 onion • bouquet garni • 4 tbsp. (55 g) butter • 6 tbsp. (60 g) flour • 2 cups (½ liter) milk • 8 tbsp. (115 g) shrimp butter • 5 oz. (140 g) shrimp • ½ cup (1.2 dl) cream • 1 lemon • salt, pepper, cayenne, whole peppercorns.*

Serves 4

Time: *preparation 20 min. • cooking 50 min.*
Ingredients: *1 porgy or gilt-head (or other sea bream), 1½–2 lb (800–900 g) • 1 cup stale breadcrumbs • 2 eggs • 2 onions • 2 shallots • 1 tbsp. oil • bouquet garni • several stalks parsley • about ½ cup (60 g) blanched and chopped almonds • 1 glass white wine • toasted bread crushed • salt, pepper*

• Make a court-bouillon in a fish kettle with the wine; 2 quarts (2 liters) water; the sliced carrots; the onion and bouquet garni; salt and several peppercorns. Boil for 30-40 min. and allow to cool. • Place the cleaned salmon in the pan; bring to a boil; reduce the heat and simmer as gently as possible for 20 min. • Carefully drain the salmon and place on a long oval plate. • Remove the skin, and slice thickly without spoiling the shape of the fish. • Melt the butter, stir in the flour and gradually add the milk and 2 cups (½ litre) of court-bouillon poured through a sieve. • Season with salt, pepper and cayenne, and simmer for 10 min. • Away from the heat add the cream and shrimp butter. Reheat slowly. • Cover the salmon with some of the sauce and decorate with ''bouquets'' of shrimps and slices of lemon. Serve the remaining sauce separately.

• Hard boil 1 egg. • Soak the stale breadcrumbs in a little milk and squeeze as dry as possible. • Finely chop the onions and shallots and cook gently in butter. • Add the bouquet garni, season and cook for a little longer until the onions are soft but not browned. • Chop the hard-boiled egg and mix with the soaked crumbs. • Removing the bouquet garni, add the onions and shallots to the egg-crumb mix and put through a sieve or food-mill. Bind together with the other lightly beaten egg. • Insert this stuffing into the fish's stomach and carefully sew up the opening. Brush with oil and cover with the crushed, toasted bread. • Place in an ovenproof dish with the remaining stuffing around the fish. • Pour the glass of wine into the dish and sprinkle the fish with the almonds. Cover with buttered greaseproof paper. • Cook in a moderate oven (375˚F; 190˚C; **5**) for about 50 min, basting occasionally.

FRESH SARDINES WITH SPINACH
✱ SARDINES FRAICHES AUX EPINARDS

Serves 6

Time: *preparation 30 min.* • *cooking 25 min.*
Ingredients: *18–24 sardines* • *2 eggs* • *1 cup (75 g) soft breadcrumbs* • *⅔ cup (150 g) butter* • *2 cloves garlic* • *1 lemon* • *3–3½ lb (1.5 g) spinach* • *salt, pepper*

• After washing the spinach thoroughly, cook for 15 min. in a large pan of boiling, salted water. • Drain and press hard to squeeze out all the moisture. • Return to the heat together with the butter which has been mashed with the crushed garlic. Simmer over a very low heat without stirring. • Remove the heads and tails from the sardines and cut them open; take out the bones and close again. • Dip the sardines into the beaten eggs then roll in the breadcrumbs. • Brown gently in butter in a large frying pan. • Put the spinach on a hot serving dish and arrange the sardines around the edge. • Serve very hot.

FILLETS BERCY
✱ FILETS DE COLIN A LA BERCY

Serves 4

Time: *preparation 20 min.* • *cooking 25 min.*
Ingredients: *2 lb. (1 kg) hake or cod fillets* • *generous ½ cup (125 g) butter* • *3 shallots* • *1 glass dry white wine* • *1 lemon* • *1 tbsp. flour* • *2 tbsp. dried breadcrumbs* • *1 stock cube* • *salt, pepper* • *2 tbsp. chopped parsley*

• Make up the stock and poach the fillets gently for approximately 10 min. • Melt butter in a large frying pan and add the chopped shallots; do not let them brown. • Add the white wine and 1 cup (2.5 dl) of stock, lemon juice, salt and pepper. • Make a beurre manié with the softened butter and flour by rolling them into little balls; add one by one to the pan, away from the fire, stirring gently. • Put the fillets in a buttered ovenproof dish and pour in the sauce which you have brought to a boil two or three times. • Sprinkle with dried breadcrumbs and brown under the grill or in a hot oven for about 15 min. • Just before serving sprinkle with chopped parsley.

WHITING IN WHITE WINE
✳ MERLANS AU VIN BLANC

Serves 4

Time: *preparation 25 min.* • *cooking 20 min.*
Ingredients: *8 whiting 4–4½ oz. (125 g) each* • *2 cups (½ liter) dry white wine* • *2 onions* • *2 carrots* • *bouquet garni* • *several sprigs parsley* • *5 tbsp. (70 g) butter* • *1 tbsp. flour* • *salt, pepper*

• Chop the onions and cut the carrots into rounds. • In a thick-bottomed pan melt half the butter and cook the onions until softened but not browned; add the carrots. • Let them cook over a low heat for a few minutes; sprinkle with flour, stir and leave for another minute. • Pour in the wine and bring to the boil, stirring. Add the bouquet garni and parsley; cover and simmer for 20 min. • Meanwhile sprinkle the fish both inside and out with salt and pepper, and arrange in an ovenproof dish. • When the vegetables are cooked, take out the bouquet garni and parsley. Add 1 glass of cold water and pour over the fish. • Place in a hot oven (400˚F, 200˚C′ 6) and cook for 20 min., basting occasionally. • Turn off the heat but leave the fish in the oven for a few minutes. • Put little pieces of the remaining butter over the fish and serve.

CREAMED COD
✳ MORUE A LA CREME

Serves 6

Time: *preparation 30 min. + soaking* • *cooking 25 min.*
Ingredients: *2½ lb. (1.2 kg) cod or 1¼ lb. (600 g) fillets* • *1¾ lb. (800 g) potatoes* • *2 onions* • *1 rounded tbsp. (20 g) butter* • *1 cup (2.5 dl) cream* • *1 tbsp. flour* • *2 tbsp. chopped parsley* • *salt, pepper*

• Skin the cod; slice and leave in water for about 4 hr. to remove some of the salt. • Drain, arrange in a large saucepan and cover with cold water. Bring to a boil, turn off the heat and leave, covered, for 15 min. • Meanwhile boil the potatoes without letting them disintegrate. • Chop the onions very finely and cook them in butter until soft; do not let them brown. • Add the flour and stir until it has become slightly golden. Moisten with a little liquid from the cod; stir and then add the cream. • Season lightly. • Drain the cod, wipe each piece lightly and put into the onion sauce. Heat without boiling. • Put the sliced potatoes into a deep dish, place the fish in the center, pour over the sauce and sprinkle with chopped parsley. • Serve at once.

POLLACK WITH SAUERKRAUT
✻ LIEU A LA CHOUCROUTE

COD MORNAY
✻ CABILLAUD MORNAY

Serves 6

Time: *preparation 15 min.* • *cooking 45 min.*
Ingredients: *2–2½ lb. (1 kg) pollack (other saltwater fish such as turbot or halibut can be substituted)* • *6 frankfurters or other mild sausages* • *6 thin slices bacon* • *2½ lb (1 kg) cooked sauerkraut with juniper berries or a few drops of gin* • *2 cups (½ liter) dry white wine* • *4 tbsp. (55 g) butter* • *1 onion* • *bouquet garni* • *salt, pepper*

Serves 6

Time: *preparation 10 min.* • *cooking 45 min.*
Ingredients: *2½ lb. (1.2 kg) cod* • *1 bouillon cube* • *2½ cups (⅔ liter) Bechamel sauce* • *½ cup (50 g) grated gruyère* • *12 mussels*

• Roll the slices of bacon around the fish and tie like a roast of meat. • Put the butter in a saucepan and cook the finely chopped onion. • Add the fish and brown it on both sides. • Pour in wine to cover, and add the bouquet garni. • Season; cover and cook over a moderate heat for 45 min. • Meanwhile, reheat the sauerkraut with the remainder of the wine. Brown the sausages without additional fat. • Serve the pollack on a large, heated dish surrounded with sauerkraut and frankfurters.

• Make up the stock and pour over the cod. • Bring to a boil; lower the heat immediately and simmer very gently for 10 min. • Meanwhile, make a béchamel sauce (recipe no. 272) and add to it some of the grated gruyère. • Remove the pan from the heat and leave the fish, covered, to cool in the liquid for about 8 min.; then take it out of the pan and carefully remove the bones and skin. Cut the fish into pieces the size of an egg. • Arrange the fish in a gratin dish. • Steam the mussels for a few minutes. • Remove from their shells and place between the pieces of cod. • Cover with the sauce. Sprinkle with the rest of the cheese. • Put into a pre-heated moderate oven for about 20 min. to brown gently.

HERRINGS IN MUSTARD SAUCE
⚜ HARENGS SAUCE MOUTARDE

Serves 6

Time: *preparation 10 min. • cooking 15 min.*
Ingredients: *6 herrings • 2 tbsp. oil • 2 tbsp. strong white mustard • 1 glass dry white wine • 3 tbsp (40 g) butter • 2 tbsp. flour*

• Brush the herrings all over with the oil and grill under a lively heat for 5 min. on each side. • Arrange in a flameproof dish. • Make a mustard sauce by mixing the softened butter and the mustard together to a creamy paste; stir in the flour and then dilute with the wine, stirring all the time. • When the sauce is very smooth, pour it over the fish and put into a very hot oven, (475°F; 250°C; **9**) for 5 min. • Serve immediately in the dish in which they were cooked.

MACKEREL BOULOGNE
⚜ MAQUEREAUX A LA BOULONNAISE

Serves 4

Time: *preparation 40 min. • cooking 30 min.*
Ingredients: *8 medium sized mackerel • 1 quart (1 liter) mussels • 8-9 oz. (250 gr) shelled shrimps • 1 bouillon cube • 4 tbsp. (55 g) butter • 2 tbsp. flour • 1 cup (2.5 dl) cream • 1 egg yolk • salt, pepper*

• Make up the bouillon. • Cut the mackerel into slices 3 in. (8 cm) long, and simmer in the stock for 10 min. • Meanwhile, thoroughly clean the mussels, and steam them open in a thick-bottomed pan over a low flame. • Remove them from their shells and keep warm in a pan over hot water. • Drain the fish and remove the skin and all the bones, and keep warm in another dish in a pan of hot water. • Melt the butter and stir in the flour. • Add some of the stock in which the fish has cooked. • Season and stir continuously to avoid lumps. • Away from the heat stir in the egg yolk and the cream; reheat without boiling and check the seasoning. • Arrange the fish and mussels on a serving dish with the shrimps clustered in scallop shells around the edge. Pour the sauce over the fish and serve at once.

TUNA BRETON
❋ THON A LA BRETONNE

BASS MARINIERE
❋ BAR A LA MARINIERE

Serves 4

Time: *preparation 20 min.* • *cooking 1 hr.*
Ingredients: *1 ¾ lb. (800 gr) fresh tuna (tunny) fish* • *13-14 oz. (400 g) fresh white shell (haricot) beans* • *1 tbsp. oil* • *2 tbsp.tomato paste* • *2 shallots* • *1 onion* • *2 cloves* • *bouquet garni* • *1 clove garlic* • *2 carrots* • *several sprigs parsley* • *salt, pepper*

Serves 4

Time: *preparation 25 min.* • *cooking 45 min.*
Ingredients: *1 bass, 2-2½ lb. (1 kg)* • *3 tbsp. olive oil* • *2 tbsp. (30 g) butter* • *2 onions* • *1 fresh carrot* • *1 leek* • *1 stick celery* • *1 bay leaf* • *1 glass dry white wine* • *salt, pepper*

• Cook the beans in a very large saucepan with plenty of water, the bouquet garni, the onion stuck with the 2 cloves, the sliced carrot, the crushed garlic, salt and pepper. Bring to the boil, cover and simmer for about ¾ hr. • Meanwhile, skin the fish. • Chop the shallots finely and let them soften in the oil in a large pan. • Place the fish in the same pan and brown it gently on all sides. • Add several tbsp. of hot water and cover. Simmer for approximately 30 min. • At the end of this time, stir in the tomato paste and add the well-drained beans • Cook for another 10 min. taking, care that the pan does not become too dry and the fish does not stick to the bottom. If necessary, add a little more hot water. • Put the tuna on a warmed serving dish surrounded by the beans; remove the bouquet garni and the garlic (if possible) and sprinkle with chopped parsley.

• NB If dried beans are used they must be soaked for at least 2 hr before cooking, and then cooked for 1-1¼ hr. • If a larger quantity of tomato sauce is desired serve some separately after having covered the fish.

• Clean the vegetables; chop them finely and cook gently with the bay leaf in a mixture of butter and oil. • When they have taken color add the wine, salt and pepper. Simmer for 10 min. • Meanwhile, clean the fish through its gills or through a small incision in its stomach. Scrape the scales but do not break the skin. • Put the fish in an ovenproof casserole and cover with the vegetables. • Check the seasoning and cook in a moderate oven (375˚F; 200˚C; **4)** for 30 min. • Serve in the casserole. • Plain boiled or steamed potatoes make a good accompaniment to bass.

CREAMED FILLETS OF SOLE
✲ FILLETS DE SOLE A LA CREME

Serves 4

Time: *preparation 25 min.* ● *cooking 35 min.*
Ingredients: *4 sole, ¾-1 lb. (400 g) each* ● *½ cup (125 g) butter* ● *½ cup (1.2 dl) fresh cream* ● *2 glasses dry white wine* ● *1 lemon* ● *1 onion* ● *1 carrot* ● *bouquet garni* ● *1 tbsp. oil* ● *salt, pepper*

● Have the fish filleted, and ask for the bones, skin and scraps of fish. ● Heat 1 tbsp. olive oil and 2 tbsp. (30 g) butter in a saucepan and add the chopped onion and carrot. ● When the vegetables are soft but not brown, add the fish bones, skin and scraps, the bouquet garni, a glass of white wine and 1 quart (1 liter) of water. Season and cook for 15 min. ● Place the fillets in a buttered oven-proof dish. Cover with a glass of white wine, the juice of a lemon and a little of the strained stock. The fillets should be just covered. ● Cook in a moderate oven (350°F, 180°C; **4**) for about 20 min. ● Remove the fish from the liquid and keep warm. Pour the strained stock and the liquid in which the fish was cooked into a saucepan and boil until 4-5 tbsp. of thick liquid remain. ● Add the cream and boil for 5 min. beating continuously with a whisk. ● Remove from the heat, add the rest of the butter a little at a time, whisking the mixture continuously. ● Pour the sauce over the fish and serve at once.

LOTTE OR BURBOT ARMORICAIN
✲ LOTTE A L'ARMORICAINE

Serves 6

Time: *preparation 15 min.* ● *cooking 35 min.*
Ingredients: *1 lotte (or burbot), 3 lb. (1.5 kg) after cleaning and boning* ● *2 shallots* ● *3 onions* ● *2 cloves garlic* ● *bouquet garni* ● *5 large tomatoes* ● *1 tbsp. tomato paste* ● *½ bottle Muscadet (or similar white wine)* ● *1 small glass cognac* ● *1 glass olive oil* ● *2 small sugar lumps* ● *6 tbsp. (85 g) butter* ● *3 oz. (1 dl) cream* ● *3 tbsp. (30 g) flour* ● *salt, pepper, cayenne* ● *2 tbsp. chopped parsley*

● Chop the onions, shallots and garlic. Cook gently in 1 tbsp. olive oil over a very low heat; stir repeatedly. ● Meanwhile, cut the fish into serving sized pieces, sprinkle with flour and brown in olive oil in another pan. ● Either evaporate by boiling, or else spoon away the water which the fish gives out during cooking, and replace with a little more oil. ● Moisten with cognac and flame. ● Add the white wine, bouquet garni, the chopped, peeled and seeded tomatoes, the sugar and the tomato paste. ● Season, cover, and leave to simmer gently for 25 min. ● Make a "beurre manié" by working the softened butter and flour into little balls. ● Take the fish from the pan, but keep warm. Remove the bouquet garni from the liquid in the pan and add the "beurre manié," stirring constantly. ● Let the sauce boil gently for a few minutes. ● Away from the heat, stir in the cream, add a pinch of cayenne and reheat. Pour the sauce over the fish and sprinkle with chopped parsley.

SKATE IN BLACK BUTTER
✳ RAIE AU BEURRE NOIR

TURBOT WITH SHELLFISH
✳ TURBOT AUX FRUITS DE MER

Serves 6

Time: *preparation 10 min • cooking 30 min*
Ingredients: *1 skate (ray) 2½-3 lb (1.200-1.500 kg) • 1 bouillon cube • ½ cup (1.2 dl) vinegar • 1 scant cup (200 g) butter • 5 tbsp. capers • 4 tbsp. chopped parsley • salt, pepper, lemon quarters*

Serves 6

Time: *preparation 1½hr • cooking 15 min*
Ingredients: *1 turbot 2½-3 lb (1.8 kg) • 6 scallops • 2 pints (1 liter) mussels • 12 small prawns • generous ½ lb. (250 g) peeled cooked shrimps • ½ lb. (250 g) mushrooms • scant 2 cups (225 g) flour • 1 cup (2.5 dl) cream • 4 tbsp. (55 g) butter • 1 egg yolk • 1 lemon • parsley • chopped shallot*

• Make up the stock and put the cleaned fish to cook in it for 20 min. without boiling (the liquid must barely simmer). • Leave to cool, then take out the skate. Remove the skin from both sides and trim the edges of the "wings" or pectoral fins. • Keep warm on the serving dish. • Heat the butter in a saucepan until it changes color. • Away from the heat stir 1 cup of half vinegar and half stock (filtered), pouring slowly into the side of the pan. • Add the capers and bring to the boil. • Pour this sauce over the fish, sprinkle with chopped parsley and serve with quarters of lemon and plain boiled or steamed potatoes.

• Clean the mussels and the scallops; wash the prawns. • Cook the mussels over a high flame with the parsley and shallots. When the shells open, pour the liquid through a sieve and reserve. • Remove the mussels from their shells. • Poach the turbot and the scallops in a court-bouillon for 5 min. and the prawns for 10 min. • Slice the mushrooms and cook gently in a little butter. • Melt the rest of the butter in a saucepan and stir in the flour until smooth. Slowly pour in the liquid from the mussels, stirring constantly. • Beat the egg yolk and cream together, add a tbsp. or two of the sauce, then gradually stir the cream mixture back into the sauce, taking care not to cook the egg yolk. • Pour into a deep dish, add the mussels, scallops, shrimps and mushrooms. • Remove the skin from the turbot and lay the fish on a hot serving dish; decorate with slice of lemon and the prawns. • Serve the sauce separately.

MUSSELS MARINIERE
✳ MOULES MARINIERE

Serves 6

Time: *preparation 30 min.* • *cooking 10 min.*
Ingredients: *7 pints (3 liters) mussels* • *7 tbsp. (100 g) butter* • *2 cups (½ liter) dry white wine* • *2 onions* • *parsley* • *1 lemon* • *salt, pepper*

• In a large, heavy saucepan melt the butter over a low heat, and cook the finely chopped onions without letting them brown. • Add a generous tbsp. chopped parsley. • Pour in the wine, bring to the boil and remove from the fire. • Meanwhile wash, scrape and debeard the mussels very carefully. • Discard those that are slightly open, unless they close again when tapped sharply with the handle of a knife. • Put them into the saucepan; add a little lemon juice and leave for a few minutes for the mussels to absorb the flavor of the liquid; stir occasionally. • 15 min. before serving, place the pan over a high flame to open the mussels. • Serve as soon as they have all opened.

STUFFED MUSSELS
✳ MOULES FARCIES

Serves 6

Time: *preparation 30 min.* • *Cooking 5-10 min.*
Ingredients: *7 pt (3 liters) mussels* • *1 scant cup (200 g) butter* • *parsley* • *6 cloves garlic* • *1 large slice stale bread* • *salt, pepper*

• Wash, scrape and debeard the mussels carefully • Cook in a little liquid over a high flame, to open. • Shell, but reserve 1/4 of the shells. Leave the mussels to cool. • Meanwhile, mash the butter with a fork, adding the finely chopped parsley and minced garlic, salt and pepper until you have a smooth paste. • Add the bread which has been soaked in a little milk and squeezed dry. • Put 2 mussels into each shell and cover generously with the garlic-butter. • Arrange in a gratin dish and place in a preheated oven (425° F; 220° C; **7**) for 10 min. to brown on the surface. • Serve at once.

SCALLOPS IN VERMOUTH
✻ COQUILLES SAINT-JACQUES AU VERMOUTH

SCALLOPS WITH MUSHROOMS
✻ COQUILLES SAINT-JACQUES FORESTIERE

Serves 6

Time: *preparation 20 min. ● cooking 30 min.*
Ingredients: *12 scallops ● ¾ lb. (350 g) mushrooms ● 1 large onion ● 2 egg yolks ● 5 oz. (1.6 dl) cream ● 1 cup white vermouth ● 2 glasses dry white wine ● ½ cup (15 g) butter ● 2 tbsp. flour ● salt, pepper. ● 1 lemon*

Serves 4

Time: *preparation 30 min. ● cooking 40 min.*
Ingredients: *12 large scallops ● ½ lb. (225 g) button mushrooms ● 8 large mushrooms ● 7 tbsp (100 g) butter ● 2 tbsp oil ● 2 tbsp chopped parsley ● 3 cloves garlic ● 2 eggs ● 1 slice stale bread ● salt, pepper ● 1 lemon ● dried breadcrumbs*

● Wash the mushrooms in water mixed with a little lemon juice; slice. ● Melt 5 tbsp. (7 g) butter in a frying pan and add the mushrooms, scallops and vermouth. ● While they simmer gently, chip the onion finely and put into a small saucepan with the white wine. ● Bring to a boil; lower the heat immediately and simmer for about 15 min. Then add to the mushrooms and scallops; stir and continue cooking. ● Make a beurre manié with the remaining butter and flour and add piece by piece to the scallops. ● Stir continuously until the mixture thickens. ● Season with salt and pepper and simmer (if necessary on an asbestos mat) for another 10 min. ● Meanwhile beat the egg yolks with the cream. Away from the heat add very gradually to the sauce, stirring all the time. ● Reheat for a few minutes; transfer to a warmed dish. Serve at once.

● Wash and drain the scallops. ● Wash and slice the button mushrooms. Cook slowly in a pan with a quarter of the butter. ● Season, and add 1 tbsp. chopped parsley with a clove garlic. ● Hard-boil 1 egg; cool and chop. ● Soak the bread in a little milk; squeeze out all the surplus. ● Away from the heat add the chopped egg and bread to the mushrooms. Bind with the other uncooked, lightly beaten egg. ● Soak the 8 large mushrooms in oil; place in a gratin dish and put into a hot oven for 5-10 min. ● Remove and fill with the mushroom-egg preparation. ● Sprinkle with dried breadcrumbs and return to the oven for about 10 min. (do not overcook). ● Meanwhile, slice the scallops and cook in butter. Add the coral, if available, towards the end of the cooking. ● Season and arrange on a serving dish in their shells. ● Place the stuffed mushroom caps around them, and sprinkle with the remaining parsley mixed with the 2 finely chopped cloves of garlic.

ROCK LOBSTER IN BANYULS WINE
✳ LANGOUSTES AU VIN DE BANYULS

Serves 4–6

Time: *preparation 30 min.* • *cooking 1½ hr.*
Ingredients: *2 rock or spiny lobsters, about 2 lb. (1 kg) each* • *1 bottle Banyuls wine or Madeira* • *½ cup (1.2 dl) whisky* • *4 tomatoes* • *4 onions* • *3 shallots* • *1 clove garlic* • *bouquet garni* • *generous ½ lb. (250 g) Bayonne ham or prosciutto* • *4 tbsp. (55 g) butter* • *5 tbsp. (50 g) flour* • *1 eel or fish (cod) head* • *generous ½ lb. (250 g) fish scraps or small fishes* • *1 carrot* • *salt, pepper, cayenne* • *1¼ cup (3 dl)oil*

• Make a fish "fumet" with the fish head, fish scraps or small fishes, the chopped carrot and 2 quarts (2 liters) of cold salted water. Bring to a boil; skim and simmer, covered, for 40 min. (this can be done the day before). • Meanwhile, cut the lobster into pieces, splitting the heads and keeping the coral and the green matter for thickening the sauce. • Heat ⅔ of the oil in a large pan and sear the pieces of lobster. • Pour in the whisky and flame. • Add the Vin de Banyuls or Madeira and bring to the simmering point. • In another pan, put the finely chopped onions, shallots and garlic to soften in the rest of the oil. When they are soft but not brown, add the peeled, seeded tomatoes cut into quarters and the finely chopped ham. • Simmer for 5 min., then pour over the lobster with 2 cups (4–5 dl) of the strained fish "fumet." • Season with salt, pepper and a pinch of cayenne. • Cover and simmer gently for 20 min. • Put the lobster pieces in a dish and keep warm. • Take the bouquet garni out of the sauce; then reduce it over a high flame. • Rub the lobster coral and green matter through a sieve into a bowl. • Make a "beurre manié" with the flour and butter. • Stir bit by bit into the mixture in the bowl, then empty into the sauce, stirring all the time as you bring it to the boiling point. • Pour the sauce over the lobster and serve at once.

CRAYFISH OR PRAWNS BORDEAUX
✳ ECREVISSES A LA BORDELAISE

Serves 6

Time: *preparation 20 min.* • *cooking 40 min.*
Ingredients: *3 doz. crayfish, jumbo shrimp or prawns* • *2 carrots* • *1 onion* • *2 shallots* • *2 tomatoes* • *1 large glass dry white wine* • *1 small glass brandy* • *7 tbsp. (100 g) butter* • *2 tbsp. olive oil* • *1 tbsp. chopped parsley* • *1 sprig tarragon* • *1 sprig thyme* • *salt, pepper, cayenne*

• Dice the carrots. • Chop the onions and shallots finely. • Cook together gently in a covered pan with 2 tbsp. butter and the tarragon and thyme for 20 min. • Meanwhile, prepare the crayfish or prawns by removing the central vein. Sauté in the oil with 1 tbsp. butter until they have turned a rosy red. • Flame with the brandy. • Add the cooked vegetables, the tomato pulp, and half the chopped parsley. • Pour the white wine over the mixture; season with salt, pepper and a pinch of cayenne. • Quickly bring to the boiling point; reduce the heat; cover and simmer for 8–10 min. • Remove the crayfish but keep them warm. • Simmer the sauce very gently for another 10 min. • Away from the heat, check the seasoning and add the remaining butter in little pieces while stirring continuously. The sauce should be perfectly smooth. • Put the crayfish in a warmed dish and cover with the sauce. Sprinkle with the rest of the parsley and serve.

SCAMPI FRITTERS
✻ BEIGNETS DE LANGOUSTINES

Serves 6

Time: *preparation 30 min.* • *cooking 10 min.*
Ingredients: *36 large crayfish (or jumbo shrimp or prawns)* • *2 tbsp. olive oil* • *2 cups (250 g) flour* • *2 egg whites* • *salt, pepper*

• Bring 4 quarts (4 liters) of heavily salted water to a boil. • Plunge the crayfish into the boiling water; return to the boil and cook for 4 min. • Remove the crayfish and run under cold water. Shell and dry. • Mix the flour with 1 cup (2 dl) warm water until it forms a smooth paste; add the salt and oil; then fold in carefully the stiffly beaten egg whites. • Roll the scampi in this mixture and drop into hot but not smoking oil. • When nicely browned, remove from the oil and drain on absorbent paper. • Serve alone or accompanied by slices of lemon or tartar sauce.

LOBSTER TIMBALE
✻ HOMARD EN TIMBALE

Serves 4

Time: *preparation 20 min.* • *cooking 50 min.*
Ingredients: *1 live lobster, 3-3½ lb. (1.8 kg)* • *1 bouillon cube* • *2 cups (½ liter) dry white wine* • *2 liqueur glasses Grand Marnier* • *4 tbsp. (55 g) butter* • *½ cup (1.2 dl) cream* • *1 egg yolk* • *bouquet garni* • *salt, pepper*

• Plunge the live lobster head first into boiling salted water, allowing 12-15 min. for cooking after the water has come to a boil for the second time. • Take off the heat and allow to cool. • Separate the tailpiece from the body and slice it; remove the sand sac near the head; crack the claws; remove the coral; extract the meat from the body after splitting it open. • Cook the claws and the meat in butter in a deep pan with salt and pepper until the shells turn rosy. • Meanwhile, make up the bouillon cube and add the wine and liqueur. • Pour over the lobster; put the bouquet garni into the pan and cook for 20 min. • Drain the lobster and remove all the meat left inside the claws. • Put it in a bowl and keep in warm in a pan of hot water while you reduce the stock by boiling fast until there is only about 1½ cups (⅓ liter) left. Take out the bouquet garni. • Gradually pour in the stock stirring constantly. • Check the seasoning, reheat without boiling and pour over the lobster which should be in a timbale or large round bowl. Serve at once.

STUFFED SQUID
✳ ENCORNETS FARCIS

Serves 6

Time: *preparation 30 min.* ● *cooking 50 min.*
Ingredients: *8 squid* ● *6 oz. (150 g) fat salt pork* ● *½ cup (100 g) rice* ● *8 small onions* ● *8 tbsp. olive oil* ● *3 glasses white wine* ● *2 tbsp. tomato paste* ● *½ glass brandy* ● *1 egg yolk* ● *3 tbsp. chopped parsley* ● *2 cloves garlic* ● *bouquet garni* ● *1 small piece orange peel* ● *½ tsp. powdered thyme* ● *salt, pepper, cayenne*

● Choose whole squid, of equal size if possible, enough for 6 large helpings. ● Clean carefully under running water and cut off the heads. ● Chop these up with the 6 onions, the salt pork, 2 whole squid and the garlic. ● Cook this mixture in 1 tbsp. oil for about 5 min., then add the washed and drained rice. Season. ● Stuff the remaining 6 squid with this mixture and fasten them securely with toothpicks. ● In a heavy-bottomed saucepan heat 2 tbsp. oil over a very low heat, using an asbestos mat if necessary. Add the remaining 4 onions, chopped, and the piece of orange peel. ● In another pan quickly cook the squid in oil and, as soon as they are nicely brown, add them to the onions. ● Pour in the brandy and flame. ● Add the white wine, the garlic, thyme, bouquet garni and tomato paste. ● Add a very little salt and a pinch of cayenne and simmer 40 min. ● Make a mayonnaise with the egg yolk and remaining olive oil and pour into the serving dish. Mix in several tbsp. of the wine sauce and put the squid in this dish. ● Serve at once with the rest of the sauce in a bowl.

VEGETABLES

. . . we must cultivate our gardens.

Voltaire

ARTICHOKES WITH BEANS
✻ BARBOUILLADE D'ARTICHAUTS AUX FEVES

Serves 4

Time: *preparation 20 min.* • *cooking 50 min.*
Ingredients: *12 small greenish-purple artichokes • lemon juice • 2 lb. (1 kg) young fava (broad) beans • 10 small onions • 2 oz. (50 g) lean bacon • 1 tbsp. olive oil • 2 glasses dry white wine • 1 glass water • 2 springs thyme • 1 sprig mint • 1 spring savory • 1 lemon • salt, pepper*

• Break off the artichoke stems; remove the tough filaments and slice thinly. Quickly sprinkle with lemon juice to prevent blackening. • Cut the small base leaves off the artichokes. • Cut the top third off the leaves and slice the artichokes into quarters; sprinkle with lemon juice. • Shell the beans. • Heat the oil in a large frying pan, and let the bacon soften without browning. • Add the onions, the artichokes and the sliced stems. When they have absorbed a good quantity of the fat, add the beans and herbs. Season. • Add the wine and water and reduce the heat. • Cook for about 20 min., stirring occasionally very gently so as not to crush the beans. • When the sauce has been reduced, cover the pan and cook for a further 5-10 min. • Serve hot with lamb or veal.

ASPARAGUS SOUFFLE
✻ SOUFFLE AUX ASPERGES

Serves 4

Time: *preparation 40 min.* • *cooking 50 min.*
Ingredients: *1¾ lb. (800 g) asparagus • 6 eggs separated • 3 tbsp. (40 g) butter • 3 tbsp. (30 g) flour • 1 cup (¼ liter) milk • salt, pepper, nutmeg*

• Wash and scrape the asparagus, discarding the tough, woody ends of the stalks. Tie them into small bundles with soft string and cook in boiling salted water uncovered (to keep the color) for 25 min. • Drain carefully and purée in a food processor, or pass through a sieve. • Melt the butter; slowly stir in the flour and when smooth gradually add the milk stirring constantly. Remove from the heat and allow to cool. • Meanwhile beat 6 egg whites until they form peaks. • Add 4 egg yolks one at a time to the cooled sauce stirring vigorously without stopping. • Add salt, pepper and a little nutmeg. • Add the puréed asparagus to the sauce and when well mixed carefully fold in the egg whites. • Pour this mixture into a well-buttered soufflé dish deep enough for the soufflé to fill it only ⅔ full. If the dish is not deep enough tie a band of greaseproof paper around the outside so that it stands about 2 in. (6 cm) above the top of the dish. • Place in the middle of a preheated oven (400°F, 200°C; 5-6) and cook for 20-25 min. • The soufflé is ready when a thin knitting needle plunged through the side of the puff, comes out clean. Serve instantly. • It is better to make your guests wait for the soufflé as it will not wait for them but will collapse within about 5 min.

CARROT PUREE
* MOUSSELINE DE CAROTTES

CARDOONS AU GRATIN
* GRATIN DE CARDONS

Serves 4

Time: *preparation 25 min. • cooking 35 min.*
Ingredients: *2 lb. (1 kg) baby carrots • 1 tbsp. cooked rice • 1 lump sugar • 3-4 tbsp. cream • 5 tbsp. (70 g) butter • salt, pepper*

Serves 6

Time: *preparation 45 min. • cooking 1½ hr.*
Ingredients: *2 medium sized cardoons • 7 tbsp. (100 g) butter • 2 lemons • 2 tbsp. (20 g) flour • 2 cups (½ liter) Béchamel sauce • 2 tbsp. oil • 1 cup (110 g) grated cheese (⅔ gruyère; ⅓ parmesan) • salt, pepper, mixed herbs*

• Wash the carrots and plunge into boiling salted water with the cube of sugar. Cook for 35 min. • Drain and put through a food mill or sieve with the rice. • Pile this purée in a pan and place in a pan of water over a gentle heat. • In another pan melt the butter, then add it to the purée beating continuously with a wooden spoon. • Add the cream working the mixture all the time. • Transfer the purée to a hot serving dish, check the seasoning and serve hot.

• Remove the hard stems from the cardoons. Then take off the tender stalks, one at a time and slice into 3 in. (8 cm) sections. • Carefully remove the stringy parts and soak the pieces in water mixed with some lemon juice. • Prepare a salted white court bouillon: gradually mix 1 tbsp. flour with 2 cups (½ liter) water and some salt and bring to a boil, stirring frequently. • Put in the cardoons; lower the heat; cover the pan and simmer for 1¼ hr. The cardoons are cooked when the flesh comes away easily. • Meanwhile, prepare a béchamel sauce (recipe no. 272) flavored with mixed herbs or, if possible, nigella seeds. • Drain the cardoons and arrange in a well-buttered ovenproof dish, alternating a layer of vegetables with a layer of grated cheese. Cover with the béchamel sauce and sprinkle the surface with small knobs of butter. • Cook in a moderate oven (400°F; 200°C; **5-6)** and allow to brown slowly. • Serve hot when the top is nicely golden.

CREAMED SALSIFY
* SALSIFIS A LA CREME

Serves 6

Time: *preparation 30 min. • cooking 1 hr.*
Ingredients: *2 lb. (1 kg) salsify • 5 tbsp. (70 g) butter • ½ cup (1.2 dl) cream • 2 tbsp. vinegar • 2 tbsp. flour • 1 tbsp. chopped parsley • 1 tbsp. chopped fresh mixed herbs • salt, pepper*

• Carefully wash the salsify; scrape and soak in vinegar to prevent blackening. Cut in lengths of about 3 in. (8 cm); split lengthwise if they are too thick. • Prepare a white court bouillon by mixing 2 tbsp. of flour to a smooth paste with a little cold water, and gradually adding 2 quarts (2 liters) of salted water. • Throw the salsify into the "blanc" and boil for about 50 min. • Drain carefully and put into a large frying pan with the butter. • In another pan, heat the cream slightly and pour onto the salsify. Allow to simmer for 5-10 min.; add salt and pepper. • Turn into a heated serving dish, sprinkle with the parsley and herbs and serve.

FENNEL WITH BACON
* FENOUILS AUX LARDONS

Serves 6

Time: *preparation 15 min. • cooking 1 hr.*
Ingredients: *4 large bulbs fennel • 2 onions finely chopped • 6 oz. (150 g) thick strips of bacon • 2 cups (½ liter) bouillon • 4 tbsp. (55 g) butter • 1 bouquet garni • salt, pepper*

• Remove the very hard outer shell of the fennel; cut the bulbs in quarters and blanch in boiling salted water for 5 min. Drain well. • Put the onions in a thick-bottomed pan and cook in butter until transparent. • Cut the bacon into short, thick strips and add to the onion. Brown on all sides. • Meanwhile chop the fennel into bite-sized pieces and add to the browned bacon and onion mixture. • When they are beginning to turn gold add the bouquet garni, seasoning, and bouillon. • Simmer gently for 50-60 min. • Remove the bouquet garni; check the seasoning and serve as an accompaniment to grilled or roast meat.

POTATOES WITH GRUYERE
⚜ GRATIN DAUPHINOIS

Serves 6

Time: *preparation 20 min. • cooking 1 hr.*
Ingredients: *4-4½ lb. (2 kg) potatoes • 1 cup (¼ liter) milk • 1½ cups (3.8 dl) light cream • 6 tbsp. (85 g) butter • 1½ cups (165 g) grated gryère • 1 clove garlic • salt, pepper, nutmeg*

• Peel, wash and dry the potatoes. Slice thinly. • Rub a shallow ovenproof dish thoroughly with a cut clove a garlic; butter generously. • Cover the bottom with a thin layer of cream, then a layer of sliced potatoes sprinkled with salt, pepper and a pinch of nutmeg and cover with grated gruyère. • Continue arranging alternate layers of potatoes and gruyère finishing with cheese, but keeping some back for the final cooking. • Pour in the milk and the remainder of the cream. • Cook in a moderate oven for approx 1 hr. About 10 min. before taking from the oven sprinkle the surface with the last of the gruyère and raise the oven temperature slightly to brown the surface quickly. • Serve hot in the baking dish.

POTATOES DAUPHINE
⚜ POMMES DAUPHINE

Serves 6

Time: *preparation 30 min. • cooking 40 min.*
Ingredients: *2 lb. (900 g) boiling potatoes • 1 glass milk • 1 cup + 2 tbsp. (140 g) flour • 7 tbsp. (100 g) butter • 4 eggs. salt, pepper • oil or fat for frying*

• Cook the potatoes, drain and purée. • Add a little milk (the purée must be thick) and season. • In a saucepan put 1 cup (¼ liter) water with the butter and salt. Bring to a boil and remove from the heat. • Add all the flour at once to the liquid and mix well. • Replace on a low flame stirring continuously until the paste comes away from the sides of the pan. Remove from the heat and cool. • Add the whole eggs, one by one, beating vigorously after each egg. You should obtain a very smooth paste. • Mix 1/3 of this paste with 2/3 puréed potatoes (if necessary, weigh them). • Taking spoonfuls the size of a nut of this mixture, fry them in the oil or fat. When they are golden brown on all sides, take them out and drain on absorbent paper. • Serve at once.

MUSHROOMS WITH CREAM
✻ CEPES A LA CREME

STUFFED ONIONS
✻ OIGNONS FOURRES

Serves 6

Time: *preparation 20 min.* ● *cooking 30 min.*
Ingredients: *2 lb. (1 kg) mushrooms (if possible, Boletus)* ● *juice of 1 lemon* ● *2 shallots, chopped finely* ● *1 wine glass oil* ● *2 tbsp. (30 g) butter* ● *1 cup (2.5 dl) cream* ● *2 tbsp. chopped parsley* ● *salt, black pepper*

Serves 6

Time: *preparation 20 min.* ● *cooking 1¼ hr.*
Ingredients: *12 large white onions* ● *½ lb. (225 g) minced veal or pork* ● *several strips of bacon* ● *1 egg slightly beaten* ● *3 tbsp. (40 g) butter* ● *2 cups (½ liter) bouillon* ● *1 tbsp. (15 g) sugar* ● *2 tbsp. mixed chopped herbs and parsley* ● *salt, black pepper*

● Wash the mushrooms very quickly in water to which you have added the lemon juice. Pat them dry and cut in pieces. ● Stir them into a pan with the melted butter, oil and seasonings. Add the shallots, cover and simmer gently for 20 min. ● Add the cream and simmer for 2 more min. ● Check the seasoning and turn into a heated serving dish. ● Sprinkle with the parsley and serve.

● Choose onions of equal size. ● Peel and plunge into boiling water for 10 min. to whiten. ● Drain and press gently in a cloth to remove the excess liquid without spoiling the shape. ● Make a small cavity about the size of a nut in each onion. ● Brown the meat in butter, briefly; add the herbs, parsley and seasoning. ● Bind this mixture with the egg and put it into the cavities in the onions. ● Cover the base of a flame-proof pan with the bacon strips and place the onions on them. Sprinkle with the sugar to "glaze". ● Cook over a high flame for 5 min. (do not brown). ● Half-fill the pan with the bouillon and continue cooking gently for approx 1 hr. ● Serve the onions in a very hot dish, sprinkled with the rest of the bouillon which has been reduced over a high flame and skimmed of fat.

BEANS SOISSONAISE
❋ PUREE SOISSONAISE AUX CROUTONS

SPINACH TART
❋ TARTE AUX EPINARDS

Serves 4

Time: *preparation 10 min.* ● *cooking 1¼ hr.*
Ingredients: *1 generous lb. (500 g) fresh white navy or other shell beans* ● *1 carrot* ● *1 onion stuck with a clove* ● *1 bouquet garni* ● *½ cup (120 g) butter* ● *2 slices stale bread* ● *scant ½ cup (1.2 dl) light cream* ● *salt, white pepper*

Serves 6

Time: *preparation 20 min.* ● *cooking 50 min.*
Ingredients: *4 lb. (2 kg) spinach* ● *a little over 1 lb. (500 g) puff pastry* ● *1 cup (2.5 dl) heavy cream* ● *4 tbsp. (55 g) butter* ● *4 eggs well beaten* ● *2 tbsp. (20 g) flour* ● *salt, pepper, nutmeg*

● Put the beans into cold water with the carrot, the onion, the bouquet garni, salt and pepper. ● Bring to a boil and cook for 1-1¼ hr. (depending on the size and quality of the beans). ● Remove the bouquet garni, the carrot and the onion and put the beans through a sieve or food mill twice to obtain a smooth purée. ● Add the cream and half the butter and beat well. If necessary, to make the purée more creamy, add a little of the water in which the beans have cooked. ● Reheat slowly, stirring to avoid burning. ● Fry triangles of bread in butter and arrange around the edge of the dish in which the purée is served.

● Make the pastry according to recipe no. 253 or use frozen pastry. ● Wash the spinach very thoroughly and remove the hard stalks. ● Plunge into a deep saucepan of boiling salted water and cook uncovered for 5 min. Drain and press in a tea-towel to remove all excess liquid. ● Melt the butter in a saucepan, add the flour and cook for 2 min. stirring all the time. Gradually add the cream. ● When the sauce has thickened slightly, season and add a little nutmeg. ● Remove from the heat and, when cooled, add the beaten eggs stirring briskly. ● Mix ⅔ of this sauce with the spinach and check the seasoning. ● Roll out the pastry to ¼ in. (½ cm) thick. ● Generously butter and flour a 10 in. (26 cm) baking dish. ● Line with pastry. Prick with a fork and fill with the spinach mixture. ● Cover the top with the remainder of the egg sauce. ● Cook in a preheated moderate oven for approximately 40 min. ● When the tart is cooked, turn off the oven and wait 5–10 min. before taking out the tart.

TOMATOES FRANCHE-COMTE
❋ TOMATES FRANC-COMTOISES

Serves 4

Time: *preparation 25 min.* ● *cooking 25 min.*
Ingredients: *8 large tomatoes* ● *3 egg whites* ● *4 egg yolks* ● *1 cup (¼ liter) milk* ● *4 tbsp. (40 g) flour* ● *1 generous cup (125 g) grated gruyère* ● *6 tbsp. (85 g) butter* ● *salt, pepper, nutmeg*

● Wash and dry the tomatoes. ● With the point of a small, sharp knife cut a small lid off the top of each tomato and scoop out the interiors. Sprinkle a little salt into the cavities and turn the tomatoes upside down on absorbent paper to drain. ● Melt ⅔ of the butter in a saucepan, add the flour and stir until smooth. ● Add a little milk, mixing with a wooden spoon; season with salt, pepper and nutmeg; add the remainder of the milk stirring all the time. ● Take from the heat and leave to cool. ● Add a knob of butter and the egg yolks, one at a time, mixing well.1bAdd most of grated gruyère, reserving some for the top. ● Beat 3 egg whites until stiff and fold into the mixture. ● Place the tomatoes in a deep oven-proof dish, fill with the sauce and cover with the remainder of the grated cheese and a small piece of butter. ● Cook in a moderate oven for 20-25 min.

BEETS IN SAUCE
❋ BETTES SAUCE MOUSSEUSE

Serves 6

Time: *preparation 15 min.* ● *cooking 30 min.*
Ingredients: *3 lb. (1½ kg) beets* ● *1 ¾ cups (400 g) butter* ● *5 egg yolks* ● *3 tbsp. (30g) flour* ● *juice of 2 lemons* ● *salt, pepper, cayenne*

● Carefully peel the beets and remove the stringy parts. Wash and cut into 3 in. cubes. ● Stir a little cold water in the flour and mix until smooth. Gradually add 3 quarts (3 liters) water. ● Bring this "white consomme" to a boil and throw in the beets. Leave to cook for at least 30 min. ● In a thick-bottomed saucepan put the 5 egg yolks, 3 half egg shells of cold water, salt, pepper and a pinch of cayenne. ● Place in a pan of hot (not boiling) water and beat constantly until the mixture thickens to the consistency of a creamy custard. ● If the cooking is too rapid, take the saucepan from the hot water and keep beating until the sauce has cooled a little. ● Clarify the butter and add gradually to the sauce, beating all the time. ● Place the beets in a hot dish; add the lemon juice to the sauce and pour at once over the beets. ● Serve right away.

POTATOES AUVERGNE
✤ ALIGOT

STUFFED ZUCCHINI
✤ COURGETTES FARCIES

Serves 6

Time: *preparation 20 min.* • *cooking 45 min.*
Ingredients: *3 lb. (1.5 kg) potatoes* • *1⅓ lb. (600 g) Cantal (a hard strong cheese from the Auverge)* • *½ cup (1.2 dl) light cream* • *½ cup (110 g) butter* • *1 clove garlic, crushed* • *salt*

Serves4

Time: *preparation 15 min.* • *cooking 50 min.*
Ingredients: *4 zucchini (courgettes)* • *9 oz. (250 g) sausage meat* • *1 onion chopped finely* • *1 egg slightly beaten* • *1 glass milk* • *2 slices stale bread* • *several strips of bacon* • *4 tbsp. (55 g) butter* • *2 tbsp. hopped parsley* • *salt, pepper*

• Peel the potatoes and boil in salted water until very soft. • Cut the Cantal in fine slices. • Drain the cooked potatoes and pass through a sieve or food mill. • Add the butter and mix with a wooden spoon or spatula over a low heat. Add the garlic. • Away from the heat add the Cantal bit by bit by lifting the puree with the spatula and inserting the cheese underneath so that it melts and forms strings. • Add the cream and return to the fire for 10 or 15 min., mixing all the time with the spatula. • Keep taking the saucepan off the heat to prevent the ''aligot'' from sticking to the bottom of the pan. • When the Cantal has blended thoroughly into the potatoes, serve immediately. • This is a good accompaniement to beef or pork.

• Wash and dry the zucchini and cut in halves lengthwise. • Scrape out the seeds in the center and remove part of the flesh with a small spoon. Take care not o break the skin. • Mix the chopped flesh with the onion and cook gently in butter. Add the sausage meat and cook, stirring to brown all over. • Soak the bread in the milk, until very soft. Squeeze well to remove excess liquid. • Mash with a fork and add to the sausage mixture together with the parsley. • Remove from the heat, cool slightly and bind together with the beaten egg. • Fill the zucchini halves with this mixture and place in a frying pan which you have lined with the strips of bacon. Cover and cook over a gentle heat for about 45 min. • Lift carefully onto a hot dish and serve at once.

EGGPLANT CATALAN-STYLE
* AUBERGINES A LA CATALANE

SPRING GARDEN
* JARDINIERE PRINTANIERE

Serves 4-6

Time: *preparation 30 min.* • *cooking 45 min.*
Ingredients: *4 eggplants (aubergines)* • *3 tomatoes* • *2 cloves garlic, finely chopped* • *1 tbsp. breadcrumbs* • *1 tbsp. olive oil* • *salt, pepper* • *cooking oil (olive oil or vegetable oil may be used)*

Serves 4

Time: *preparation 15 min.* • *cooking 1 hr.*
Ingredients: *½ lb. (225 g) small new potatoes* • *1 lb. (450 g) new peas (petit pois)* • *6 oz. approximately (1¼ cups; 150 g) green beans* • *½ lb. (225 g) baby carrots* • *⅓ lb. (150 g) baby turnips* • *1 lettuce* • *4 tbsp. (55 g) butter* • *1 tbsp. chopped parsley* • *2 tbsp. cream* • *salt, pepper*

• Cut the eggplants into slices lengthwise, leaving them joined at the stalk. • Sprinkle the slices with coarse salt and leave to "sweat" for 1 hr. • Carefully rinse and dry them without separating the slices. • Spread them fan-wise in a large frying pan and brown them in the cooking oil. • Drain on absorbent paper, arrange them in a gratin dish and season. • Cut the tomatoes in half and seed them; sprinkle with half of the parsley, garlic and breadcrumbs mixture. • Place the tomatoes between the eggplants, sprinkle with the olive oil and cook in a hot oven for 30 min. • Just before serving, cover the dish with the remainder of the parsley mixture, finish the cooking and serve hot.

• Wash and dry the lettuce. • Shell the peas, string the beans if necessary, and lightly scrape the other vegetables. • Melt the butter in a saucepan and add the peas, beans, carrots and turnips. • Stir until all the vegetables are coated with butter; add the lettuce, a glass of water, the parsley and seasoning. • Cook gently for 20 min. • Then add the whole potatoes (those that are slightly larger may be cut in 2 or 3 pieces). • Cook for another 35 min. adding a little hot water occasionally if necessary. • Remove from the heat, add the cream and serve on a very hot plate.
• NB This dish makes a good garnish for meat.

BRAISED LETTUCE WITH ANCHOVIES
❋ LAITUES BRAISEES AUX ANCHOIS

CAULIFLOWER MOUSSE
❋ MOUSSE DE CHOU-FLEUR

Serves 4

Time: *preparation 15 min.* • *cooking 30 min.*
Ingredients: *4 very fresh heads of lettuce (Boston, etc.)* • *anchovies in oil* • *12 pitted black olives* • *2 tbsp. capers* • *2 large tomatoes* • *7 oz. (200 g) gruyère* • *8 tbsp. olive oil (or vegetable oil)* • *2 tbsp. (30 g) butter* • *salt, pepper*

Serves 6

Time: *preparation 20 min.* • *cooking 1½ hr.*
Ingredients: *1 large white cauliflower* • *1 lb. (½ kg) potatoes* • *2 tbsp. (20 g) flour* • *½ cup (115 g) butter* • *4 eggs* • *salt, pepper* • *sauce mousseline*

• Remove the coarser outer leaves of the lettuce and carefully wash and dry the hearts. • In between the leaves place the halved olives, the chopped anchovies, the capers, the thinly sliced tomatoes and the gruyère cut as finely as possible. • Generously butter a fireproof dish just large enough to hold the lettuce closely together so that the leaves will remain closed. • Pour 2 tbsp. oil over each lettuce; season. • Cover the dish and cook in a moderate oven for 30 min. • Serve the lettuce very carefully so that the stuffing does not fall out.

• Cut the cauliflower into flowerets, discarding the hard center stalk and coarse outer leaves. Wash well. • Moisten the flour with a little cold water. Gradually add 2 quarts (2 liters) water and bring to a boil. • Throw in the cauliflower and bring quickly back to the boiling point. Lower the heat and simmer, uncovered, for 30 min. • Meanwhile, peel the potatoes and cook in salted water (approximately 20 min.) until soft enough to be puréed through a sieve or food mill. • Drain the cauliflower, pass under running cold water and return to the saucepan with 6 tbsp. (85 g) of the butter. • Mash to a purée. • Mix the puréed potatoes with the cauliflower and add the eggs one at a time, beating well. • Butter a gratin dish or fairly shallow Pyrex dish and spoon in the ''mousse.'' Dot the surface with small knobs of butter and place in a pan of hot water. • cook in a hot oven (450°F; 230° C; **7·8**) for 1 hr. Serve with mousseline sauce (recipe no. 274).

TOMATO TART
✻ TARTE AUX TOMATES

Serves 6

Time: *preparation 40 min.* ● *cooking 40 min.*
Ingredients: *1 scant lb. (400 g) puff pastry* ● *1 cup (¼ liter) Mornay sauce* ● *1 tbsp. butter* ● *1½ lb. (700 g) tomatoes* ● *salt, pepper*

● Make the pastry in advance (recipe no. 253) or use frozen pastry which you have allowed to thaw at room temperature according to instructions. ● Line a buttered pie plate with the thinly rolled out pastry pressing it up against the sides of the dish. Flute the edges and chill. ● Then brush with a little lightly beaten egg yolk and bake "blind" in the oven (425/F; 220°C; **7**) for about 15 min. until the crust is set without being browned. ● Meanwhile peel and seed the tomatoes, and cut into segments. ● Put a layer of tomato over the bottom of the slightly cooled pastry; season. Cover with the Mornay sauce (recipe no. 278) and place the remaining tomato slices over this; season. ● Return to the oven for 10-12 min. or until the top layer of tomatoes is slightly blackened at the edges. ● Take straight to the table and serve at once.

SALADS

Salad refreshes without enfeebling
and fortifies without irritating.

Brillat-Savarin

PARIS CUP
✳ COUPE PARISIENNE

Serves 4

Time: *preparation 20 min.* • *cooking 20 min.*
Ingredients: *1 cup (200 g) rice* • *7 oz. (200 g) green beans* • *3½ oz. (100 g) lettuce* • *3½ oz. (100 g) mushrooms* • *1 scant cup (100 g) grated carrots* • *2 avocadoes* • *12 large prawns* • *1 red onion* • *2 lemons* • *salt, pepper, cayenne* • *fresh thyme, bay, chopped parsley* • *1 scant cup (2.2 dl) light cream*

• Put the whole peeled onion into a saucepan, with a sprig of thyme, 1 bay leaf, ½ lemon and 2 quarts (2 liters) water. • Bring to a boil, and throw in the prawns. Add salt and pepper and bring again to the boiling point. • Cook for 3 min. over a moderate heat. Remove from the flame and allow to cool. • Place the rice in 2 cups cold water with salt, pepper and ¼ tsp. cayenne and bring to a boil. Reduce the heat; cover the pan and simmer very gently (without stirring) until all the water is absorbed (approx 15-20 min). • Transfer the rice to a dish to cool. • Cook the beans in boiling salted water (do not overcook; they should still be slightly firm); drain and rinse under cold running water. • Peel the avocadoes; slice thinly and sprinkle with salt, pepper and lemon juice. • Peel and wash the mushrooms; slice and sprinkle with salt, pepper and lemon juice. • Wash and dry the lettuce; break into pieces and mix together with the beans, rice and other ingredients. • Place in individual salad bowls and garnish with the shelled prawns. • Serve sprinkled with a little cream lightly beaten with salt, pepper and chopped parsley.

PERIGORD SALAD
✳ SALADE A LA PERIGOURDINE

Serves 6

Time: *preparation 40 min.* • *cooking 25 min.*
Ingredients: *1 lb. (½ kg) green beans* • *1 lb. (½ kg) green asparagus* • *2 artichoke hearts* • *1 small head chicory (in England, curly endive)* • *7 oz. (200 g) foie gras (goose liver pâté)* • *2 canned truffles* • *1 lemon* • *salt, pepper* • *olive oil* • *wine vinegar*

• Remove the outside leaves from the artichokes; trim them evenly; rinse in lemon juice and cook uncovered in water to which a little lemon juice or vinegar has been added for approximately 20 min. Allow to cool and divide into 6 portions. • Boil the beans, uncovered, in plenty of water with a little salt. When they are just cooked but still a little crisp, drain and rinse under running cold water. • Cook the asparagus in the same way, but tied together in bunches, standing upright with the tips just above the water. • Wash the endive; pat dry in a clean tea towel and break into pieces. • Cut the truffles (reserve the juices in the cans) and the pate into thin slices. • Divide the beans, asparagus, artichoke hearts and endive among individual salad dishes and garnish with slices of truffle and foie gras. Set aside in a cool place. • Just before serving, cover with the following sauce: 6 tbsp. olive oil, the juice from the truffles, 2 tbsp wine vinegar, salt and pepper stirred together until well blended.

NORMANDY SALAD WITH SHRIMPS
✸ SALADE NORMANDE AUX CREVETTES

DANDELION SALAD WITH BACON
✸ SALADE DE PISSENLIT AU LARD

Serves 4

Time: *preparation 20 min.*
Ingredients: *3 apples • 1 escarole (curly endive or Belgian chicory can be substituted) • 7-8 oz. (200 g) cooked and shelled shrimps • 2 tbsp. French mustard • ⅜ cup (1.6 dl) light cream • salt, pepper • 1 lemon*

Serves 6

Time: *preparation 15 min. • cooking 5 min.*
Ingredients: *1¼ lb. (550 g) young fresh dandelion leaves (young spinach leaves may be substituted) • 10 oz. (300 g) smoked bacon • 3 tbsp. olive oil • 1 tbsp. vinegar • 1 tsp. prepared (or French) mustard • salt, pepper*

• Peel and core the apples, and cut into slices or dice. Sprinkle with the juice of ½ lemon. • Wash the escarole and break the leaves into pieces. • Mix the cream and mustard together in a bowl; add the juice of ½ lemon and stir well; add salt and freshly ground black pepper. • Pour over the apple slices, escarole and shrimps which have been arranged in a flat dish and serve.

• Clean the dandelion leaves; pull the roots apart to get at the tender little central leaves and wash in several changes of water (wash spinach if used, in the same way). • Make the vinaigrette in the salad bowl with the salt and pepper, mustard, vinegar and olive oil. • Chop the bacon in little pieces and fry until golden and crisp in 1 tbsp. oil. • Toss the salad in the vinaigrette and, as soon as the bacon is ready, empty the pan over the salad. • Mix well and serve immediately.

FISH SALAD
✢ SALADE AUX POISSONS

SALADE NICOISE

Serves 6

Time: *preparation 20 min. • cooking 20 min.*
Ingredients: *1¾ lb. (800 g) mixed white fish (cod, hake, turbot, etc.) • 1 ½ cups (300 g) rice • ½ lb. (225 g) canned or frozen crabmeat • 1 lettuce • 2 large tomatoes • 1 green pepper • saffron • 1 recipe mayonnaise (recipe no. 281) • 1 recipe green mayonnaise (recipe no. 282)*

Serves 6-8

Time: *preparation 45 min. • cooking 20 min.*
Ingredients: *4 tomatoes • 4 potatoes • ½ lb. (225 g) green beans • 1 small lettuce • 2 green or red peppers • 2 hard boiled eggs • 1 bunch celery • 1-2 cans (about 14 oz; 400 g) tuna fish in oil • ½ lb. (225 g) anchovies in oil • ¾ oz. (100 g) black olives • olive oil, wine vinegar, salt, pepper, mustard for the vinaigrette (recipe no. 290)*

• Cook the rice in salted water with ½ tsp. saffron. • In another pan or fish kettle, bring the fish to a boil; lower the heat; simmer for 5 min. and set aside, covered, to cool (the fish will continue to cook while the water gets cold). • Wash and pat dry the lettuce; peel the tomatoes and slice. Remove the seeds from the green pepper and slice lengthwise (see illustration). • Chop up the crabmeat. • Prepare the two mayonnaises and set aside in a cool place. • Just before serving, cover a large platter with lettuce; unmold the rice onto the leaves and fill the center of the ring with the remainder of the lettuce torn into small bits, the sliced tomato and the drained fish cut into egg-sized pieces and mixed with the crabmeat. • Arrange the strips of pepper over the top. • Serve the mayonnaises separately.

• Peel the potatoes and boil in salted water for approximately 20 min. (do not let them break apart). • Cook the beans separately. • Remove the seeds from the peppers and slice. • Peel and quarter the tomatoes; remove some of the seeds. • Wash and dry the lettuce; set aside the white inner leaves. • Clean the celery and cut the tender inner leaves into fine slices. • Drain the oil from the tuna and break the fish into pieces. • Shell the eggs and cut in quarters. • In a large flat salad bowl arrange the sliced, cooled potatoes; put a layer of beans over the top, then the lettuce and the celery. Cover with tomato quarters, sliced peppers, anchovies and some olives. The final layer should consist of the tuna, the quartered eggs and the remaining olives. • Make a vinaigrette in another bowl. Pour it over the salad and toss lightly just before serving.

MIXED RICE SALAD
✤ SALADE DE RIZ

Serves 4

Time: *preparation 20 min. • cooking 30 min.*
Ingredients: *1 generous lb. (500 g) cooked chicken • ¼ lb. (110 g) mushrooms • 1 small bunch green celery • 3 tbsp. (40 g) butter • 3 tomatoes • about ½ cup (125 g) cooked peas • 1 onion • 1¼ cups (250 g) rice • 2 cups (½ liter) stock • oil vinegar, mustard, salt, pepper for the vinaigrette (recipe no. 290)*

• Wash the celery and cut the outer stalks into fine slices. Reserve the hearts. • Cook the sliced celery in the butter with the chopped onion for 3-4 min. stirring frequently. • Add the sliced mushrooms and cook for a further 3 min., stirring all the time. Season. • Add the rice; mix well. • When the rice is just beginning to turn golden pour in the stock. • Still stirring, bring to the boiling point; lower the heat; cover the pan and simmer very gently for 20 min. until all the liquid is absorbed. • Allow the rice to cool a bit. Make the vinaigrette and pour over the warm rice. • Leave until cold, then add the chicken cut into small pieces; the peeled and quartered tomatoes; the peas and finely sliced heart of celery. • Mix well, cover and leave in the refrigerator for 1 hr. • Serve very cold.

TUNA FISH SALAD BRETON
✤ SALADE DE THON A LA BRETONNE

Serves 6

Time: *preparation 20 min. • cooking 20 min. + 1 hr. for the beans*
Ingredients: *1-2 cans tuna fish packed in water (about 14 oz.; 4000 g) • 10 oz. (33 g) navy beans or other small white shell (haricot) beans • 3½ oz. (100 g) pickled cucumber (1 dill pickle) • 4 tomatoes • 2 red or green peppers • 2 tbsp. chopped chives • 3 eggs • oil, vinegar, mustard, salt, pepper for the vinaigrette (recipe no. 290)*

• Cook the beans for 1 hr. (this can be done the day before). • Hard-boil the eggs. • Remove the seeds from the peppers and slice lengthwise. • Slice the tomatoes and the pickled cucumber into rounds. • Crumble the tuna; shell and quarter the cooled eggs. • Make a vinaigrette in the salad bowl using a little extra mustard for a more piquante sauce. • Put in all the ingredients (except for a few slices of tomato and the egg to be used as a garnish) and mix well. • Garnish with the quartered eggs and tomato slices, and sprinkle with chopped chives. • Leave in the refrigerator until serving time.

SALADE ECOLE BUISSONNIERE

SALADE ARGENTEUIL

Serves 4

Time: *preparation 15 min. + 1 hr. marinating • cooking 10 min.*
Ingredients: *1 head chicory (in England, curly endive) • Several stalks of celery • 5 oz. (150 g) shelled hazel nuts • 2 eggs • oil, vinegar, mustard, salt, pepper for the vinaigrette (recipe no. 290)*

Serves 6

Time: *preparation 20 min. • cooking 25 min.*
Ingredients: *1 Romaine lettuce • 1 lb. (500 g) asparagus • 1 generous lb. (500g) mushrooms • 2 eggs • 2 lemons • ½ cup (1.2 dl) light cream • salt, pepper*

• Hard boil the eggs. Cut the celery into very fine slices. • Make a vinaigrette. Pour this over the celery and leave to marinate for 1 hr. • Wash and dry the curly endive. • Shell the eggs and slice thickly as shown in the illustration. • Chop the hazel nuts coarsely. • Make a piquante vinaigrette (using a little extra mustard) and pour it over the endive in the bottom of a salad bowl. • Stir the celery and its marinade; add the eggs and nuts and pour onto the endive. • Chill until serving time.

• Clean, then cook the asparagus in boiling salted water (the stalks should be tied together so that the asparagus can stand up with the tips out of the water). • Hard boil the eggs. • Wash the lettuce, pat the leaves dry and arrange them in a circle in a flat salad bowl. • Wash the mushrooms in water with a little lemon juice or vinegar in it and slice. • Make a dressing with the cream, the juice of 1 lemon, salt and pepper. Stir the mushrooms into this sauce and pour into the center of the lettuce. • Quarter the eggs and arrange on top of the mushrooms. • Cut off the hard woody ends of the asparagus and place the stems in a circle around the mushrooms. • Serve very cold.

ALSATIAN SALAD
✤ SALADE ALSACIENNE

BELGIAN ENDIVE SALAD WITH WALNUTS
✤ SALADE DE CHICOREE AUX NOIX

Serves 6

Time: *preparation 15 min.* • *cooking 20 min.*
Ingredients: *2-2 ¼ lb. (1 kg) potatoes* • *1 thick slice cooked ham, approximately ½ in. (1 cm) thick* • *2 cervelat sausages (or other mild finely-textured smoked sausage)* • *1 thick slice tongue* • *2 small beetroot* • *3 pickled cucumbers* • *1 tbsp. capers* • *1 glass dry white wine* • *2 eggs* • *1 shallot* • *several stalks of parsley* • *oil, vinegar, salt, pepper for the vinaigrette (recipe no. 290)*

Serves 6

Time: *preparation 20 min.*
Ingredients: *about 1 lb. (500 g) endive (in England, white chicory)* • *3-4 oz. (100 g) shelled walnuts* • *1 apple* • *½ lb. (225 g) gruyère* • *2 tbsp. light cream* • *oil, vinegar, mustard, salt, pepper for the vinaigrette (recipe no. 290)*

• Wash the potatoes and boil in their skins for approximately 20 min. (do not overcook). • Simmer the sausages over a low heat for 10 min. • Hard boil the eggs. • Chop together finely the capers, shallot and parsley. • Peel the beetroot and dice. • Slice the pickled cucumber; cut the sausages, the ham and the tongue into small pieces. • Peel the warm potatoes; slice thickly and cover with the wine. • Mix together all the other ingredients and add to the potatoes. • Make a vinaigrette; pour it over the salad, toss and serve.

• Cut the base off the stalks of endive (chicory); wash and dry and slice into rounds. • Dice the apple and the gruyère. • Make a vinaigrette and add the cream. • Put the endive, apple, gruyère and walnuts into a salad bowl; cover with the dressing and toss. • This salad must be served fresh and cannot be kept in the refrigerator.

HAM SALAD
✿ SALADE AU JAMBON

"SWEET" SALAD
✿ SALADE "DOUCE"

Serves 6

Time: *preparation 20 min.*

Ingredients: *3 red apples • 1 bunch celery • 1 small bunch radishes • 1 thick slice ham, 12 oz. (350 g) • 2 tbsp. fresh mixed herbs, chopped • 1 tbsp. light cream • oil, vinegar, mustard, salt, pepper for the vinaigrette (recipe no. 290)*

Serves 6

Time: *preparation 25 min. • cooking 10 min.*

Ingredients: *3 large handfuls mixed salad greens • 5 oz. (150 g) bacon • 1 thick slice ham, 1/2 lb. (200 g) beetroot • 15 whole walnuts • 2 tbsp. vinegar • salt, pepper • oil • 2 tbsp. (30 g) butter • 3 slices stale bread*

• Slice the apples thinly but do not peel. • Wash and halve the radishes. • Wash the celery keeping only the tender inner stalks and heart; slice finely. • Dice the ham. • Put all these ingredients together in a salad bowl and sprinkle with the fresh chopped herbs (chives, thyme, savoury, etc). Make a vinaigrette and stir in the cream; pour it over the salad; toss and leave for 10 min. before serving. • This salad must be served fresh and not chilled.

• Hard-boil the eggs. Wash and dry the salad and toss together. Remove the skin from the salami; dice the salami and the ham. Peel and cube the beetroot. Shell the eggs and cut into quarters. Cube the bacon and fry until crisp in a little oil. Put all the ingredients, except the bacon, into a salad bowl; season with salt and pepper then empty the pan of cooked bacon over the salad. Fry the bread in the same pan in a mixture of butter and oil; cut into triangles. Deglaze the frying pan with the vinegar; simmer for a few minutes then pour over the salad. Mix well; arrange the fried bread round the sides of the bowl and serve.

FARMER'S SALAD
✳ SALADE FERMIER

Serves 6

Time: *preparation 15 min.* • *cooking 20 min.*
Ingredients: *10 oz. (300 g)boiled beef (leftovers can be used)* • *1 ¾ lb. (800 g) potatoes* • *3 onions* • *2 eggs* • *2 large tomatoes* • *3 small cucumbers (or 1 large one)* • *oil, vinegar, mustard, salt, pepper for the vinaigrette (recipe no. 290)*

• Boil the potatoes in their skins for approx 20 min. (do not over-cook). • Hard-boil the eggs. • Slice the tomatoes and the onions into thin rounds. • Slice the beef. • Shell the eggs and chop the whites (reserve the yolks). • Peel and slice the potatoes. • Put the meat, tomatoes, onions, chopped egg whites, potatoes and sliced cucumber into a large salad bowl. • Make a vinaigrette by mashing the egg yolks with the oil and vinegar; add the seasonings and pour over the salad. Toss and serve.

CAMARGUE SALAD
✳ SALADE CAMARGUE

Serves 6·8

Time: *preparation 30 min.* • *cooking 20 min.*
Ingredients: *1¼ cups (250 g) rice* • *2¼ lb. (1 kg) mussels* • *12 large prawns* • *about ½ lb. (250 g) shrimps, cooked and shelled* • *about ½ lb. (250 g) mushrooms* • *3 eggs* • *1 lemon* • *1 recipe mayonnaise (recipe no. 281)* • *1 recipe vinaigrette (recipe no. 290)*

• Cook the rice in plenty of boiling salted water. • Scrape and thoroughly wash the mussels; steam them open and remove from the shell. • Hard-boil the eggs. Cool and shell. • Wash the mush-rooms in water to which a little vinegar or lemon juice has been added. Slice very finely. • Put all these ingredients and the shrimps (but not the eggs) into a salad bowl and cover with a vinaigrette. Toss. • Garnish the surface with the hard-boiled eggs cut into quarters; sprinkle with herbs and keep in a cool place until time to serve. • Serve the mayonnaise separately.

SWEETCORN SALAD WITH SHRIMPS
❊ SALADE DE MAÏS AUX CREVETTES

Serves 6

Time: *preparation 25 min. + 30 min. marinating*
Ingredients: *1 large can sweetcorn ● 1 avocado ● ½ cup (75 g) raisins ● 1 egg yolk ● 5 oz. (150 g) shrimps cooked and shelled ● 1 lemon ● 1 recipe mayonnaise ● 1 tsp. paprika ● 1 glass rum*

● Soak the raisins in the rum for 30 min. ● Drain the corn. ● Dice the flesh of the avocado (replace the pit in the flesh to prevent it from blackening). Make a mayonnaise (recipe no. 281) and add 1 tsp. paprika. ● Put the ingredients, including the drained raisins, into a salad bowl, add the mayonnaise and mix gently. ● Serve very cold.

LEEK SALAD
❊ SALADE AUX POIREAUX

Serves 6

Time: *preparation 20 min. ● cooking 10 min.*
Ingredients: *6 leeks ● 6 tomatoes ● 4 eggs ● 3-4 oz. (100 g) smoked ham diced ● 1 recipe vinaigrette (recipe no. 290)*

● Hard-boil the eggs. ● Meanwhile, thoroughly wash the leeks and slice into rounds (discard the tough green ends). ● Peel and slice the tomatoes. When the eggs have been cooled under cold running water, shell and slice. ● Put all the ingredients into a salad bowl and make a vinaigrette using a little extra mustard. Pour over the salad, toss and serve.

EXOTIC SALAD
⚜ SALADE EXOTIQUE

Serves 6

Time: *preparation 15 min.*
Ingredients: *1 can hearts of palm (about 8 oz.; 225 g) • 1 avocado • 1 grapefruit • ½ lb. (225 g) shrimps, cooked and shelled • ⅔ cup (100 g) raisins • 2 small pickled (or canned) red peppers • 1 lemon • olive oil, cider vinegar, mustard, salt, pepper, cayenne for the vinaigrette (recipe no. 290)*

• Soak the raisins in warm water for a few minutes. • Drain the hearts of palm and cut into rounds. • Peel the avocado and slice; sprinkle with lemon juice to prevent blackening. • Peel and slice the grapefruit. • Slice the peppers. • Drain the raisins and put all the ingredients into a salad bowl. • Make the vinaigrette (if preferred, use a little curry powder instead of cayenne to add extra spice) and pour over the salad. • Keep in the refrigerator until serving time.

DESSERTS

A superb meal, shared, is the cause of
greater happiness than the marriage of true minds.

APPLE UPSIDE-DOWN TART
❊ TARTE TATIN

Serves 6

Time: *preparation 15 min. + 2 hr. standing ● cooking 30 min.*
Ingredients: *10-11 oz. (300 g) pie dough ● 6 apples ● 1 cup (200 g) sugar ● 7 tbsp. (100 g) butter ● 1 egg*

● Prepare the pie dough in advance (recipe no. 252) and let it stand in a cool place for 2 hr. (frozen pastry may be used instead). ● Thickly butter a heavy round pie dish, deep enough to contain the filling. Sprinkle the butter with a generous layer of sugar. ● Peel and quarter the apples, taking care to remove all the seeds and hard pieces of core. Slice each quarter in two ● Lay the slices in the sugared dish in circles, pressing them as close together as possible. When the surface is covered, arrange the remaining slices evenly on top of the others. ● Sprinkle with the remainder of the melted butter and the sugar ● Roll out the pastry and cover the pie. Tuck the edges between the apples and the edge of the dish, down to the base if possible. ● Brush with beaten egg and place in a preheated hot oven (400°F; 200°C; **6-7**) and cook for approximately 30 min. ● During the baking, look at the surface of the pastry and cover lightly with a piece of aluminum foil if it begins to burn. ● When the pastry is cooked, turn the tart upside down onto a serving dish. The apples should look carmelized and be soft and buttery.

NUT CHARLOTTE
❊ CHARLOTTE AUX NOIX

Serves 8

Time: *preparation 30 min. + 1 day refrigeration*
Ingredients: *30 sponge finger biscuits (lady fingers) ● 1 ¾ cups (200 g) finely-ground nuts (walnuts, hazelnuts or a mixture) ● 1 cup + 1 tbsp. (250 g) butter ● 1 ¼ cup (250 g) sugar ● 2 eggs ● whole nuts for decorating ● 1 small glass kirsch ● whipped cream (optional)*

● Work the butter lightly with a fork in a bowl over warm water but do not let it melt. ● Add the sugar and continue to work to a smooth paste. Add the powdered nuts and mix thoroughly. ● Separate the eggs and add the yolks one at a time, stirring well. ● Beat the egg whites until they stand up in stiff peaks and fold very gently into the nut mixture. ● Butter a charlotte mold. ● Mix the kirsch with the same amount of water and sprinkle over each finger biscuit; then, as quickly as possible, line the base and sides of the mold with them. If necessary, trim some of the biscuits to fit between the gaps at the top of the mold. ● Pour the nut mousse into the biscuit-lined mold and cover the top with a layer of moistened biscuits. ● Put a plate with a heavy weight on it on top of the mold and put in the refrigerator until the next day. ● Just before serving, wrap a tea towel, soaked in very hot water and wrung out, around the mold and invert the charlotte onto the serving dish. ● Decorate with whipped cream and whole nuts.

DIPLOMAT CHOCOLATE PUDDING
✵ DIPLOMATE AU CHOCOLAT

KUGELHUPF
✵ KUGELHOPF

Serves 6

Time: *preparation 20 min. + 1 day refrigeration • cooking 10 min.*
Ingredients: *30 sponge finger biscuits (lady fingers) • 3 ½-4 oz. (100 g) dark cooking chocolate • ½ cup (100 g) sugar • 3 eggs • 1 glass whisky • 1 pint (½ liter) vanilla cream*

Serves 8

Time: *preparation 40 min. + 4-5 hr. for rising • cooking 50-60 min.*
Ingredients: *3 ⅓ cups (400 g) flour • 3 eggs • 11 tbsp. (150 g) butter • ½ cup (100 g) sugar • ½ tsp. salt • 1 package granulated yeast • 1 ⅓ cups (⅓ liter) milk • 1 cup (160 g) raisins • 3 oz. (100 g) chopped almonds • 1 small glass rum • several tbsp. confectioners sugar for decoration*

• Heat 4-5 tbsp. whisky in a small heavy saucepan. • Away from the fire, add the chocolate, broken into very small bits; place the pan over hot water and stir continuously with a wooden spoon until the chocolate is melted. • Add the softened butter a little at a time with the sugar. Keep stirring until the mixture is thick, smooth and shiny. • Away from the heat stir in the egg yolks one by one. • Beat the egg whites until very stiff and fold carefully into the mixture. • Mix the remainder of the whisky with the same amount of water, and quickly dip the biscuits into the liquid, one at a time, before using them to line the base and sides of a buttered charlotte mold. • Empty the chocolate mixture into the mold; cover the top with the remaining biscuits. • Place a plate with a heavy weight on it on top of the mold and leave in the refrigerator until the next day. • Make a vanilla cream (recipe no. 240) and have in the refrigerator until needed. • Just before serving, turn the charlotte onto a large plate, cover with vanilla cream and, if desired, grated chocolate or glacé cherries.

• Soak the raisins in a mixture of rum and warm water. • Dissolve the yeast in 3 tbsp. warm milk, then add 1 tbsp. sugar and about ¾ cup (100 g) flour. • Mix well with your fingers and leave, covered with a warm cloth, to rise in a warm place for 1 hr. • Add the remaining flour, sugar, salt, the beaten eggs and the milk. Knead well until the dough is smooth and elastic and detaches itself easily from your fingers (about 20 min). • Add the drained raisins. • Cover the bowl again with a warmed towel and leave in a warm place for 1 hr. • Generously butter a kugelhopf mold (these are fluted ornately with a center funnel) and sprinkle with the chopped almonds making sure that they stick to all the grooves. • Put the dough into the mold (it should come about ⅔ up the sides); cover and leave for at least a further 2 hr. to rise until it reaches the top of the tin. • Preheat the oven to 375°F (190°C; **5**) for 20 min. before placing the kugelhopf inside. Leave for 20-25 min. before opening the oven door. • When it is golden, cover with a piece of buttered greaseproof paper and cook for another 30-40 min. • The kugelhopf is ready when a skewer comes out clean when inserted. • Unmold and sprinkle with powdered sugar. Eat while warm.

GRAND MARNIER SOUFFLE
❋ SOUFFLE AU GRAND MARNIER

Serves 6

Time: *preparation 15 min.* • *cooking 35–45 min.*
Ingredients: *1 cup (¼ liter) milk* • *4 tbsp. (55 g) butter* • *5 tbsp. (50 g) flour* • *¼ cup (50 g) sugar* • *1 rounded tbsp. (15 g) potato flour or cornstarch* • *½ tsp. vanilla extract* • *5 eggs* • *2 small glasses Grand Marnier* • *1 large sponge finger biscuit (lady finger)*

• Melt the butter gently in a large saucepan. When it bubbles, remove from the heat, add the flour and the potato flour or cornstarch, and stir until smooth. • Add the warmed milk to which the sugar and vanilla have been added. • Return to the heat and let the mixture cook slowly while stirring continuously so that it does not stick. Put aside to cool. • Separate the eggs; beat the yolks well and stir into the cooled mixture until smooth. • Add 1½ glasses Grand Marnier. • Beat the egg whites until they are stiff and fold gently into the batter. • Crumble the lady finger and soak in ½ glass Grand Marnier. • Pour half the soufflé mixture into a well-buttered and sugared soufflé dish. Cover with the crumbled biscuit and pour the rest of the soufflé batter in. • Place in a preheated moderate oven (350˚F; 180˚C; **4**) for 35–45 min. until the soufflé is puffed high and golden. • Eat immediately.

PROFITEROLES SEVIGNE
❋ PROFITEROLLES GLACEES SEVIGNE

Serves 6

Time: *preparation 20 min.* • *cooking 30 min.*
Ingredients: *1½ pt. (¾ liter) vanilla ice cream* • *1¼ cups (150 g) flour* • *⅓ cup (150 g) butter* • *4 eggs* • *1 tbsp. sugar* • *1 pinch salt* • *5 oz. (150 g) cooking chocolate* • *1 tsp. powdered instant coffee*

• Put 7 tbsp. (100 g) butter, the sugar and the salt into a saucepan with 1¼ cups (3 dl) water and bring to a boil. • Take off the heat and pour all the flour into the saucepan at once. • Stir well with a spatula and return to the heat, continuing to stir until the pastry forms a compact mass that rolls easily away from the sides of the pan. • Away from the stove make a well in the center of the mass and break an egg into it; beat vigorously with a wooden spoon or spatula and continue in this way with all the eggs until they are completely absorbed. • Preheat the oven to 425˚F (220˚C; **6·7**). • On a buttered baking sheet drop small knobs of the pastry with a spoon about 2 in. apart and cook for approximately 20 min. • When the profiteroles are done, take from the oven and pierce the side of each puff with a sharp knife. This insures that they do not become soggy as they cool. • Just before serving, slowly melt the chocolate (broken into small pieces) with the rest of the butter. • Mix the powdered coffee with 2 tbsp. hot water and add to the chocolate. • Open the profiteroles; fill each with a spoonful of ice cream; arrange in a pyramid on the serving dish and pour the chocolate sauce over them. • Serve at once.

CHAMPAGNE SHERBET
❈ SORBET AU CHAMPAGNE

Serves 6

Time: *preparation 20 min. + several hr. freezing ● cooking 10 min.*
Ingredients: *1 jar of preserved fruit in syrup ● 1 cup (¼ liter) dry champagne ● ¾ cup (150 g) sugar ● 1 lemon*

● Make a syrup by simmering the sugar and the juice from the preserved fruit for 10 min. ● Cool, then add the juice of the lemon and the champagne. ● If possible, measure with a syrup hydrometer (glucometer); the sugar density should not be more than 15˙. ● Pass half the fruit through a food mill or sieve and dice the remainder. ● Combine the fruit with the champagne mixture (there should be equal quantities of each). ● Put into the freezer. ● An hour or two before serving, put the dishes in which you are to serve the sherbet into the refrigerator so that they become very cold. ● Once you remove the sherbet from the freezer, serve at once.

● NB A syrup hydrometer (glucometer) is a great aid in the making of sherbet, as the sugar density will affect the texture of the sherbet.

NORMANDY SHERBET
❈ SORBET "TROU NORMAND"

Serves 18

Time: *preparation 10 min. ● cooking 10 min.*
Ingredients: *1 quart (1 liter) Calvados or apple brandy ● 3 lb. (1½ kg) sugar ● 2 lemons ● about 1½ quarts (1½ liters) water*

● Cook the water and the sugar together for about 10 min. or until it begins to thicken slightly into a syrup. Cool. ● Add the Calvados and the juice of the lemons. ● If possible, check the sugar density with a syrup hydrometer (glucometer). It should be 15˙. ● Taste and, if necessary, stir in a little more sugar. ● Put into the freezer, which should be as cold as possible because of the alcohol content of the sherbet. ● Chill the serving dishes for an hour or so before serving and serve as soon as you take the sherbet from the freezer.

EPIPHANY CAKE WITH FRANGIPANE
✤ GALETTE DES ROIS A LA FRANGIPANE

Serves 8

Time: *preparation 20 min.* • *cooking 50 min.*
Ingredients: *about 2 lb. (1 kg) puff pastry* • *7 tbsp. (100 g) butter* • *½ cup (100 g) sugar* • *⅔ cup (100 g) ground almonds* • *1 small glass rum* • *3 eggs*

• Prepare the puff pastry in advance (recipe no. 253) or use frozen pastry and allow it to thaw sufficiently. • With a fork work together the softened (but not melted) butter, the ground almonds, the sugar and the rum. • When the mixture is creamy, add 2 whole eggs, one at a time, and beat into the butter mixture as vigorously as possible. • Divide the pastry into 2 balls and roll them out on a floured surface to a thickness of ¼ in. (½ cm), keeping their circular shapes. • Place one of the rolled out circles on a baking sheet; spread the surface with the almond mixture (frangipane), leaving a margin of about ¾ in. (2 cm) around the outside. • Brush this border with the white of the third egg and cover the whole with the second circle, pressing down hard on the edge so that the two stick firmly together. • With the point of a knife draw lines across the pastry to form squares or rectangles. • Use a skewer or knitting needle to pierce the cake 5 or 6 times all the way through. • Brush the surface with the yolk and what remains of the white of the third egg and place in a hot oven (425°F; 220°C; 6-7) which has been preheated for 20 min. • After 20 min., brush the cake again with the rest of the egg and let it cook for another 40 min. but do not let it burn. • Serve hot.

• NB The traditional Epiphany Cake contains a bean or a porcelain figure of a baby. The finder is "king" for the year.

CREPES SUZETTE

Serves 6 (18 pancakes)

Time: *preparation 20 min.* + *2 hr. standing time* • *cooking 10 min.*
Ingredients: *2 cups (250 g) flour* • *4 eggs* • *2 cups (½ liter) milk* • *1 tbsp. oil* • *4 tbsp. Cointreau or Curaçao* • *a pinch of salt* • *For the "suzette:" ½ cup + 1 tbsp. (125 g) butter* • *1 orange* • *⅔ cup (125 g) sugar* • *1 liqueur glass Curaçao* • *½ cup (1.2 dl) brandy or rum*

• Two hours before you wish to cook the pancakes, prepare the batter: Put the sifted flour, a pinch of salt and the whole eggs into a bowl. Beat together while adding the milk slowly to obtain a smooth thin batter without lumps. • Strain through a sieve. • Add the oil and leave to stand. • Meanwhile, prepare the "suzette:" Cream the butter and sugar together and add the juice of an orange with the finely grated peel. • When ready to serve, add the Cointreau or Curaçao to the pancake batter. If it is not fluid enough, add a little more milk. • Use about 2 tbsp. batter for each pancake; tilt the pan so that the batter thinly covers the whole surface. Make the pancakes as thin as paper. • Stack them without sugaring them on a warm plate. • Put the orange-flavored butter in a pan and cook gently until it bubbles. • Dip each pancake in this mixture, fold in four and arrange on the serving dish. • Add the liqueur glass of Curaçao and the brandy or rum to the remaining butter sauce. • Heat and flame the liquid. While it is still flaming, pour it over the crêpes and serve as soon as the flames die down.

• NB The batter for the crêpes can be made a day in advance.

VANILLA MOUSSE
✻ CRÈME MOUSSEUSE

Serves 6

Time: *preparation 15 min.* • *cooking 15 min.*
Ingredients: *2 cups (½ liter) milk* • *4 eggs* • *⅓ cup (75 g) sugar* • *½ tsp. vanilla extract*

• Put the milk, sugar and vanilla in a pan and bring to a boil. Cool. • Separate the whites from the yolks of the eggs; add 1 tbsp. milk to the yolks; beat hard and continue beating while adding the rest of the milk gradually. • Return to the heat and cook very gently while stirring all the time. It is essential not to let the mixture boil. • Remove from the heat when the mixture coats the back of the spoon. • Beat the egg whites until they form stiff peaks; add to the tepid custard, gently lifting the mass of whites so that they do not break up too much. • Refrigerate until time to serve.

COFFEE BAVARIAN CREAM
✻ BAVAROIS AU CAFÉ

Serves 6

Time: *preparation 30 min.* + *several hr. chilling* • *cooking 10 min.*
Ingredients: *1 cup (¼ liter) milk* • *4 egg yolks* • *1 cup (200 g) sugar* • *4 tbsp. (50 g) freshly ground coffee* • *1 quart (1 liter) crème Chantilly* • *1 tbsp. unflavored gelatine*

• Bring the milk to a boil and add the very finely ground (pulverized) coffee. Cover and let it brew. • Dissolve the gelatine in a little cold water. • Work the egg yolks and the sugar together with a wooden spoon until the mixture becomes very pale and creamy. • Pour the cooled coffee through a fine sieve onto the egg yolks, stirring all the time. • Put into a saucepan over a very low heat and bring slowly to the boiling point without letting the mixture actually boil. Stir continuously. • Remove from the heat when the custard coats the back of the spoon. • Cool slightly, add the dissolved gelatine, stir well and leave to get cold. • Then mix in the crème Chantilly (recipe no. 260). • Take an ordinary round mold with a hole in the center, deep enough to hold the mixture, and rinse in cold water. Drain but do not dry the mold. • Sprinkle the inside with sugar and pour in the Bavarian cream. Keep in the refrigerator (not the freezer) until ready to serve. • Unmold onto a serving dish, sprinkle with finely grated chocolate or fine grains of coffee and sugar and serve.

CLAFOUTI
✻ CLAFOUTIS LIMOUSIN

Serves 6

Time: *preparation 15 min.* • *cooking 30 min.*
Ingredients: *Scant 2 cups (225 g) flour* • *¾ cup (150 g) sugar* • *1 pinch salt* • *4 eggs* • *2 cups (½ liter) milk* • *1 liqueur glass kirsch* • *1 generous lb. (500 g) cherries (if possible, black)*

• Mix the flour, salt and sugar in a bowl. • In another bowl beat the eggs with the milk; add the kirsch. • Pour slowly into the flour stirring to make a smooth and creamy batter. • Butter an ovenproof dish and cover the bottom with the cherries. • Pour in the batter and bake at 400°F (200°C; **6-7**) for 30-40 min. The pudding should be golden and puffed up (like a Yorkshire pudding). • Sprinkle with granulated or powdered sugar, and serve warm.

• NB This pudding may be flamed if, just as it is being served, a glass of warm kirsch is poured over it and set alight.

DANNEMARIE CHARLOTTE
✻ MARQUIS DE DANNEMARIE

Serves 8

Time: *preparation and cooking 1¼ hr. (prepare the day before)*
Ingredients: *9 oz. (250 g) dark cooking chocolate* • *1 can (approximately 15 oz.; 400 g) sweetened chestnut purée* • *40 sponge finger biscuits (lady fingers)* • *1 scant cup (100 g) ground almonds* • *¾ cup (100 g) chopped almonds* • *1 tsp. powdered coffee diluted in 1 tbsp. water* • *scant ½ cup (1 dl) rum* • *1 cup + 5 tbsp. (300 g) butter* • *1½ cups (300 g) sugar* • *6 eggs* • *¾ cup (2 dl) milk*

• Bring the milk and 1 cup (200 g) of the sugar to a boil. Remove from the heat. • Separate 5 eggs. • Beat the yolks and slowly add the cooled milk, beating all the time with a wooden spoon. • Cook slowly over a very low heat, stirring continuously; do not allow to boil. • When the custard coats the back of the spoon, take the pan off the heat. Allow to cool. • Meanwhile, in a double boiler melt the chocolate with the coffee. • When the chocolate is soft, add 1 scant cup (250 g) of the butter in small lumps; let the mixture cool slightly, then add it to the custard. Mix well until you have a stiff, beige-colored cream. • Combine the chestnut purée and the ground almonds. • Add the remaining egg yolk and the rest of the butter, which has been melted. • Bring the rest of the sugar and ⅔ glass of water to a boil and cook for 6 min. • Add the rum and allow to cool. • Line the bottom of a charlotte mold with buttered greaseproof paper. Butter the sides of the mold. • Dip each lady finger briefly into the rum syrup and line the sides and base of the mold. • Pour in the chocolate mixture and press it down lightly but firmly. Sprinkle with chopped almonds. • Cover with a layer of rum-soaked finger biscuits. • Add the chestnut purée. • Finish with a layer of finger biscuits soaked in rum. • Cover the mold with a plate that has a heavy weight on it and leave in the refrigerator overnight. • Unmold just before serving. • If desired, sprinkle with powdered sugar and decorate with chocolate-coated almonds.

RICE A L'IMPERATRICE
✳ RIZ A L'IMPERATRICE

FLOATING ISLAND
✳ ILE FLOTTANTE

Serves 8

Time: *preparation and cooking 1 hr. 25 min.*
Ingredients: *2½ cups (500 g) rice • 1½ cups (300 g) sugar • 2 quarts (2 liters) milk • ½ vanilla bean or ½ tsp. vanilla extract • 8-9 oz. (250 g) crystallized or candied fruit • 8-9 tbsp. apricot jam or jelly • peel of 1 lemon • 7 tbsp. (100 g) butter • 1 pint (½ liter) vanilla cream • 2 tbsp. (2 g) unflavored gelatine • 2 cups (5 dl) Chantilly cream • 8 oz. (250 g.) gooseberry jam or jelly • 1 small glass kirsch*

Serves 6

Time: *preparation and cooking 50 min*
Ingredients: *8 eggs • 15 sugar coated almonds (preferably pink) • ½ tsp. salt • ¾ cup (150 g) caster sugar • 1 tbsp. (15 g) vanilla flavored sugar (or a few drops vanilla extract) • 20 small lumps sugar*

• Bring the milk to a boil with the sugar. • Remove from the heat; add the vanilla and set aside, covered, to cool. • Wash the rice in cold water to remove some of the excess starch; then boil for 3 min. in a large panful of water; drain; rinse; drain once more and put into a metal casserole with the vanilla-flavoured milk, the piece of lemon peel, butter and a pinch of salt. • Bring quickly to a boil, then place in a preheated oven (300°F; 150°C; **1·2**) and cook, covered, for 35-40 min. *Do not stir during cooking.* • Make the vanilla cream or custard (recipe no. 240), incorporating the gelatine dissolved in 3 tbsp. cold water before cooking. Leave to cool. • When the rice has absorbed all the liquid, it is ready to leave the oven. Set aside to cool, and take out the lemon peel. • Meanwhile, make the Chantilly cream (recipe no. 260). • Mix the rice and the vanilla custard gently together with the diced crystallized fruits and the sieved apricot jam. • Add the Chantilly cream and pour the mixture into a well-buttered mold. • Leave in the refrigerator for several hours before serving. • Just before serving, unmold the pudding onto a dish. • Serve with a gooseberry sauce made by beating the jam or jelly with the kirsch.

• Separate the whites from the yolks of the eggs and beat until very stiff, adding the sugar 1 tbsp. at a time. Reserve the yolks. • Gently fold in the crushed almonds and empty the mixture carefully into a buttered charlotte mold; it should reach ¾ way up the side of the mold. • Place in a pan of water and cook in a moderate preheated oven (350 F; 180 C; **3·4**). The meringue is cooked when a knitting needle inserted in the center comes out clean. • Leave for 5 min. in the oven with the door ajar before removing. Unmold while still warm, into a deep dish or a wide bowl. • While the "island" is cooking, prepare a vanilla cream (recipe no. 240) with the egg yolks. • Make a caramel sauce with the sugar lumps and just enough water to dampen them, cooking them over a low heat without burning. When the sugar has melted and begun to turn pale gold, pour it over the still warm egg whites. • Keep in the refrigerator until time to serve. Then pour the vanilla cream over and around the meringue and take the "floating island" to the table. • Serve cold.

STRAWBERRY SHERBET CHARLOTTE
✳ CHARLOTTE AU SORBET DE FRAISES

Serves 6

Time: *preparation 30 min. + 2 hr. refrigeration*
Ingredients: *1 generous lb. (500 g) fresh strawberries • 3 cups (300 g) confectioners sugar • 2 lemons • 1 pint (½ liter) heavy cream • 2 tbsp. unflavored gelatine • 24 sponge finger biscuits (lady fingers) • ½ lb. (225 g) firm, whole strawberries for decorating • scant ½ cup (1 dl) whipped cream • several tbsp. strawberry liqueur, kirsch or cognac*

• Sieve the strawberries to obtain a thick purée. • Dissolve the sugar in a little boiling water; when cool, mix with the purée. • Add the juice of the lemons. • If possible, measure the sugar density with a syrup hydrometer (glucometer). This fruit ice should have a sugar density of not more than 18˚. • Put into the freezing compartment of the refrigerator. • Soften the gelatine in a little cold water, then add a few tbsp. hot water to dissolve. • Beat the cream until it forms peaks and add sugar to taste; carefully stir in the gelatine. • Mix with the partially frozen fruit ice. • Butter the sides of a charlotte mold and line the base with buttered greaseproof paper. • Make a syrup with sugar and a little water and add kirsch or the liqueur of your choice. • Quickly dip each finger biscuit, one at a time, into the liquid so that they are moistened, not drenched, and line the base and sides of the mold. • Carefully pour the cream and fruit mixture into the mold and put on the top shelf of the refrigerator for at least 2 hrs. • Just before serving, turn out the mold onto a dish and decorate the charlotte with the whipped cream and whole strawberries.

CHEESE CAKE
✳ GATEAU MOUSSEUX AU FROMAGE BLANC

Serves 6

Time: *preparation 20 min. • cooking 1½ hr.*
Ingredients: *1 generous lb. (500 g) farmers cheese, well drained • 4 eggs • 1 cup (200 g) sugar • 1¼ cups (⅓ liter) milk • 5 tbsp. (50 g) flour • 1 lemon*

• Put the well-drained cheese and the egg yolks into a bowl. • Beat well and add half the sugar and the flour. • Stir in the milk to obtain a smooth, creamy batter. • Add the finely grated lemon rind. • Beat the egg whites until they form peaks, gradually adding the remainder of the sugar. • Fold in the cheese batter by carefully scooping up the egg whites in order not to break them. • Butter a large, deep mold and pour in the mixture; take care that it does not fill the mold to the top, as it will rise. • Cook in a pan of water in a fairly hot oven (400˚F; 200˚C; **6**), for ½ hr. then lower the heat to moderate (325˚ F; 160˚C; **2-3**) for about 1 hr. • Be careful not to let the top burn. • Let the pudding cool in the mold, then turn out onto a dish to serve.
• NB This cake is delicious with a raspberry sauce (recipe no. 268).

QUEEN OF SABA CHOCOLATE CAKE
✢ REINE DE SABA

PEARS BELLE-HELENE
✢ POIRES BELLE-HELENE

Serves 6

Time: *preparation 20 min.* • *cooking 30 min.*
Ingredients: *6 eggs* • *9 oz. (250 g) unsweetened cooking chocolate* • *1 scant cup (100 g) ground almonds* • *1 cup + 2 tbsp. (250 g) butter* • *½ tsp. vanilla extract (or 2 sachets vanilla-flavored sugar)* • *½ tsp. baking powder* • *2 rounded tbsp. potato flour or cornstarch* • *4 oz. (125 g) dark sweet chocolate* • *¾ cup (100 g) confectioners sugar*

Serves 4

Time: *preparation 30 min.* • *cooking 20 min.*
Ingredients: *4 large perfect pears* • *1 pint (½ liter) vanilla ice cream* • *1 cup (200 g) sugar* • *½ tsp. vanilla* • *7 oz. (200 g) dark sweet chocolate*

• Break the cooking chocolate into small pieces and put in a small, heavy pan with 2 tbsp. water. Place in a double boiler over a very low heat to melt. • Beat the egg yolks with the sugar until they become pale and creamy. Add them slowly to the chocolate away from the heat, stirring all the time with a wooden spoon. • Reserve ¼ cup (50 g) butter for the icing. • Soften the rest of the butter without melting it and mix it with the ground almonds, the cornstarch and the baking powder. • Combine these two mixtures stirring to obtain a smooth creamy paste. • Beat 3 egg whites with a pinch of salt until they form peaks. • Fold carefully into the chocolate mixture. • Butter a mold and sprinkle with sugar; pour in the mixture but do not fill more than ¾ full. • Put into the oven, which has been preheated 20 min. in advance to 425°F (220°C; **6-7**), and cook for 25-30 min. • Let the cake cool in the pan and unmold when it is quite cold. • Just before serving, make the icing: melt the sweet chocolate with 1 tbsp. water and the reserved butter in a double boiler. Stir with a wooden spoon while gradually adding the confectioners sugar. • As soon as the mixture resembles a thick paste, spread it over the cake with a spatula. • The cake may be decorated with shaved chocolate. Serve when the icing has set.

• NB The cake should cook quickly to retain a soft creamy center.

• Make the vanilla ice cream following recipe no 240. • Put 1 cup (¼ liter) water in a pan with the sugar and bring to a boil. Cook for 10 min. • Add the vanilla. • Peel the pears and cut in half lengthwise; remove the seeds and cook very gently for 2-3 min in the vanilla flavored syrup. • Let the fruit cool in the syrup; then take out, drain and set aside in the refrigerator with the dishes or cups in which the pears will be served. • Just before serving melt the chocolate, broken into small pieces, with the butter in a double boiler. • Put 2 scoops of vanilla ice cream in each cup along with 2 pear halves placed upright. • Pour the chocolate sauce over the pears and serve at once.

APPLE MOUSSE WITH NORMANDY SAUCE
✳ MOUSSE DE POMMES SAUCE NORMANDE

PEAR AND ALMOND TART
✳ TART BOURDALOUE

Serves 6

Time: *preparation and cooking 1 hr. 20 min. + refrigeration*
Ingredients: *2¼ lb. (1 kg) firm crisp apples • 5 egg whites • 1½ cups (300 g) sugar • cinnamon • 1 pint (½ liter) cream • 1 small glass Calvados or apple brandy*

Serves 6

Time: *preparation 30 min. • cooking 30 min.*
Ingredients: *A 10" (25.4 cm) pre-cooked pie crust shell • 3 cups (¾ liter) custard filling (crème patissiere) • 6 pears • ½ tsp. vanilla extract • 1 ¼ cup sugar • 9 tbsp. (125 g) butter • 1¾ cup (200 g) ground almonds • 4 eggs • 1 pinch powdered vanilla (or a 1-2 drops vanilla extract) • 1 small glass Kirsch • 5 tbsp. (50 g) powdered sugar*

• Peel and core the apples; cut in pieces. • Put them into a large saucepan with ⅔ cup (135 g) sugar, a pinch of cinnamon and a few tbsp. water. Cover and cook over a very low heat, taking care that the apples do not burn. • When they are cooked, purée them, replace in the pan and return to the heat to get rid of some of the excess liquid, stirring all the time with a wooden spoon. • Allow to cool; then put in the refrigerator for at least 1 hr. • Just before taking the purée out of the refrigerator, beat the egg whites until they form peaks, gradually adding ½ cup (100 g) sugar. • Whip the apple purée until it becomes frothy; then fold very gently into the beaten egg whites and return to the refrigerator for 1 hr. • Just before serving, put the cream with the rest of the sugar into a small pan and bring slowly to the boiling point; add the Calvados. • Serve the pudding very cold, in a bowl, accompanied separately by the hot sauce.

• Prepare the custard filling (recipe 242) and keep in the refrigerator until needed. • Make a syrup with 1 cup (¼ liter) water, ⅔ cup (125 g) sugar and the vanilla extract. • Peel the pears; remove the seeds and cut in half lengthwise; poach gently in the syrup for a few minutes. When they are cooked, drain carefully. • Mash the softened butter in a bowl with the ground almonds, the rest of the sugar, a pinch of powdered vanilla (or 1-2 drops vanilla extract) and the kirsch. • When the mixture is smooth and creamy, beat in the eggs one at a time. • Put into the pre-cooked pastry shell (recipe no. 252) and bake for 15 min. in a moderate oven. Cool slightly. • Place the pear halves on top of the pie, cover with the crème patissiere and sprinkle with powdered sugar.
• Put under a very hot grill for 2 seconds to brown the sugar.

LEMON TART
✳ TARTE AU CITRON

Serves 6

Time: *preparation 25 min. • cooking 30 min.*
Ingredients: *about 1 lb. (500 g) pie dough • ¾ cup (150 g) sugar • ⅔ cup (150 g) butter • 3 eggs • 3 lemons*

• Make the pie dough (recipe no. 252). • In a bowl, beat the eggs lightly with a fork, add the sugar and then mix with an egg-beater. • Add the finely grated lemon peel and the juice. When the sugar has almost dissolved in the juice, add the softened butter and beat until smooth. • Line a buttered pie pan with the pastry and pour in the lemon mixture. • Cook in a slow oven for 25-30 min. or until the mixture has set. Cool before serving. • Decorate with very thin slices of lemon.
  • NB The tart may be covered in meringue: beat the whites of 2 eggs until stiff and add 5-6 tbsp. (75 g) sugar. Cover the already cooked tart with the meringue and return to the oven for a few minutes to brown.

RUM BABA
✳ BABA AU RHUM

Serves 8

Time: *preparation 30 min. + 4 hr. rising time • cooking 40 min.*
Ingredients: *scant 2 cups (250 g) flour • 4 eggs • salt • 1 tbsp. (15 g) baker's yeast • 1 glass milk • 5 rounded tbsp. (75 g) butter • 2½ cups (500 g) sugar • 8 oz. (250 ag) apricot jam • 1 glass dark rum (Jamaican if possible)*

• Soften the yeast in tepid milk, then stir in 1 heaping tbsp. flour and a pinch of salt. Form this into a ball, cover with a cloth and leave for 30-40 min., until it has doubled in volume. • Then add 6 tbsp. (60 g) flour, the lightly beaten eggs, the melted butter and, little by little, the rest of the flour. • Mix carefully with your fingers, kneading and twisting the dough (an electric beater may be used) until it no longer sticks to the side of the bowl or to your fingers. • Butter a savarin or ring mold and pour in the dough which should reach halfway up the side. Cover with a cloth and put in a warm place away from drafts. • When the dough has risen to the top of the mold, put it in a preheated oven (400° F; 200° C; **6)** for 10 min.; then reduce the heat to 350° F (177° C; **4)** and cook for about another 30 min. The baba should be a rich brown color, but not burnt. It is cooked when a toothpick or skewer comes out clean after being inserted in the top. • To unmold, invert onto a cake rack and leave for 10 min.; loosen the sides with a knife and turn out onto a serving dish. • Make the syrup with 1 quart (1 liter) water and 1 lb. (450 g) sugar. Simmer together until it thickens. Take off the heat and stir in the rum. • Prick the baba all over with a toothpick or skewer and carefully pour the rum over it. Spoon up the syrup that collects in the dish and spoon it over the baba again until all has been absorbed (about 2 hr.). • Before serving, spread the baba with apricot jam that has been thinned with a little hot water and (if necessary) sieved.

PINEAPPLE "BELLE-DE-MEAUX"
❖ ANANAS BELLE-DE-MEAUX

PEARS IN RED WINE
❖ POIRES AU VIN

Serves 4

Time: *preparation 25 min.*
Ingredients: *1 large pineapple • about ½ lb. (200 g) strawberries • 3 tbsp. kirsch • 2 cups (½ liter) Chantilly cream*

Serves 8

Time: *preparation 20 min. + 1 day refrigeration • cooking 25 min.*
Ingredients: *8 large pears • 1 quart (1 liter) Bordeaux wine • 1 cup (200 g) sugar • 8 oz (200 g) black currant preserves • a small piece of cinnamon stick or ½ tsp. powdered cinnamon*

• Slice the pineapple in half lengthwise. Carefully scoop out the pulp taking care not to break the skin of the pineapple. • Dice the pulp, removing the pieces of hard core from the center. • Put the strawberries (which have been hulled and gently wiped clean) to soak with the pineapple in the kirsch. • When they have had time to absorb the flavor of the kirsch, fill the pineapple halves with the mixture and put on the lowest shelf in the refrigerator. • Make the Chantilly cream (recipe no. 260). • Just before serving cover the filled pineapple halves with the cream and decorate with a few strawberries that have been set aside.

• Peel the pears but do not remove the stalks. • Arrange in a wide saucepan with the cinnamon and black currant preserves; cover with wine. • Bring to a boil, lower the heat, cover and simmer for 20 min; do not let the pears break. • When they are cooked, remove carefully from the pan and place in a serving bowl. • Reduce the syrup over a high heat to about ⅓; pour over the pears and, when cool, put into the refrigerator until the next day. • Turn the pears over occasionally, so that they are thoroughly soaked in the sauce.

FOUR-PART CAKE WITH PRUNES
✲ QUATRE-QUARTS AUX PRUNEAUX

PEACHES CHEVREUSES
✲ PECHES CHEVREUSES

Serves 6

Time: *preparation 25 min.* • *cooking 50 min.*
Ingredients: *5 medium eggs* • *the same weight of flour, butter and sugar* • *a pinch of salt* • *10-11 oz (300 g) prunes*

Serves 4

Time: *preparation 20 min. +4 hr. refrigeration* • *cooking 40 min.*
Ingredients: *¾ cup (125 g) semolina* • *1⅓ cups (275 g) sugar* • *¾ cup (2 dl) sweet wine* • *4 eggs* • *1¾ oz. (50 g) candied fruits* • *4 large peaches* • *1 vanilla bean* • *1 jar black currant jelly (approximately 8 oz.; 220 g)* • *1 glass cherry brandy* • *1 scant cup (100 g) chopped almonds*

• Weigh the eggs. • Measure equal weights of flour, butter and sugar. • Remove the pits from the prunes using a small pointed knife. • Mix the sifted flour, the softened butter, the sugar and the eggs in a large bowl; add a pinch of salt. • When you have a smooth paste, spread half of it over the bottom of a buttered cake pan. Cover with the prunes and put the rest of the batter on top. • The pan should be only ¾ full. • Smooth the top of the mixture with a spatula. • Put into a preheated oven (425° F; 220° C; **7**) for 15 min.; then reduce the heat to 400° F (200° C; **6**) for 10 min.; and, finally, reduce again to 350° F (180° C; **4**) for a final 25 min. Take care not to let the top burn. • Cool for 5 min. before removing from the pan.

• NB Before the stated cooking time is up, test the cake by piercing with a skewer or toothpick. The cake will lose its springy texture if it is overcooked. • Although it can be eaten as soon as it is cool, this cake tastes better after 24 hr.

• Pour the wine and the same quantity of water into a saucepan; add the vanilla bean broken in halves. • Boil over a high flame for a few minutes; then pour in the semolina and 9 tbsp. (125 g) sugar. • Lower the heat and stir all the time with a wooden spoon to prevent the semolina from becoming lumpy. • After 20 min., remove from the heat and take out the vanilla bean. • When the semolina has cooled a little, add the egg yolks, beating well after each one. • Beat the egg whites until they form stiff peaks and fold carefully into the semolina; then pour the mixture into a buttered savarin or ring mold. • Put into the refrigerator for at least 4 hr. • Make a syrup with enough water to cover the peaches and ¾ cup (150 g) sugar. • Poach the peaches in this syrup, letting them simmer for 3 min. • Peel the peaches and let them get cold. • Combine the black currant jelly and the cherry brandy in a pan and dissolve over a gentle heat. • Just before serving, unmold the semolina pudding, place the peaches in the center of the ring, cover with black currant sauce and sprinkle with the candied fruit and almonds.

SOUFFLEED ORANGES
✻ ORANGES SOUFFLEES

Serves 6

Time: *preparation 15 min. • cooking 15 min.*
Ingredients: *6 oranges • 4 eggs • 5 tbsp. (50 g) flour • ½ cup (100 g) sugar • 1 small glass orange liqueur (Curaçao or Cointreau)*

• Slice off the tops of the oranges and carefully scoop out the insides, reserving the pulp and juice. • In another bowl beat together the egg yolks and the sugar until the mixture is thick and lemon-colored. • Add the flour, the liqueur and the orange juice and pulp. • Beat the egg whites very stiff and fold gently into the orange batter. • Fill the orange "shells" with the souflée mixture and bake in a moderate oven for 15 min. • Serve at once.

BURGUNDIAN RIGODON
✻ RIGODON

Serves 8

Time: *preparation 15 min. • cooking 30 min.*
Ingredients: *3 cups (¾ liter) milk • ¾ cup (150 g) sugar • salt • ½ tsp. powdered cinnamon • about 3-4 (150 g) stale brioche • 6 eggs • 2 tbsp. cream of rice • 3 tbsp. (40 g) butter • 1½ cup (150 g) chopped walnuts and hazelnuts • 1 cup (100 g) chopped almonds • 1 small jar (4-5 oz.; 125 g) fruit jam or jelly of your choice*

• Boil the milk with the sugar, a pinch of salt and the cinnamon. Take from the heat; cover and set aside to infuse. • Cut the brioche into very small pieces; sprinkle with several tbsp. of the flavored milk and leave to soak. • Beat the eggs with 2 tbsp. of cream of rice; then very slowly add the cooled milk, beating continuously. • Stir with a wooden spoon while adding the brioche. • Add the chopped walnuts and hazelnuts and stir well. • Butter an ovenproof dish and pour the mixture into it. • Dot the surface with small knobs of butter and cook in a preheated moderate oven (350°F); 180°C; **4**) for 30 min. • While the cake is still warm, spread the surface with a thin layer of fruit jelly and sprinkle with chopped almonds.

• NB In season, a layer of fresh puréed strawberries or peaches can be substituted for the jam.

LARGE APPLE PANCAKE
✤ CREPIAU DE POMMES

Serves 6

Time: *preparation 15 min. • cooking 15 min.*
Ingredients: *1½ cup (20 g) flour • 1 cup (¼ liter) milk • salt • 3 large apples • 4 eggs • 9 tbsp. (125 g) butter • 5 tbsp. (75 g) sugar*

• Peel the apples, slice thinly, place in a saucepan and sprinkle with sugar. Cover the pan and shake so that all the pieces are well covered with sugar. • Set aside while you prepare the pastry. • Put the flour, a pinch of salt and the eggs in a bowl and mix until the flour has absorbed the eggs; then add the cold milk. • The result should be a rather thick pancake batter; if it is too thick add a little water. • Heat half the butter in a frying pan. • Pour in a generous ladle of batter and let it run all over the bottom of the pan. As it begins to set, put in the apples. • Cover with the remaining batter, and cook over a moderate heat, taking care that the pancake does not stick to the frying pan. • Lift the edge carefully and, when it looks nicely golden, turn the pancake with a large spatula to brown the other side. • Do this very gently so that the apples can cook inside. • Serve at once, sprinkled with sugar, or with a little honey.

STUFFED APPLES
✤ POMMES FOURREES

Serves 6

Time: *preparation 20 min. • cooking 30 min.*
Ingredients: *6 apples • about 6 brioche (300 g) • 4 tbsp. (55 g) butter • 2 cups (300 g) raisins • 1 glass rum • ½ cup (100 g) sugar*

• Wash and dry the raisins and soak in the rum. • Wipe the apples but do not peel. Remove the seeds with an apple-corer and scoop out the flesh without damaging the skins. • Cut the brioche into thin slices and lay over the bottom of a buttered ovenproof dish. Sprinkle with rum. • Crumble the brioche that is left and put it with the raisins in the rum. • Mix together the apple pulp with the raisins and breadcrumbs and carefully fill the apple skins with the mixture. • Put a small piece of butter on top of each apple and arrange them in the dish on the layer of bread. • Sprinkle generously with sugar and bake in a preheated oven (325°F; 160°C; 2-3) for 20-30 min., according to the size and type of the apples. • Serve in the cooking dish while still hot.

CHOCOLATE DELIGHT
❋ DELICE AU CHOCOLAT

Serves 8

Time: *preparation 20 min. + 12 hr. refrigeration • cooking 5 min.*
Ingredients: *2 cups (250 g) sweetened powdered chocolate or cocoa • 1 cup + 2 tbsp. (250 g) butter • 4 eggs • 4 rounded tbsp. sugar • 1 cup heavy cream (optional)*

• Melt the chocolate, the sugar and the butter cut into small pieces in a double boiler over very low heat. • Stir constantly with a wooden spoon until you have obtained a smooth and shiny cream. • Away from the heat, add the whole eggs, one at a time, stirring well after each one. • Beat the mixture with an electric mixer for 15 min. (be sure the mixer does not overheat). • Pour the chocolate mixture into an oiled mold and leave in the refrigerator overnight. • To unmold, pass the blade of a knife around the sides of the mold and invert onto a plate. • For a lighter dessert, before pouring into the mold, fold in 1 cup of heavy cream which has been whipped until stiff but not grainy. • This dessert may be served alone or accompanied by a coffee cream or decorated with Chantilly cream, shaved chocolate, and nuts.

DIJON ICE CREAM
❋ DIJONNAISE

Serves 6

Time: *preparation 25 min. + several hr. freezing • cooking 10 min.*
Ingredients: *14 oz. (400 g) black currants • 1½ cup (300 g) sugar • ¾ cup (1.8 dl) heavy cream • ½ glass crème de cassis (black currant liqueur) • 1 tsp. cornstarch*

• Carefully rinse and drain the black currants; remove any pieces of stalk. • Sieve or purée in a food mill. • Lightly beat the cream with 1½ cup (250 g) sugar. Add the black currant purée and mix thoroughly. • Put into the freezing compartment of the refrigerator and leave for several hours. • Meanwhile, make a sauce by mixing the rest of the sugar and the cornstarch with a glass of water and bringing to a boil. • Take off the heat, add the liqueur and allow to cool. • When ready to serve, unmold the ice cream and cover with the sauce. • Serve immediately.

ORANGE MOUSSE WITH STRAWBERRY SALAD
❋ MOUSSELINE A L'ORANGE

Serves 6

Time: *preparation and cooking 35 min. + several hr. chilling*
Ingredients: *3 oranges ● 1½ oz (3½ tbsp; 50g) chopped pistachio nuts ● 6 eggs ● 2 cups (½ liter) milk ● ¾ cup (150 g) sugar ● 4 tbsp. (40g) cornstarch ● 2 bananas ● 24 large firm strawberries ● ½ lemon*

● Grate the rind of the oranges. ● Bring the milk to a boil and add the orange peel. ● Remove from heat, cover, and let stand for 10 min. ● Separate the whites from the yolks of the eggs and put the yolks in a bowl with the sugar. Beat together until the mixture is thick and lemon-colored. ● Add the cornstarch softened in 2 tbsp. milk and mix well. ● Very gradually add the rest of the milk, stirring continually. Bring slowly back to the boiling point without ceasing to stir with a wooden spoon. ● Allow the custard to simmer very gently for 1 min. only, then pour into a deep dish. Leave to cool, stirring occasionally. ● Beat the eggs until stiff with a pinch of salt. ● Fold carefully into the tepid custard without breaking up the whites. ● Pour into a deep bowl and sprinkle with chopped pistachios; leave in the refrigerator for several hours. ● Meanwhile peel the bananas and slice. Sprinkle with lemon juice. ● Halve the strawberries and slice the oranges from which you have removed any remaining peel. ● Mix all the fruit together in a deep bowl and sprinkle with sugar. ● Chill and serve with the cold soufflé.

CREAMS, PASTRY DOUGHS AND SAUCES

Gourmets can be happy in the knowledge
that they live longer and more contentedly
than those abstemious people who do not find
pleasure in good food and wine.

VANILLA CREAM
✲ CREME DE VANILLE

Serves 6

Time: preparation 5 min. • cooking 15 min.
Ingredients: *1 quart (1 liter) milk • 6 egg yolks • 1 pinch salt • ½ cup (100 g) sugar • 1 vanilla bean (or 1 tsp. vanilla extract)*

• Bring the milk to a boil with the vanilla bean cut in halves lengthwise, and a pinch of salt. • Allow to cool, covered, away from the heat. • Beat the egg yolks in a bowl with the sugar until they are pale and frothy. • Pour the cooled milk slowly into the eggs stirring all the time; return the pan to the heat and cook, stirring constantly with a wooden spoon. • Do not let the mixture boil; remove from the heat as soon as the cream sticks to the back of the spoon. • Pour into a serving bowl and leave to cool. Stir several times to prevent a skin from forming on the surface during the cooling process. • This cream, which can be served as it is, can also be used as the base for many other desserts, and as a decoration.

CUSTARD FILLING
✲ CREME PATISSIERE

Makes 1 quart (1 liter) of custard

Time: preparation 15 min. • cooking 10 min.
Ingredients: *1 quart (1 liter) milk • 6 eggs • 1 cup (200 g) sugar • about ¾ cup (100 g) flour • ½ tsp. vanilla extract or 1 sachet vanilla flavored sugar • 1 pinch salt • butter*

• Put 5 egg yolks and the sugar into a deep bowl and beat until the mixture is pale and frothy. • Add, a little at a time, the sifted flour (use less flour for a thinner custard). • Beat in the remaining whole egg, and whisk until the custard is thick and smooth. • Scald the milk with a pinch of salt and the vanilla or vanilla sugar. • Cool a little, then pour slowly onto the egg mixture, whisking all the time to prevent the eggs from scrambling. Place over a low heat and bring to boiling point, while stirring continuously with a wooden spoon. • When the custard has bubbled 2 or 3 times, remove from the heat and allow to cool, covered with a piece of buttered greaseproof paper to prevent a skin from forming on the surface. • This custard filling may be put into choux pastry puffs, or used as a base for fruit flans or trifles.

CHOCOLATE CREAM
✲ CREME AU CHOCOLAT

Serves 6-8

Time: preparation 20 min. • cooking 10 min.
Ingredients: *½ lb. (250 g) dark chocolate broken into squares • 1 cup (2.5 dl) heavy cream • 6 egg yolks • 8 tbsp. (80 g) flour • 1 cup (200 g) sugar • ½ tsp. vanilla extract or 1 sachet vanilla flavored sugar • 1 quart (1 liter) milk*

• Put the egg yolks in a deep bowl with the sugar and beat until the mixture is lemon-colored and frothy. • Add the sifted flour a little at a time, beating continuously. • Scald the milk with the vanilla extract or vanilla-flavored sugar. • Melt the chocolate pieces in a double boiler with 3-4 tbsp. water; stir constantly with a wooden spoon. • When the chocolate has melted, slowly add the hot milk still stirring. • Pour this mixture gradually into the egg yolks beating vigorously. • Return to the heat and cook gently, stirring still, until the mixture thickens. Bring slowly to boiling point and allow to simmer for 1 min. • Remove from the heat. • Allow to cool, stirring occasionally, and cover with greaseproof paper to prevent a skin from forming on the surface. • Meanwhile beat the cream until it forms peaks (do not let it become hard and gritty) and fold gently into the cold chocolate until the mixture is perfectly smooth and creamy.

KIRSCH CUSTARD
✲ CREME AU KIRSCH

Serves 6

Time: preparation 20 min. • cooking 10 min.
Ingredients: *1 quart (1 liter) milk • 6 eggs • 1 cup (125 g) plain flour • 1 vanilla bean • 1 pinch salt • 1 ¼ cup (3 dl) heavy cream • 1 cup (200 g) sugar • 2 tbsp; (30 g) butter • 1 small glass kirsch*

• Put the vanilla, broken in two lengthwise, into the milk with a pinch salt, and bring gently to a boil. • Remove from the heat and leave covered, to cool. Remove the vanilla. • Meanwhile, beat the eggs adding the sifted flour, a little at a time, and the sugar. • Gradually add the cooled milk stirring briskly with a wooden spoon; return to the heat and continue stirring until the mixture coats the back of the spoon. • Take away from the heat and pour through a fine sieve. • Butter a sheet of greaseproof paper and place over the custard to prevent a skin from forming on the surface. • Just before serving, whisk the cream until it forms soft peaks and fold into the cold custard using a lifting and turning movement so that it retains its light, frothy texture. • Add the kirsch, stir again, and serve very cold.

CARAMEL CUSTARD
❋ CREME RENVERSEE

Serves 6-8

Time: *preparation 10 min.* • *cooking 1 hr.*
Ingredients: *1 quart (1 liter) milk* • *8 eggs* • *1 scant cup (180 g) sugar* • *1 pinch salt* • *1 vanilla bean* • *18 sugar lumps (about 100 g)*

• Scald the milk with the vanilla bean split lengthwise, a pinch salt and the sugar. • Remove from the fire and cool to lukewarm. • Meanwhile, in a metal mold (or several small molds), make a caramel topping with the sugar lumps (caster or granulated sugar will do just as well) soaked in water. • Place the mold over a low heat and when the sugar is dark brown remove from the heat and dip the base of the mold into cold water, then turn it around in your hands so that the caramel coats the sides. • Return the mold to the bowl of cold water. • Beat the eggs and gradually add the milk pouring it through a fine sieve. • Pour the custard into the caramelized mold and place in a pan of water. • Cook for approx 1 hr. at (300°F; 150°C; **2**). • The custard is ready when a toothpick or fine pointed knife inserted into the center comes out clean. • Chill before unmolding onto a serving dish. Put the dish over the top of the mold before reversing. It may be necessary to run a knife gently around the sides of the mold first.

CREAM FRITTERS
❋ CREME FRITE

Serves 6-8

Time: *preparation 20 min. + 12 hr. chilling* • *cooking 10 min.*
Ingredients: *3 cups (¾ liter) milk* • *scant 1½ cups (200 g) flour* • *6 eggs* • *1¼ cups (250 g) sugar* • *½ tsp. vanilla extract or 1 sachet vanilla flavored sugar* • *2 tbsp. rum* • *fine bread crumbs* • *2 eggs* • *olive oil*

• Beat 3 whole eggs with the sugar and the vanilla extract or vanilla sugar, until the mixture is thick and creamy. • Add the sifted flour a little at a time, being careful not to form lumps. • When the batter is smooth, whisk in 3 egg yolks, one at a time, beating hard. • Bring the milk to a boil and pour very slowly into the eggs, beating continuously (the eggs must not cook). • Place the mixture over a low heat and bring to a boil; allow it to bubble for just 3 seconds and stir all the time. This is essential. • Add the rum. • Pour this batter into an oiled cake tin and chill for 12 hr. Turn the batter out onto a table or large pastry board, and cut into strips approximately 1-1½ in. (3-4 cm) wide, using an oiled knife. • Cut the strips into rectangles, dip them in the beaten egg; roll in bread crumbs. • Place in a deep fry basket and deep fry very quickly so that the fritters do not soften in the hot oil. • Serve hot or warm, sprinkled with sugar.

CUSTARD PIE
✳ TARTE AU FLAN

RASPBERRY OR STRAWBERRY ICE
✳ GLACE A LA FRAMBOISE OU A LA FRAISE

Serves 6

Time: *preparation 20 min. • cooking 1½ hr.*
Ingredients: *about 1 lb. (500 g) pie dough • 5 cups (1¼ liters) milk • 5 eggs • ½ tsp. vanilla extract or 1 sachet vanilla flavored sugar • 1 scant cup (125 g) flour • 1¼ cups (250 g) sugar • butter*

Serves 6

Time: *preparation 35 min • cooking: none*
Ingredients: *1 generous lb. (500 g) mashed raspberries or strawberries • 2 lemons • 2 oranges • 1 lb. (450 g) sugar*

• Make the pie dough (recipe no. 252) or thaw out the frozen variety. • Roll out to ¼ in. (½ cm) thickness and line a lightly buttered and floured pie pan. • Do not prick the pastry, but place in the coldest part of your refrigerator for 20 min. to prevent it from shrinking during cooking. • Scald the milk with the vanilla. • Mix the sugar and 3 whole eggs in a deep bowl; when the mixture is thick and smooth, add the sifted flour. • Beat the 2 remaining egg yolks and lightly whisk into the mixture. • Add the warm (but not boiling) milk, stirring constantly. • Pour into the pastry shell and cook in a preheated oven (475° F; 250° C; **9**) for 30 min., then lower the heat to 300° F (150° C; **2**) and continue cooking for another hour. • Serve cold.

• Whisk the pulped fruit in a food processor or beat hard with a whisk. • Stir in the juice of the oranges and lemons. • Dissolve the sugar in a little boiling water and add to the fruit. • If possible, measure with a syrup hydrometer; the sugar density should not be more than 18°. • If it is too high, add a little water; if too low, stir in a small quantity sugar. • Pour into a container and put in the freezing compartment of the refrigerator. • Do not freeze too quickly; fruit ices should freeze slowly if they are to attain the delicate consistency between being too soft and rock hard. • Other fruit ices can be made by the same method, but never forget to add lemon juice which brings out the flavor of the fruit being used.

BUTTER CREAM
�֎ CREME AU BEURRE

Serves 6

Time: *preparation 30 min.* • *cooking 15 min.*
Ingredients: *1 lb. + ¾ cup (600 g) butter • 1 ¾ cup sugar (350 g) sugar • 5 egg yolks • 1 ¼ (150 g) cocoa powder • 1 tsp vanilla extract (or 2 sachets vanilla flavored sugar)*

• Dissolve the sugar in a little water over a low heat. When it begins to form threads when lifted with a fork, remove immediately from the heat. • Beat the egg yolks and whisk into the hot sugar, beating continuously as for a mayonnaise. The mixture should become thick and pale and fall back upon itself in wide "ribbons" when lifted up by the whisk. • Mash the butter with a fork until it is soft and creamy; add the egg and sugar mixture gradually, whisking hard all the time; add the vanilla or vanilla flavored sugar and the cocoa powder mixing all together thoroughly. • Put in a cool place or on the lowest shelf of the refrigerator to harden slightly. • Butter cream is an excellent filling or decoration for cakes and desserts, and is always used for the traditional "Yule Log" served at Christmas in France.

CHOCOLATE MOUSSE
✾ MOUSSE AU CHOCOLAT

Serves 6

Time: *preparation 20 min.* • *cooking a few min.*
Ingredients: *½ lb. (250 g) bitter chocolate • 4 tbsp. (55 g) butter • 4 eggs • ⅔ cup (125 g) sugar • a pinch of salt*

• Beat 3 egg yolks with the sugar until the mixture is thick and frothy. • Break the chocolate into small pieces and melt with 3-4 tbsp. water in the top of a double boiler. • When it is smooth and creamy, take away from the heat and stir in the softened butter to form a thick shiny paste. • Stir the chocolate into the egg and sugar mixture until very smooth. • Beat 4 egg whites with a pinch of salt until they form peaks, then fold into the chocolate mixture using a lifting and turning movement so as not to break up the whites too much. • Pour carefully into a bowl and leave in the refrigerator for several hours.

CREPE BATTER
✾ PATE POUR CREPES

Makes 15 pancakes

Time: *preparation 10 min + 2 hr resting*
Ingredients: *2 cups + 1 tbsp. (250 g) flour • 2 cups (½ liter) milk • 4 eggs • 1 tbsp. vegetable or peanut oil • a pinch of salt • 1 lemon • 3 tbsp. rum*

• Put the flour in a deep bowl and make a well in the center. Into this drop the eggs and a pinch of salt. • Mix well together, then gradually add the milk, stirring constantly. • When the batter is free from lumps, add the oil and the finely grated lemon rind. • Stir in 3 tbsp. rum and leave to stand for at least 2 hr. • If the batter is not sufficiently thin, add a little milk just before using.

BASE FOR ICE CREAMS
✾ BASE POUR LES GLACES

Serves 8

Time: *preparation 20 min.* • *cooking 10 min.*
Ingredients: *3 cups (¾ liter) milk • 1 cup (200 g) sugar • 6 egg yolks • 1 vanilla bean • ½ tsp. vanilla extract or 1 sachet vanilla flavored sugar*

• Bring the milk to a boil with the vanilla bean split lengthwise. • Remove from the heat and leave, covered, to infuse. • Beat the egg yolks with the sugar and the vanilla extract or vanilla sugar, until they become pale and thick enough to fall back on themselves in wide ribbons when lifted up on the whisk. • Add the tepid milk gradually to the egg mixture while continuing to beat without stopping. • Return to the heat and cook, while still stirring, until the sauce coats the back of the spoon. • Do not let the sauce boil. • Take away from the heat, cool and transfer to a freezing container. • Fresh cream may be used in place of milk, either in part or completely. This will make a richer ice cream.

• NB This recipe serves as the base for many kinds of ice creams: the addition of 3 tbsp. strong black coffee makes coffee ice cream; 5 oz. (150 g) chocolate melted in a double boiler and added to the sauce makes chocolate ice cream. The addition of 5 oz. (150 g) toasted ground almonds or hazelnuts makes almond or praline ice cream. To make a crème plombières mix in 5 oz. (1.6 dl) fruit syrup flavored with kirsch. This basic ice cream can also be mixed with rum-soaked raisins; pieces of marrons glacées or coconut.

248

251

250

249

PIE DOUGH
❊ PATE BRISEE

PUFF PASTRY
❊ PATE FEUILLETEE

Makes approximately 1 lb. (500 g) pastry

Time: *preparation 15 min. + 2 hr. resting*
Ingredients: *2½ cups (300 g) all-purpose flour* • *½ lb. (250 g) butter* • *a pinch of salt* • *3 eggs*

Makes approximately 1 lb. (500 g) pastry

Time: *preparation 2 hr.*
Ingredients: *2½ cups (300 g) all-purpose flour* • *1 rounded cup (250 g) unsalted butter* • *a pinch of salt* • *1 cup (¼ liter) water*

• Put the sifted flour into a deep bowl. • Make a well in the center and put in a pinch of salt, the softened butter and the whole eggs. • Mix together lightly with your fingers to form a malleable paste. • If the result is too dry and crumbly, add a little boiled water which has cooled to lukewarm. The pastry should not stick to the sides of the bowl and the flour should be completely absorbed. • Form the pastry into a ball, cover with a cloth and leave to rest for at least 2 hr.

• Put the sifted flour into a deep bowl and make a well in the center. • Pour in the water with a pinch of salt and gradually mix into the flour with your fingertips. Form into a soft heavy ball. Work as quickly as possible. • Place the ball on a floured board and flatten it slightly with your hands. • Work the butter until it is soft and malleable. • Roll out the dough into a long rectangle, about ½ in. (1 cm) thick and place the flattened butter in a square in the center. • Fold first one end of the dough, then the other, over the butter (like folding a letter). • Leave to stand for 15 min. • Working from one of the open ends of the folded dough to the other, roll the pastry into a long rectangle. Use quick strokes of the rolling pin and do not roll over the edges of the pastry. • Fold the pastry into thirds as before and allow to rest for another 15 min. • Repeat this process 4–5 times, rolling from open end to open end each time. The more often the pastry is rolled in this way, the flakier it will be. • Finally, put into the refrigerator until ready to use, although it is better to use it immediately.

CHOCOLATE CUSTARD
✻ CREME RENVERSEE AU CHOCOLAT

Serves 6

Time: *preparation 20 min. + 6 hr. refrigeration • cooking 1 hr.*
Ingredients: *1 quart (1 liter) milk • 10 eggs • ½ lb. (250 g) dark chocolate broken into pieces • ½ tsp. vanilla or 1 sachet vanilla flavored sugar • sugar • 1 vanilla bean*

• Bring the milk to the boiling point with the vanilla bean broken in two lengthwise. Remove from the heat, cover and leave to infuse. • Meanwhile, melt the broken chocolate with 1 tbsp. water in a double boiler over a low heat or in a very low oven. • Remove the vanilla bean from the tepid milk and stir the milk carefully into the melted chocolate. • Add 5 egg yolks beaten with 5 whole eggs; whisk hard. • Add sugar to taste (this depends on the sweetness of the chocolate), but do not make the custard too sweet. • Pour the mixture through a fine sieve into a buttered charlotte mold and put in a pan of water in a very slow oven for 1 hr. The water in the pan must not boil. • Allow to cool in the mold then leave in the refrigerator for at least 6 hr. before unmolding. • Make a vanilla cream (recipe no. 240). • Just before serving unmold the custard and cover with the vanilla cream.

SAND TARTS
✻ PATE SABLEE

Makes approximately 1 lb. (500 g) of pastry

Time: *preparation 15 min. • cooking 10–12 min.*
Ingredients: *1⅔ cups (200 g) flour • 9 tbsp. (125 g) butter. 1 egg. 1 pinch salt. scant ½ cup (80 g) sugar*

• Work the butter with a fork in a slightly warmed bowl, until it is soft. Add a pinch salt, the sugar, the sifted flour and the yolk of an egg. • Mix these ingredients together as quickly as possible with your finger tips. • Form the pastry into a ball, cover with a lightly floured cloth and chill for 20 min. before rolling out and cutting into various shapes. • Sand tarts should be cooked for 10–12 min. in a 350°F (180° C; **3–4**) oven.

FRITTER BATTER
✱ PATE POUR BEIGNETS

Makes 20 fritters

Time: *preparation 10 min. + 1 hr. resting.*
Ingredients: *2 cups (250 g) flour • 5 eggs • 1 pinch salt • 2 tbsp. vegetable or olive oil • 1 cup (2.5 dl) water.*

• In a bowl beat together 2 egg yolks and 1 whole egg; add the flour with a pinch of salt a little at a time, mixing well. • Pour in 1 cup water and whisk until smooth. The batter should be liquid and should not stick to your fingers. • Add the oil and leave the batter in a warm place to rest for 1 hr. • Just before cooking, add the flavoring and ingredient you have chosen to incorporate into the fritters and 4 stiffly beaten egg whites.

CREAM PUFF PASTRY
✱ PATE A CHOUX

Makes approximately 18 profiteroles

Time: *preparation 15 min. • cooking 25 min.*
Ingredients: *1 cup (¼ liter) water • 1¼ cups (150 g) flour • 7 tbsp. (100 g) butter • 4 eggs • 1 pinch salt • 1 egg • 1 tbsp. sugar (only if the profiteroles are to be filled with a sweet cream).*

• Bring the water slowly to a boil with the salt, butter and sugar (if used). • Add the flour all at once, remove from the fire and stir briskly until the mixture is thoroughly blended. • Return to a high heat for 1 min. and beat with a wooden spoon until the mixture is dry enough to roll away from the sides of the pan. Remove from heat. • Make a well in the center of the pastry and break an egg into it; beat vigorously. Repeat with the remaining 3 eggs beating very hard each time (it will take longer to absorb the 3rd and 4th eggs). • Cream puff pastry should be used at once, while it is still warm. If this is not possible, rub butter over the surface and cover with greaseproof paper to prevent a skin forming. • To cook the puffs, either drop small teaspoonfuls of the pastry onto a buttered baking sheet, or, even better, squeeze through a pastry bag with a ½ in. nozzle. • Bake in a hot (425°F; 220°C; **7**) oven for about 20 min. The puffs should double in size and be golden brown. • To prevent the puffs from becoming soggy, remove from the oven, quickly, pierce each puff once with the prongs of a fork or the point of a sharp knife and return to the oven, which has been turned off, for a further 5 minutes. • Fill the puffs or profiteroles with custard filling (recipe no. 242), Chantilly cream (recipe no. 260) or with a savory filling such as cheese, creamed mushrooms or chicken.

BRIOCHE

SPONGE CAKE
✻ BISCUIT DE SAVOIE

Makes approximately 1 lb. (450 g) dough

Time: *preparation 30 min. + overnight rising*
Ingredients: *2½ cups (300 g) flour • ⅔ cup (150 g) butter • salt • 1 tbsp. sugar • 4 eggs • 1 tbsp. (10 g) yeast • ½ cup (1.2 dl) warm milk*

Serves 6

Time: *preparation 20 min.*
Ingredients: *⅔ cup (125 g) sugar • ⅞ cup (100 g) flour • 4 eggs • 1 lemon*

• Using ¼ of the flour, the yeast and a little warmed milk, make a fairly stiff paste and put into a bowl with approximately ¼ cup warm water. • In 20 min. the mixture should have doubled in volume. • Put the remaining flour in a large bowl and make a well in the center; put in a pinch of salt and the sugar. Pour in the rest of the warmed milk and 3 whole eggs. • Using your hands, work into the flour; this should take 10 min. • Add the yeast mixture. If the dough is too dry, add a little more tepid water. • Take the dough from the bowl and place on a floured board or table top. • Knead it well, pulling it out and twisting it and slapping it down hard onto the floured surface. This will help to get as much air as possible into the dough. • Work the softened butter well into the dough. • When it is smooth and elastic, place it in a clean bowl and cover with a tea towel. • Leave for 4-5 hr.; then beat down, flatten it into a rectangle, fold in thirds like a letter and leave to rise in a cool place overnight. • Just before using, break the brioche down gently so it will remain light. • Use either one large fluted brioche mold or several small ones. • Butter the inside before placing the brioche dough in the tins. Brush with beaten egg and leave to rest for 30 min. before baking. • A large brioche should take 30 min. in a 450°F (230°C; **8**) oven; small ones 10-15 min. at the same temperature. • The dough will keep for 3 days in the refrigerator if wrapped in aluminum foil.

• Put 4 egg yolks and the sugar into a bowl and whisk to a foamy cream. • Add the finely grated rind of 1 lemon. • Throw in the flour and beat again until the mixture is free of lumps. • Beat the egg whites until they form stiff peaks and fold them gently into the batter. • This sponge should be cooked in a moderate oven (325°F; 160°C; **2-3**). The time will depend on the type of mold used. • "Savoie" is used as a base for many sweets and puddings: sponge fingers, jam sandwich cakes, Yule logs, etc. It is the batter used for lady fingers which are used in "charlottes" and "diplomats."

CHANTILLY CREAM
❀ CRÈME CHANTILLY

Makes 1 quart (1 liter) cream

Time: *preparation 20 min.*
Ingredients: *2 cups (½ liter) heavy cream • 3 tbsp. sugar • ½ tsp. vanilla extract or 1 sachet vanilla flavored sugar*

• Put the cream in a bowl and leave in the refrigerator for 1 hr. before making the Chantilly. The secret of success lies in having the cream at the right temperature. • In hot weather put the bowl of cream inside a larger bowl of ice cubes when whipping. • Beat the cream with an electric beater (or with a whisk) • When it is forming peaks, use the whisk to beat in the sugar 1 tbsp. at a time • Chill until ready to use.

CARAMEL SAUCE
❀ SAUCE AU CARAMEL

Serves 6

Time: *preparation and cooking 25 min.*
Ingredients: *¾ cup (150 g) sugar • 2 cups (½ liter) milk • 1 vanilla bean • 3 egg yolks*

• Melt the sugar in a heavy saucepan with 1 small glass of water, until it has turned to a pale gold syrup. • Meanwhile, bring the milk to the boiling point with the vanilla bean broken in two lengthwise. Cool slightly; remove the vanilla and pour into the hot caramel, beating all the time with a whisk. • Beat the egg yolks in a bowl, then very slowly pour in the milk mixture, still beating very hard • Return to the saucepan and replace over the heat. Let the sauce thicken over a very gentle heat; stir all the time with a wooden spoon. • When the sauce coats the back of the spoon, pour it through a fine sieve or strainer and leave to cool. Stir it occasionally to prevent a skin from forming on the surface. • This is a delicious sauce to serve with rice cake, ice creams, custards, etc.

CHERRY SAUCE
❀ SAUCE AUX CERISES

Serves 6

Time: *preparation and cooking 15 min.*
Ingredients: *1 jar Morello cherries • ½ cup (100 g) sugar • 2 glasses cherry brandy*

• Put the cherries through the coarsest blade of your food processor. • Put into a saucepan with the juice from the jar and the sugar. • Place over a low heat to dissolve the sugar, then simmer for a little while to reduce the sauce, and remove from the heat. • Add the cherry liqueur and leave to cool.

RUM ZABAGLIONE
❀ SABAYON AU RHUM

Serves 6

Time: *preparation and cooking 15 min.*
Ingredients: *6 egg yolks • 1 ¼ cups (250 g) sugar • 3 glasses rum • ½ tsp. vanilla extract*

• Whisk the egg yolks and the sugar together in a metal bowl (special copper bowls with rounded bases are used by professional chefs for zabaglione, but they are expensive for an ordinary household) until the mixture is very thick and pale, and forms wide ribbons when lifted up on the whisk. • Add the vanilla and put in a double-boiler over simmering water; whisk all the time until the mixture thickens. • Remove from the heat and lightly beat in the rum. • Serve warm or cold.
• NB Marsala, Port or Madeira can be substituted for the rum.

BLACK CURRANT SAUCE
❀ COULIS DE CASSIS

Serves 6

Time: *preparation 5 min.*
Ingredients: *2 cups (½ liter) black currant syrup • 3 liqueur glasses clear spirit (e.g. kirsch, grappa, schnapps)*

• Mix the syrup and the spirit thoroughly. In summer fresh fruit can be added: black currants, raspberries etc. The syrup should be made of fresh fruit and sugar only, without coloring or other additives. • Black currant sauce may be served over ice cream and other desserts.

PUNCH
❀ SAUCE AU PUNCH

Time: *preparation and cooking 10 min.*
Ingredients: *2 level tsp. potato flour or cornstarch • 1 lemon • ½ cup (100 g) sugar • ½ tsp. vanilla extract or 1 sachet vanilla flavored sugar • 5 tbsp. rum*

• Grate the lemon peel very finely. • Stir the cornstarch or potato flour into a little cold water; add 5 tbsp. more water and cook, stirring all the time. • As soon as the sauce begins to simmer, add the grated lemon peel, the sugar, the vanilla extract or sugar, and the rum. Stir well. • Cool, strain and serve as a separate accompaniment to desserts.

264

261

260

265

262

263

CHOCOLATE SAUCE
✻ SAUCE AU CHOCOLAT

Serves 6

Time: *preparation and cooking 15 min.*
Ingredients: *14 oz (400 g) dark chocolate* • *3 generous tbsp. heavy cream* • *½ tsp. vanilla extract or 1 sachet vanilla flavored sugar* • *4 tbsp. (55 g) unsalted butter*

• Break the chocolate into small pieces and melt in a double-boiler with 2 tbsp. water • When the chocolate is smooth and satiny, remove from the heat and stir in the butter. Add the vanilla extract or vanilla sugar and cream. • Serve with profiteroles, rice cake, semolina etc.

COFFEE SAUCE
✻ SAUCE AU CAFE

Serves 6

Time: *preparation and cooking 25 min.*
Ingredients: *½ cup water* • *3 rounded tbsp. (50 g) sugar* • *1 cup (2.5 dl) strong black coffee* • *1 tsp. vanilla extract* • *2 egg whites*

• Put the water, sugar and coffee into a heavy-bottomed saucepan. Bring slowly to boiling point, stirring to melt the sugar. • Simmer until the sauce begins to turn syrupy (a drop of the sauce dropped into cold water should harden into a little ball; this takes a little while). • Remove from the heat and add the stiffly beaten egg whites. Beat again. • If desired add 1 tbsp. cream.
• This sauce is excellent with ice creams, puddings or cakes.

BERRY SAUCE
✻ SAUCE AUX FRUITS ROUGES

Serves 6

Time: *preparation and cooking 10 min.*
Ingredients: *1 generous lb. (500 g) strawberries (or raspberries or redcurrants or a mixture)* • *1 ¼ cups (250 g) sugar* • *1 lemon*

• Clean and hull the strawberries and pass through a sieve or food mill. • Put into a saucepan with the sugar and the juice of a lemon. Cook over a low heat until the sugar has dissolved; stir constantly. • Set aside to cool.
• This sauce can be poured over ice creams or steamed puddings, or served separately in a jug with rice cake or milk puddings.

APRICOT SAUCE
✻ COULIS D'ABRICOTS

Serves 6

Time: *preparation and cooking 15 min.*
Ingredients: *12 fresh or canned apricots* • *½ cup (100 g) sugar (do not use sugar if using canned apricots packed in syrup)* • *1 tsp. vanilla extract*

• Put the apricots and sugar into a saucepan with a cup of water (or use the syrup of canned fruit). Bring to a boil, lower the heat, add the vanilla and simmer for approximately 5 min. • Sieve or put through a food processor. • Transfer to a sauceboat and allow to cool.

PINEAPPLE SAUCE
✻ SAUCE A L'ANANAS

Time: *preparation and cooking 15 min.*
Ingredients: *4 slices pineapple (fresh or canned)* • *1¼ cups (250 g) sugar (use ½ this amount with canned fruit)* • *4 egg yolks* • *1 tsp. vanilla extract*

• Cut the pineapple slices into small pieces and cook over a low heat with 2 cups (½ liter) water, the sugar and the vanilla extract. • When the liquid is syrupy remove from the heat, pour through a strainer and set the bits of fruit aside. • Beat the egg yolks until creamy, then slowly add the syrup beating all the while. • Put over a low flame and cook, stirring with a wooden spoon until the sauce coats the back of the spoon. • Pour through a strainer into a serving jug; add the pineapple pieces and serve.
• This is a very good accompaniment to pineapple ice cream or banana ice cream, and can also be poured over other pineapple desserts.

CALVADOS SAUCE
✻ SAUCE AU CALVADOS

Time: *preparation and cooking 25 min.*
Ingredients: *4 or 5 apples* • *½ cup (100 g) sugar* • *1 cup calvados or apple brandy*

• Peel and core the apples, and cut into small pieces. Put the apple peel, cores (remove the seeds) and 1 cup water into a saucepan; bring to a boil and strain. • Cook the apple pieces with the sugar in the resulting juice. When the apples are soft, put through a food processor, stir in the calvados and leave to cool. • The sauce should not be too thick.
• This is an excellent sauce for baked apples, tarts, pancakes, charlottes etc.

266

271

267

268

269

270

BECHAMEL SAUCE
✿ SAUCE BECHAMEL

Time: *preparation and cooking 15 min.*
Ingredients: *3 tbsp. (40 g) butter • 4 tbsp. (40 g) flour • 2 cups (½ liter) milk • salt, pepper*

• Melt the butter slowly in a saucepan. • Add the flour, stirring constantly with a wooden spoon to obtain a smooth roux. • Add the milk gradually while continuing to stir. • Season, and bring slowly to boiling point. Lower the heat and simmer for 5 min.

ONION SAUCE
✿ SAUCE SOUBISE

Time: *preparation and cooking 45 min.*
Ingredients: *4½ lb. (2 kg) onions • 2 cups (½ liter) bouillon or milk • 2 cups (½ liter) Béchamel sauce (recipe no. 272) • 4 tbsp. (55 g) butter • salt, pepper, nutmeg*

• Chop the onions very finely and blanch for 2 min. in boiling water. Empty into a sieve and pass under running cold water. Drain thoroughly. • Put into a saucepan and cover with bouillon (or milk); simmer. • When the onions have softened almost to a purée increase the heat so that the liquid evaporates. Stir continuously to prevent burning. • Put the onions through a sieve or food mill; add a thick Béchamel sauce and return to the heat, stirring all the time. • Do not let the sauce come to a boil. • Keep hot until serving time; dice the butter and drop the pieces onto the surface of the sauce. Just before serving, stir. • This sauce is very good with lamb and can be used as a second vegetable.

SAUCE MOUSSELINE

Time: *preparation and cooking 20 min.*
Ingredients: *¾ cup (175 g) butter • 1 lemon • 3 egg yolks • salt, pepper • ½ cup (1.2 dl) heavy cream, whipped*

• Put the butter into a saucepan and place in a double boiler over a very low heat to melt. • Then add the egg yolks one at a time, mixing well. • Add 1 tbsp. water and the juice of a lemon. Season and stir well. It is important to stir all the time at the same speed. • The sauce should become thick and shiny. When it has reached the consistency of mayonnaise, take from the heat and beat in the whipped cream. • Serve with asparagus, cauliflower or poached fish.

SUPREME SAUCE
✿ SAUCE SUPREME

Time: *preparation and cooking 25 min.*
Ingredients: *3 tbsp. (40 g) butter • 4 tbsp. (40 g) flour • 2 cups (½ liter) chicken stock • 6–8 (60 g) mushrooms finely chopped. • 3 egg yolks • salt, pepper • ½ lemon*

• Melt the butter; put in the flour stirring constantly. Cook for 1 min. but do not let the flour brown. • Little by little add the bouillon stirring briskly and cook over a low heat for 10 min. • Add the mushrooms which have been sautéed in a little butter. Cook for 5 min. • Season; add the lemon juice and stir. • Scald a sauce boat and put in the egg yolks. Beat well, then add the sauce gradually, beating hard. • This sauce is served with boiled chicken.

BURGUNDY SAUCE
✿ SAUCE BOURGUIGNONNE

Time: *preparation and cooking 30 min.*
Ingredients: *2 cups (½ liter) red Burgundy • 4 tbsp. (55 g) butter • 1 tbsp. chopped shallots • about 12 (100 g) mushrooms • 3 tbsp. (30 g) flour • bouquet garni • salt, pepper, cayenne*

• Pour the wine into a saucepan with the shallots and bouquet garni and reduce by a half. • Put half the butter into a saucepan; let it brown slightly and stir in the flour. • Gradually add the wine, stirring until smooth; season with salt, pepper and a pinch of cayenne. • Simmer for 10 min. over a low heat. • Meanwhile, clean and slice the mushrooms. Cook in the remaining butter for 3 min. only; add to the sauce. • Let the sauce bubble a few times and transfer to a sauce-boat. • This sauce is for roast or sautéed meat.

HUNTER'S SAUCE
✿ SAUCE CHASSEUR

Time: *preparation and cooking 40 min.*
Ingredients: *3 shallots • bouquet garni • 4 tbsp. (55 g) butter • 7–8 oz. (200 g) trimmings of hare (or other small game) • 1 level tbsp. cornstarch or potato flour • 1 bottle red Bordeaux • 2 rounded tbsp. black currant jelly • 1 small glass cognac • salt, pepper, nutmeg*

• Let the chopped shallots and meat trimmings cook gently in a little butter until the shallots begin to turn transparent. • Pour the wine into the pan and put in the bouquet garni. Simmer, uncovered, until the wine is reduced by half. • Force through a sieve or food mill, taking care to extract all the good food juices. • Return to the heat. Season and add a pinch of nutmeg. • Mix the potato flour or cornstarch with a little cold water and stir into the sauce. • When the sauce has thickened, add the cognac and the black currant jelly. • Away from the heat, beat in the remaining butter. Serve in a sauce boat as an accompaniment to game.

MORNAY SAUCE
✳ SAUCE MORNAY

Time: *preparation 15 min.*
Ingredients: *3 tbsp. (40 g) butter • 4 tbsp. (40 g) flour • 2 cups (½ liter) milk • ½ cup (55 g) grated gruyère • salt, pepper*

• Make a Béchamel sauce (recipe no. 272) and, at the last moment, add the grated gruyère, stirring constantly. • This sauce is best used over fish, vegetables or eggs, browned in the oven or under the grill.

AURORA SAUCE
✳ SAUCE AURORE

Time: *preparation 15 min.*
Ingredients: *3 tbsp. (40 g) butter • 4 tbsp. (40 g) flour • 2 cups (½ liter) milk • 3 tbsp. tomato sauce (fresh if possible) • salt, pepper*

• Make a Béchamel sauce (recipe no. 272) adding 3 tbsp. tomato sauce to impart a deep rose color. • Serve with all white meat, fish or vegetables.

TARTAR SAUCE
✳ SAUCE TARTARE

Time: *preparation 15 min.*
Ingredients: *2 egg yolks • 1 tbsp. mustard • 1 cup (¼ liter) olive oil • salt, pepper • 3½ tbsp. (50 g) chopped capers • 3½ tbsp. (50 g) chopped gherkins • 1 clove garlic (optional)*

• Add the chopped capers and gherkins to a mayonnaise made from the egg, mustard, oil and seasoning (recipe no. 281). • A crushed clove of garlic adds savor to this sauce if you do not mind the aroma.

MAYONNAISE

Time: *preparation 10–15 min.*
Ingredients: *2 egg yolks • 1 tbsp. mustard • 1 cup (¼ liter) olive oil • salt, pepper*

• Put the salt, pepper and mustard into a large bowl. Mix well using a wooden spoon, then stir in the egg yolks. • Add the oil, one drop at a time to start with (pouring it from a jug with a little spout is far easier than pouring it straight from the bottle), stirring continuously. • As the mixture thickens, you may pour in a few drops at a time, but great patience and energy are needed. • Keep in the refrigerator until time to serve. • Mayonnaise is excellent with chopped raw vegetables, cold fish, and cold meat.

GREEN MAYONNAISE
✳ SAUCE VERTE

Time: *preparation 15 min.*
Ingredients: *2 egg yolks • 1 tbsp. mustard • 1 cup (2.5 dl) olive oil • salt, pepper • 1 tsp. each fresh tarragon, chervil, parsley, watercress*

• This is a mayonnaise to which are added several spoonfuls of fresh green herbs. • Chop the herbs; then pass them through boiling water. Drain well before adding to the mayonnaise. • Spinach may also be used to give the desired green color, and chives add piquancy.

TOMATO SAUCE
✳ SAUCE TOMATE

Time: *preparation and cooking 45 min.*
Ingredients: *2 lb. (1 kg) tomatoes • 1 onion • 1 shallot • 1 or 2 cloves garlic • 3 tbsp. olive oil • thyme, bay • salt, pepper*

• Chop together (as finely as possible) the garlic, shallot and onion. • Cook gently in the oil until soft and transparent, but do not brown. • Plunge the tomatoes into boiling water and remove the skins. Chop up the flesh, removing the seeds. • Add to the onion and shallot. Put in a sprig of thyme and a small bay leaf. Season • Cook over a very low heat for 30 min. • Remove the thyme and bay leaf before serving. • This sauce is a good accompaniment to rice dishes, pies and quiches, and eggs.

278

281

279

282

280

283

BLACK BUTTER
✳ BEURRE NOIR

Time: *preparation and cooking 5 min.*
Ingredients: *1 cup (225 g) butter • ½ small glass wine vinegar • 3 tsp. capers*

• Melt the butter over a moderate heat. When it begins to turn brown, take the pan away from the heat and slowly pour in the vinegar. • Add the capers. • Reheat, but do not boil. • Black butter is the traditional accompaniment to skate.

BORDELAISE SAUCE
✳ SAUCE BORDELAISE

Time: *preparation and cooking 15 min.*
Ingredients: *1 glass red wine (Bordeaux) • 2 shallots • 4 tbsp. (55 g) butter • bouquet garni • 1 tsp. tomato paste • 1 tsp. flour • 1 oz. (30 g) beef marrow*

• Finely chop the shallots and cook them in half the butter until transparent, then pour in half the wine. Season; add the bouquet garni and leave to simmer. • After a few minutes add a cup of water and the tomato paste. Simmer for 10–12 min. • Make a beurre manié by rolling the remaining butter and the flour into little balls. • Drop one at a time into the sauce; keep stirring. • Meanwhile dice the marrow and poach for 1–2 min. in boiling salted water. Drain and add to the sauce. • Let it bubble a little before pouring into a sauce-boat. • Serve with braised or grilled meat.

SAUCE BERCY

Time: *preparation 15 min.*
Ingredients: *1 glass dry white wine • 1 cup bouillon or fish stock • 4 tbsp. (55 g) butter • 2 shallots • salt, pepper • 1 tbsp. chopped parsley*

• Chop the shallots and cook gently in a little butter until they become transparent. • Add the white wine and bouillon. Season; boil for a few minutes. • Add the remaining butter and stir well. • Just before serving add the parsley. • Serve with fish poached in a court-bouillon.

GRIBICHE SAUCE
✳ SAUCE GRIBICHE

Time: *preparation 15 min.*
Ingredients: *3 hard-boiled eggs • 1 tbsp. mixed fresh herbs • 1 tbsp. mustard • 1 cup (2.5 dl) olive oil • 1 tsp. wine vinegar • salt, pepper*

• Mash the egg yolks with the mustard and finely chopped herbs (chives, tarragon, basil etc) until the mixture is thick and creamy. • Add the oil (from a small jug with a good spout) drop by drop stirring with a wooden spoon, as for a mayonnaise. • Add the vinegar, again stirring all the time. • Chop the egg whites finely and add to the sauce. • Beat again and keep in the refrigertor until serving time, then beat the sauce once more and serve. • This is excellent with veal, tongue, cold meat or fish.

BUTTER SAUCE
✳ BEURRE BLANC

Time: *preparation and cooking 15 min.*
Ingredients: *1 cup + 5 tbsp. (300 g) butter • 4 shallots • 1 glass dry white wine or bouillon • salt, pepper*

• Melt a knob of butter in a heavy saucepan with the finely chopped shallots and white wine; reduce over a moderate heat. • Add the remaining butter cut into small pieces, stirring all the time until the sauce is smooth and creamy. • Beat with a whisk until the mixture becomes foamy. Serve in a heated sauce-boat. • NB Never allow this sauce to boil; if necessary place the pan over hot water before adding the butter. It is an excellent accompaniment to fish poached in bouillon, especially pike.

SAUCE PERIGORD
✳ SAUCE PERIGUEUX

Time: *preparation and cooking 35 min.*
Ingredients: *2 tbsp. (30 g) butter • 3 tbsp. (30 g) flour • 1 cup (2.5 dl) tomato sauce • 1 cup (2.5 dl) Madeira • 1 cup (2.5 dl) bouillon • About 12 (100 g) mushrooms • 1 small tin truffles or truffle peelings*

• Clean the mushrooms and drop them into boiling water. • Melt the butter and stir in the flour using a wooden spoon; cook for a few minutes stirring all the time. • Add the tomato sauce and the bouillon; simmer for several minutes before pouring in the Madeira. • Cook over a low heat for 20 min. • Chop the mushrooms very finely and add to the sauce; allow to boil for just a few seconds. • Add the truffle peelings and transfer the sauce to a sauce-boat. • Sauce Perigord is a good accompaniment to roast meats, chicken or game.

VINAIGRETTE

Serves 4

Time: *preparation 5 min approx.*
Ingredients: *4 tbsp. oil ● 2 tbsp. wine vinegar ● ½ tsp. mustard ● 1 pinch powdered mixed herbs (optional) ● salt ● freshly ground black pepper*

● Stir mustard, salt and freshly ground black pepper to taste into the vinegar until dissolved. Add a pinch of herbs if desired. ● Pour in the oil, stirring all the time with a fork until the vinaigrette thickens. ● The flavor can be varied with the addition of an anchovy, which has been pounded in a mortar, or with a little finely chopped onion or chives.

ONE-DISH MEALS

The pleasures of the table are those that,
throughout time, environment, catastrophes,
and from day to day, remain
a constant consolation in all our sorrows.

LORRAINESE STEW
❖ LA POTEE LORRAINE

SAUERKRAUT
❖ CHOUCROUTE

Serves 8

Time: *preparation 30 min. + 12 hr. soaking • cooking 3 hr.*
Ingredients: *2½-3 lb. (1.2 kg) boned shoulder of mutton • 1 generous lb. (500 g) smoked pork belly • 1 Morteau sausage (or other spicy continental sausage) • 4 smoked sausages • 1 green cabbage • 2 lb. (1 kg) carrots • 6 leeks • 3 small turnips • 3 onions • 8 large potatoes • ¾ lb. (400g) navy or other white shell beans (haricots)*

• Soak the shoulder of mutton and the pork overnight in a large bowl of water; change the water twice. • The next day, let the meat cook in 4 quarts (4 liters) water. Meanwhile, clean the vegetables, and blanch the cabbage in a large pan of water for 5 min. • Put the dried beans in 3 quarts (3 liters) cold, salted water and bring slowly to a boil; let them continue simmering for 2 hr. • Then add the carrots, turnips and onions. • 30 min. before the end of the cooking time, add the cabbage and the sliced leeks. • In another pan of salted water, cook the peeled potatoes separately. • Serve the liquid from the vegetables in a soup tureen and the sliced meat on a dish surrounded by the vegetables. • Mustard, pickles and gherkins make good accompaniments.

Serves 8-10

Time: *preparation 30 min. + 12 hr. soaking • cooking 3-4 hr.*
Ingredients: *about 5 ½ lb. (2.5 kg) sauerkraut • 1 carrot • 1 onion • bouquet garni • 12 juniper berries • 3 cloves • ½ tsp. coriander seeds • 2 tbsp. goose fat (or lard) • several rinds of smoked bacon • 1 boned loin of pork • 1 generous lb. (500 g) smoked breast of pork • 1 Morteau sausage • 6 Montbéliard sausages • 1 cervelat (saveloy) sausage • 8 Strassburg sausages (a variety of spicy and mild uncooked sausages can be substituted for the above) • 4½ lb. (2 kg) potatoes • 1 bottle dry white German or Alsace wine • ½ liqueur glass kirsch*

• Leave the loin and breast of pork to soak in cold water for 12 hr. or overnight. If the sauerkraut is acid, soak it also for 1-2 hr.; rinse several times and press hard to remove the excess liquid. Then place it in a large terrine on top of the bacon rind. Melt the goose fat (or lard) in a small heavy pan and cook the chopped onions until they are transparent but not brown. Pour the onions and the cooking fat onto the sauerkraut. Put the bouquet garni, the coriander, cloves and sliced carrot into a muslin bag; tie firmly and push into the sauerkraut. Season with salt, white pepper and juniper berries. Place the loin and the shoulder of pork on top of the cabbage and pour in enough wine to cover the cabbage. Add the kirsch and put the terrine in a preheated oven (300 F; 150 C; 1-2) and cook for 3-4 hr. 1-2 hr. before the dish is done (depending on the type of sausage used) add the sausages. Morteau and Montbéliard will take about 2 hr.; cervelat, Strassburg sausages and frankfurters take about 1 hr. Meanwhile, boil the potatoes in their skins (it is better to peel them at the last minute to conserve their flavor). To serve, put the sauerkraut in a deep dish and arrange the spicier sausages on top. Serve the meat separately with the potatoes and the cervelat and Strassburg sausages cut up. Serve on warmed plates if possible.

CASSOULET

BURGUNDY FONDUE
✱ FONDUE BOURGUIGNONNE

Serves 8-10

Time: *preparation 30 min. + 11 hr. soaking • cooking 3-4 hr.*
Ingredients: *2 lb. (1 kg) dry white beans (haricots) • 14 oz. (400 g) preserved goose (confit d'oie) • 1 generous lb. (500 g) roast loin of pork or spare ribs • 1 generous lb. (500 g) shoulder of lamb • 1 garlic sausage • 2 lb. (1 kg) Toulouse sausages • 5 oz. (150 g) bacon • several bacon rinds • 1 carrot • 2 onions • 3 cloves garlic • bouquet garni • 3 large tomatoes (or 3 tbsp. tomato paste) • pepper • breadcrumbs • white wine (optional)*

Time: *preparation 1 hr. + 4 hr. marinating*
Ingredients: *approximately ½ lb. (225 g) beef (fillet or rumpsteak) per person • 1 quart (1 liter) oil • 3 tbsp. cognac • 2 tbsp. liquid caramel • 3 cloves • 6 peppercorns • salt, pepper, cayenne, nutmeg. • sauces*

• Put the beans into 3 quarts (3 liters) boiling water with the carrot, onion, 1 clove garlic and the bouquet garni. Bring back to a boil and cook rapidly for 2-3 min. • Remove from the heat and leave the beans, covered in the water for 1-1½ hr. • Meanwhile, melt 2 tbsp. goose fat in a large pan. Cube the pork and the lamb, removing excess fat and brown in the goose fat. • Slice the garlic and Toulouse sausages and add to the pan with the chunk of bacon. • Brown over a low heat; add the pulp from the peeled and seeded tomatoes (or the tomato paste), and the two remaining cloves of garlic. Simmer for at least 1 hr. • Add the chopped goose. • Drain the beans even if they are not completely cooked. Reserve some of the water. • Line a large ovenproof casserole with the bacon rinds and then fill with alternate layers of beans and meat, finishing with a layer of beans. • Pour in some of the water from the beans (white wine may be substituted) and the meat juices, and cook, uncovered in a preheated oven (300 °F; 150°C; **1-2**) for 3-4 hr. (the longer the better). • A crust will form on the surface. Break this with the back of a large spoon and baste with the cooking liquid in the terrine. This may be done several times during cooking. • If you wish to serve the cassoulet *au gratin* sprinkle a handful of breadcrumbs over the top 1 hr. before the end of the cooking time. • Serve straight from the oven.

• NB Toulouse sausage is a coarse sausage made from pork and pork fat and seasoned with pepper and a little sugar.

• Cut the beef into bite-size pieces. • Make a marinade with the cognac, caramel (which you have made by melting 2-3 tbsp.sugar over a low heat and when it is dark brown adding 1 tbsp. water), cloves, peppercorns and spices. If possible, use sea salt rather than the refined table variety. • Marinate the beef cubes for 4 hr. turning them occasionally. • Prepare at least 4 different sauces, each in a little bowl: Burgundy sauce (recipe no. 276), • Tartare sauce (recipe no. 280), • tomato sauce (recipe no. 283), • Gribiche sauce (recipe no. 287), • Perigord sauce (recipe no. 289), • sauce verte (recipe no. 282) etc. • When it is time to eat, heat the oil in the fondue pan on the heating element (put a small piece of raw potato into the oil to prevent smoking). • Drain the meat, dry it and heap on a plate, surrounded by the bowls of sauce. • Using long forks or skewers, let your guests dip each piece of meat into the hot oil then into the sauces.

SAVOY FONDUE
❋ LA FONDUE SAVOYARDE

BOUILLABAISSE

Serves 6

Time: *preparation 20 min. • cooking 8-10 min.*
Ingredients: *1¼ lb. (600 g) grated gruyère • 1¼ lb. (600 g) grated gruyère and emmenthal mixed • 3 cloves garlic • 4 glasses white Savoy wine (if possible, Chignin or Digny, but any dry white wine can be used) • 1 glass kirsch • salt, pepper, nutmeg • 2 lb. (1 kg) stale French bread*

Serves 8-10

Time: *preparation 30 min. • cooking 25 min.*
Ingredients: *1 generous lb. (500 g) small coastal fishes • 1 generous lb. (500 g) small crabs • 2lb. (1 kg) any white fish (haddock, cod, bream, sant-pierre, sea bass,etc.) • 2 rock lobsters or crayfish • 2 red mullets • 1 lb. (500 g) eel cut in 2 in. pieces • 8 tbsp. olive oil • 2 onions • 8 tomatoes • 1 large potato • bouquet garni (fennel, bay leaf, thyme, parsley, 6 cloves garlic, celery, rosemary) • ½ tsp. powdered saffron • cayenne • 1 crusty loaf of bread • 3 egg yolks • 1 clove garlic • 1 red pimento • salt, pepper • ½ cup olive oil*

• Cut the bread into 1 in. (2-3 cm) cubes. Rub the inside of the fondue pan with the cut clove of garlic. Pour in the wine and heat (this should be done over the stove). When the wine bubbles, add the grated cheese and stir continuously with a wooden spoon. When the cheese has melted, add the seasonings. Cook for 8-10 min., stirring all the time. Add the kirsch and take the pan to the table where the heater is burning. Serve the bread in a large basket and let your guests dip the pieces into the fondue on the ends of long forks or skewers.

• Clean and dry the fishes. • Peel the tomatoes and remove the seeds. • Peel the potato and slice. Heat 8 tbsp. olive oil in a very large saucepan and put in the chopped onions, the tomatoes, the crushed garlic cloves, the sliced potato and all the ingredients for the bouquet garni. Stir while adding the smaller fish and the crabs. • Reserve 1 of the rock lobsters and two of the larger fishes; cut the remaining fishes into 2 in. (5 cm) lengths. Season. • When the fishes have begun to blanch, sprinkle with saffron and add boiling water (1 glass per person + extra glass) Bring to a boil and simmer 15 min. • Very carefully add the whole fishes (which were previously set aside) and boil the bouillabaisse gently for another 10 min. • Slice and toast the bread and rub each slice with garlic. • Prepare the ''rouille'' (the traditional accompanying sauce): • make a mayonnaise with the egg yolks, the crushed and sieved pimento, 1 crushed clove of garlic, salt and olive oil. Add the oil drop by drop to the egg yolks, stirring constantly, so that the yolks do not curdle. • When the mayonnaise is thick and creamy, add a few drops of the bouillabaisse liquid to give it a rusty gold (''rouille'') color. • Take out the whole fishes, being careful not to break them, and the pieces of cut up fish. Arrange in a serving dish. • Sieve the rest of the soup, crushing the small crabs and the potato to thicken the liquid. Pour into a soup tureen. • In separate dishes, but at the same time, serve the fish, the soup, the ''rouille'' and the garlic toast.

Serves 8

Time: *preparation 30 min. + 24 hr. soaking • cooking 1 hr.*
Ingredients: *3¼ lb. (1.5 kg) fresh cod • 1 quart (1 liter) whelks or periwinkles (optional) • 1 generous lb. (500 g) baby carrots • 1 generous lb. (500 g) new potatoes • 1 generous lb. (500 g) green beans • 8 small artichokes (preferably the Italian violet kind) • 10 hard boiled eggs • 8 tomatoes • 8 cloves garlic • salt • 2 cups (½ liter) olive oil • 2 egg yolks*

Serves 8

Time: *preparation 30 min. • cooking 1¼ hr.*
Ingredients: *2 lb. (1 kg) eel • 2 lb. (1 kg) fresh cod • 8 small whiting • 1 cod or hake head • 8 leeks • 8 carrots • 8 potatoes • 1 stick celery • bouquet garni • onion stuck with 2 cloves • 4 cloves garlic • 1 small loaf French bread • 1 egg yolk • 2 tbsp. cream • sea salt, pepper*

• Desalt the cod by soaking it in cold water the day before you wish to eat it. Change the water several times. • Wash or peel the vegetables and cook in boiling salted water. • If you are using periwinkles, clean them; put them in cold salted water; bring to the boiling point and cook for 10 min. • Wash the tomatoes and the artichokes. Steam the artichokes if they are not tender enough to be eaten raw. • Put the cod into a fish kettle or long oval casserole and cover completely with water. • Place over a low heat and, as soon as the water starts simmering, turn off the heat and cover the pan. • Leave for 5-10 min.; then drain. Remove the bones and take off the skin. • To serve, arrange all the vegetables on a large dish. Place the cod on another dish surrounded by the periwinkles and halved hard boiled eggs. • With them serve the Aïoli which is prepared thus: • Peel 8 cloves garlic and cut off the hard base; crush in a mortar. When they are very soft, add a little salt and continue pounding for 1 min. • Add 2 egg yolks mixing with the pestle or with a wooden spoon. • Drop by drop, stirring all the time, add the olive oil, pouring it from a little jug. • When you have a smooth thick sauce, the aïoli is ready. • Serve in the mortar in which it was made.

• Thoroughly wash the leeks cutting off the stringy ends and all the coarse green leaves; tie the white ends in a bunch. • Wash and scrape the carrots; peel the potatoes and wash the celery. • Put 4 quarts (4 liters) water in a very large saucepan with sea salt, pepper, 2 peeled cloves garlic, the onion and the bouquet garni. Bring to a boil. • Add the leeks, carrots and the fish head. Cook, covered, for 45 min. • Add the eel, the cod (which has been cleaned) and the potatoes and simmer gently for another 30 min. • When the cooking time is almost over, place the whiting on top of the other ingredients and cook for 6-8 min. • Meanwhile, slice the bread, toast it and rub each slice generously with a cut clove of garlic. • Drain the cooked fish and arrange on a serving dish with the vegetables in the center. Keep warm. • Put the toast in a soup tureen.In a bowl beat the egg yolk with the cream and dilute slowly with a ladleful of hot soup, so that the egg does not cook. • Empty this mixture into the stockpot, stirring briskly all the time, and cook for 2 min. over a very low heat; continue stirring.
• Pour over the toast and serve at once. • The fish and vegetables may be served afterwards with mayonnaise (recipe no. 281) or Bercy sauce (recipe no. 286), or unaccompanied according to your taste.

CHICKEN IN THE POT
✷ POULE AU POT

POT·AU·FEU

Serves 6-8

Time: *preparation 25 min.* • *cooking 1½ hr.*
Ingredients: *1 chicken 4-4½ lb. (2 kg)* • *1 large veal knuckle (other veal bones may be substituted)* • *2 large bunches celery with the leaves left on* • *2 small turnips* • *4 leeks* • *6 carrots* • *2 onions* • *bouquet garni* • *salt* • *cloves*

Serves 6

Time: *preparation 30 min.* • *cooking at least 3 hr.*
Ingredients: *4½ lb. (2 kg) top ribs of beef unboned* • *1¼ lb. (600 g) gravy beef* • *2 bones without marrow* • *4 leeks* • *8 carrots* • *6 small turnips* • *2 large onions* • *1 bunch celery with leaves* • *bouquet garni* • *4 cloves* • *salt, peppercorns* • *grated gruyère*

• Put the cleaned, trussed chicken into a large stewpot with the knuckle bone and cover with cold water. • Bring to a boil; skim; lower the heat and leave to cook, covered. • Meanwhile, stick one or two cloves into each of the onions and put them into the oven to brown. • Skim the stockpot again and put in the turnips, leeks, quartered and sliced celery hearts, onions and bouquet garni. Salt. • Bring to a boil again, lower the heat and simmer gently for 1½ hr. • Serve the chicken, surrounded by the vegetables, with a bowl of the degreased bouillon on the side. • Pickled cucumbers, mustard and pickles are excellent accompaniments.

• Put the meat with the bones underneath into a large pan of cold water; salt. • Bring slowly to the boiling point until the water is merely rippling on the surface. Let the meat cook gently for as long as possible (at least 3 hr.) over a low heat, without interruption. • Meanwhile, thoroughly clean the vegetables; tie the leeks and stalks of celery into bunches; peel the onions and stick 2 cloves in each. • After 2-3 hr. cooking, add the carrots and onions with the bouquet garni. • After another 1½ hr. put in the leeks, celery and turnips with several peppercorns. • Turn the heat up very slightly so that the water is just simmering (it may be necessary to add a little more water). • When the vegetables are cooked (about 1 hr. more), skim the fat off the bouillon and serve it with a bowl of grated gruyère and slices of toast. • Slice the meat (it should fall apart) and serve decorated with the vegetables. • Mustard and pickled gherkins are good accompaniments.

NOTES ON INGREDIENTS AND MEASUREMENTS

We have tried to make the recipes in this book equally accessible to American and British readers. In general, where American and English terminology differ, the English term is given in parentheses. The following notes may, however, be helpful in clarifying some points which the limitations of space did not allow us to explain fully in the recipes themselves:

Oven Temperature.   Oven temperatures are given in Fahrenheit, Centigrade and Mark. The boldface number following the Centigrade temperature is the British oven mark number.

Measurements.   Fluid measurements are given in cups and deciliters (dl). 1 cup equals 8 oz. or 2.5 dl. 1 tbsp. equals 15 ml and 1 tsp. equals 5 ml. 1 oz. is equivalent to 25 g, and 1 lb. equals 450 g.

Sugar.   Unless otherwise specified, the ingredient sugar always refers to caster sugar. Ingredient listings of confectioners or powdered sugar refer to icing sugar.

Cream.   Light and heavy cream are synonymous with single and double cream respectively. When the recipe calls only for cream, light or single cream is indicated. It is up to the cook to decide if he or she wishes to substitute heavy or double cream for greater richness.

Shellfish.   The larger varieties of what Americans call shrimp are called prawns in Great Britain. Spiny or Rock Lobster is known in Great Britain as crawfish; and what Americans call crayfish is called Dublin Bay Prawn by the British.

INDEX OF RECIPES

121. Guinea Fowl Stuffed with Raisins
122. Turkey Braised in Champagne
123. Filleted Duck with Green Peppercorns
124. Pigeons Bordelaise
125. Goose Roasted with Apples
126. Partridge Camargue Style
127. Stuffed Quails with Croûtons
128. Thrushes Flamed in Gin
129. Christmas Turkey
130. Pheasant Grenoble
131. Hare Stew
132. Turban of Wild Boar Cutlets
133. Leg of Venison with Three Purées
134. Loin of Venison with Huckleberrie
135. Wild Duck with Cherries

Fish and Shellfish
136. Pike Fillets in White Wine
137. Eel Soup
138. Trout in Champagne
139. Shad in Sorrel
140. Salmon with Shrimps
141. Sea Bream Stuffed with Almonds
142. Fresh Sardines
143. Fillets Bercy
144. Whiting in White Wine
145. Creamed Cod
146. Pollack with Sauerkraut
147. Cod Mornay
148. Herrings in Mustard Sauce
149. Mackerel Boulogne
150. Tuna Breton
151. Bass Marinière
152. Creamed Fillets of Sole
153. Lotte or Burbot Armoricain
154. Skate in Black Butter
155. Turbot with Shellfish
156. Mussels Marinière
157. Stuffed Mussels
158. Scallops in Vermouth
159. Scallops with Mushrooms
160. Rock Lobster in Banyuls Wine
161. Crayfish or Prawns Bordeaux

162. Scampi Fritters
163. Lobster Timbale
164. Stuffed Squid

Vegetables
165. Artichokes with Beans
166. Asparagus Soufflé
167. Carrot Purée
168. Cardoons au Gratin
169. Creamed Salsify
170. Fennel with Bacon
171. Potatoes with Gruyère
172. Potatoes Dauphine
173. Mushrooms with Cream
174. Stuffed Onions
175. Beans Soissonaise
176. Spinach Tart
177. Tomatoes Franche-Comté
178. Beets in Sauce
179. Potatoes Auvergne
180. Stuffed Zucchini
181. Eggplant Catalan-Style
182. Spring Garden
183. Braised Lettuce with Anchovies
184. Cauliflower Mousse
185. Tomato Tart

Salads
186. Paris Cup
187. Perigord Salad
188. Normandy Salad with Shrimps
189. Dandelion Salad with Bacon
190. Fish Salad
191. Salade Niçoise
192. Mixed Rice Salad
193. Tuna Fish Salad Breton
194. Salade Ecole Buissonnière
195. Salade Argenteuil
196. Alsatian Salad
197. Belgian Endive Salad with Walnuts
198. Ham Salad
199. "Sweet" Salad

200. Farmer's Salad
201. Camargue Salad
202. Sweetcorn Salad with Shrimps
203. Leek Salad
204. Exotic Salad

Desserts
205. Apple Upside-Down Tart
206. Nut Charlotte
207. Diplomat Chocolate Pudding
208. Kugelhupf
209. Grand Marnier Soufflé
210. Profiteroles Sévigné
211. Champagne Sherbet
212. Normandy Sherbet
213. Epiphany Cake with Frangipane
214. Crêpes Suzette
215. Vanilla Mousse
216. Coffee Bavarian Cream
217. Clafouti
218. Dannemarie Charlotte
219. Rice à l'Impératrice
220. Floating Island
221. Strawberry Sherbet Charlotte
222. Cheese Cake
223. Queen of Saba Chocolate Cake
224. Pears Belle-Hélène
225. Apple Mousse with Normandy Sauce
226. Pear and Almond Tart
227. Lemon Tart
228. Rum Baba
229. Pineapple "Belle-de-Meaux"
230. Pears in Red Wine
231. Four-Part Cake with Prunes
232. Peaches Chevreuses
233. Souffléed Oranges
234. Burgundian Rigodon
235. Large Apple Pancake
236. Stuffed Apples
237. Chocolate Delight
238. Dijon Ice Cream
239. Orange Mousse with Strawberry Salad

Creams, Pastry Doughs and Sauces

240. Vanilla Cream
241. Chocolate Cream
242. Custard Filling
243. Kirsch Custard
244. Caramel Custard
245. Cream Fritters
246. Custard Pie
247. Raspberry or Strawberry Ice
248. Butter Cream
249. Chocolate Mousse
250. Crêpe Batter
251. Base for Ice Creams
252. Pie Dough
253. Puff Pastry
254. Chocolate Custard
255. Sand Tarts
256. Fritter Batter
257. Cream Puff Pastry
258. Brioche
259. Sponge Cake
260. Chantilly Cream
261. Caramel Sauce
262. Cherry Sauce
263. Rum Zabaglione
264. Black Currant Sauce
265. Punch
266. Chocolate Sauce
267. Coffee Sauce
268. Berry Sauce
269. Apricot Sauce
270. Pineapple Sauce
271. Calvados Sauce
272. Béchamel Sauce
273. Onion Sauce
274. Sauce Mousseline
275. Suprême Sauce
276. Burgundy Sauce
277. Hunter's Sauce
278. Mornay Sauce
279. Aurora Sauce
280. Tartar Sauce
281. Mayonnaise
282. Green Mayonnaise
283. Tomato Sauce
284. Black Butter
285. Bordelaise Sauce
286. Sauce Bercy
287. Gribiche Sauce
288. Butter Sauce
289. Sauce Périgord
290. Vinaigrette

One-Dish Meals

291. Lorrainese Stew
292. Sauerkraut
293. Cassoulet
294. Burgundy Fondue
295. Savoy Fondue
296. Bouillabaisse
297. Aioli
298. Fish Stock-Pot
299. Chicken in the Pot
300. Pot-au-Feu